THE MEANING OF COOKING

For the intense family taste
Of a certain Easter paté

THE MEANING OF COOKING

JEAN-CLAUDE KAUFMANN

Translated by David Macey

polity

First published in French as *Casseroles, amour et crises* © Armand Colin, 2005

This English edition © Polity Press, 2010
Reprinted in 2010

"Ouvrage publié avec le concours du Ministère français de la Culture – Centre national du livre"
"Published with the assistance of the French Ministry of Culture – National Centre for the Book"

Polity Press
65 Bridge Street
Cambridge CB2 1UR, UK

Polity Press
350 Main Street
Malden, MA 02148, USA

ISBN-13: 978-0-7456-4690-9
ISBN-13: 978-0-7456-4691-6(pb)

A catalogue record for this book is available from the British Library.

Typeset in 10.5 on 12 pt Sabon
by Servis Filmsetting Ltd, Stockport, Cheshire
Printed and bound in the United States by Odyssey Press Inc., Gonic, New Hampshire

The publisher has used its best endeavours to ensure that the URLs for external websites referred to in this book are correct and active at the time of going to press. However, the publisher has no responsibility for the websites and can make no guarantee that a site will remain live or that the content is or will remain appropriate.

Every effort has been made to trace all copyright holders, but if any have been inadvertently overlooked the publisher will be pleased to include any necessary credits in any subsequent reprint or edition.

For further information on Polity, visit our website: www.politybooks.com

CONTENTS

INTRODUCTION

Beginning a new survey is an adventure, albeit a modest one. The researcher sets out, armed with his hypotheses. These are indispensable instruments and represent a sort of wager on the scientific future. But he also has other ideas about what lies in store for him during a period of his life that is not as short as all that, given that it usually lasts for several years. An ambience, specific interests and relational styles: a whole world. For the sociologist, no two worlds are the same. Some propel us into a raucous exuberance and others into a realm of things that are left unspoken and have to be deciphered. Some take us into a world of brutal opinions and others into an enchanted realm of generous humanity.

I had my initial hypotheses, though it is too soon to talk about them, but I also had my own ideas before I embarked upon this survey of families and cooking. Of course I said to myself that the work would not be easy. Having spent over twenty years analysing the joys and sorrows of various domestic tasks – washing, ironing, polishing the furniture, sweeping floors – I had my reasons for putting off this study of cooking. I was, on the other hand, secretly convinced that it was an uncontroversial subject, even one that would be very enjoyable, in the same way that my study of how love affairs begin (Kaufmann 2002a) had been enjoyable. In a word, I promised myself two years of hard-working but peaceful happiness. I was mistaken. I had overlooked one major problem: the way the people I interviewed insisted on making me share their pleasures at all cost, and the interminable, loving descriptions of the creaminess and the delights of the tasty little dishes they loved so much. As I am unfortunate enough to have a formidable appetite of my own, there was a constant danger that I would begin to put on weight. So I suffered the pangs of going

1

without: day after day, my mouth watered and my stomach was empty.

I was, on the other hand, right to think it would be complex, and it soon proved to be much more complex than I had feared. I think I understand why that should be the case. It is quite simply because cooking and food are very major questions for the social sciences. Their importance is quite out of keeping with their seeming insignificance. Most authors who specialize in this area have come up against the same contradiction. They struggle to find the words to convince their readers that this is indeed an important subject and are disappointed to find that, despite all their best efforts, they are looked down on, with some condescension, as though they were smooth talkers who were simply trying to interest their readers in something that does not really matter. The list is never-ending. Michael Symons (2004), for example, proclaims that cookery is the heart of civilization – nothing less – and that, in historical terms, it lies at the origin of religions and the first political systems. In 1785, James Boswell and Dr Johnson (Johnson and Boswell 1984 [1775/1785]: 172, n. 1) were trying to find 'a perfect definition of human nature, as distinguished from the animal'. Boswell argued that: 'The beasts have memory, judgement, and all the faculties and passions of our mind, in a certain degree; but no beast is a cook.' He therefore defined man as 'a Cooking Beast'. Needless to say, his definition never really caught on. Cooking seems too ridiculous when compared with cognitive abilities or language.

But was not the same true of sexuality until Freud came along? When it was not regarded as ridiculous, or at least devoid of scientific interest, it was just something that ought to be repressed. Since then, it has emerged into the full light of day, and it explains a lot of things when it is let out of its box. Several researchers have compared the two domains and have stressed that the search for food has always been humanity's most urgent preoccupation (Fischler 1993a). The same applies to the animal kingdom, where food is much more important that sexuality: 'Those who can go without sex (bullocks, eunuchs) cannot go without food' (Rivière 1995: 189). Charles Fourier had already noted in his *Nouveaux monde amoureux*, which was written in 1816 but remained unpublished for 150 years (Fourier 1967), that the pleasures of the palate, which are dominant in childhood and old age, are less important to adults who tend to associate them with love. 'For Fourierism, learning to be wise in matters of gourmandise is no more than one stage on the road to establishing loving harmonies' (Châtelet 1977: 156). What is more relevant to our purposes (the scale of the question), the alimentary realm has always been much more socially regulated than that of sex. In the history of humanity, there have been 'many more taboos on food than sexual taboos' (Rivière 1995: 189). The social and cultural dangers are much greater. Eating has never been a minor issue.

Food is such a rich topic that it can become a trap for the researcher: when there are too many fascinating things, he or she is forced to channel his or her erudition. The researcher is constantly tempted to establish new links, to open up windows onto worlds of knowledge that are full of dazzling surprises, but he or she is pulled in opposite directions and scatters the knowledge he or she thought they were accumulating. Accumulating data can, paradoxically, kill knowledge. The more important and complex the question, the more deadly the accumulation of data. That is why I prefer to adopt a form of exposition which avoids that trap by following a narrative thread as far as I can. This is obviously not a novel and telling stories in order to explain something is not the same thing as telling a story for the sake of it. This narrative is purely there to serve the purposes of the argument. And when I find it impossible to do otherwise, I have no hesitations about breaking the narrative thread in order to say what I have to say in scientific terms. I therefore apologize in advance for the breaks and the stylistic ponderousness that may result from that decision.

As it happens, the narrative immediately comes up against a difficulty. One of the first important elements I discovered in the course of my investigations is that there is not just one story about food and cookery. There are two, and although they are very different (their religious origin is the only thing they have in common), they constantly intersect. One is quite well known in many respects but the other is much less familiar. Here is the first.

Part I

Two Stories

— 1 —

FOOD: FROM ORDER TO DISORDERS

Frogs and dogs

With all due respect to the Obélix character in the *Astérix* books, dog, rather than wild boar, was one of the Gauls' favourite foods (Goudineau 2002) until the Romans persuaded them to stop eating it. Dog is still greatly appreciated in some countries, especially in Asia (Poulain 1997), just as turtle, rat and insects are highly prized elsewhere. A world tour of different cultures' likes and dislikes provokes bewilderment, if not horror, in those who do not eat what others eat. And even if we do not compare civilizations that are far removed from one another, it reveals huge differences. It is, for example, well known that the British find it very difficult to come to terms with the fact that their French neighbours eat frogs. In a domain that is so physically intimate, cultural differences quickly make one feel sick.

It is tempting to think that this is a matter of individual taste, of local customs that are due to accidents of history, or of ancestral habits that have an astonishing ability to resist the McDonaldization of the world. But how could such different 'tastes' come into existence? In order to understand that, we have to go back to the origins of religions and human societies, and even a little further back. The animal prehistory of human beings, long before the first religions emerged, is relatively clear when it comes to food. Every animal species actually consumes only a limited range of foodstuffs and its choices are biologically determined. Taste is a rudimentary sense and its function is essentially defensive. It is a sort of alarm signal that indicates the presence of danger, especially when an animal comes into contact with something bitter (many bitter substances are toxic). Things that taste sweet or sugary, in contrast, do not trigger those defences in most species. As more highly evolved species learn what they can and cannot eat, a degree of complexity appears. Such learning processes are superimposed on the underlying biological mechanisms and are not mere extensions of them. This tendency becomes more pronounced with the earliest hominoids. Timothy Johns (1999) points out that selection and learning processes work together to extend the range of things that are good to eat. And as Christian Boudan explains (2004: 33), food was, long before the hominoids became fully human, the first medicine. 'The pharmacophagic behaviour of the generic *homo* species probably emerges much earlier than its ability to use fire and to cook food. It predates the emergence of *homo sapiens* (200,000 years ago?) and was, *a fortiori*, evident long before the species learned to cook.' Dietetics is perhaps the oldest form of knowledge.

André Leroi-Gourhan (1965) has shown how even the most modern civilizations have been unable to completely eradicate the animal nature of human beings. Every era lays down strata of cultural innovations and reformulates the long past that lives on within us but none has succeeded in putting it behind us. We simply distance ourselves from our animal nature and learn to control it better. Some elements of the old biological rules governing what we eat are still present. It is therefore no accident that contemporary societies should have found it so easy to develop a taste for sweet things. And nor is it an accident that the earliest systems of dietary laws placed such emphasis on taboos, and thus extended the animal function of taste as danger signal. The emergence of culture does, on the other hand, represent a decisive break for human beings.

As the earliest societies began to emerge, a memory capable of governing human behaviours developed. It was no longer purely physical. It became independent, was externalized and soon came to rival and then to override the biological rules (Kaufmann 2001). Even before the social fact emerged, or at the historical stage when learning was merely an individual process, human beings' new eating habits did sometimes contradict those rules. Christian Boudan (2004) points out, among other things, the paradox of bitterness. Although human beings are genetically predisposed to avoid things that are bitter, a few daring and improvised medical experiments allowed them to identify the medicinal power of some bitter plants. The social fact had, however, to be established before the categories of what could and could not be eaten could become a universal imperative, as opposed to a biological necessity. Punctilious and exhaustive lists based upon those categories became the basis for a constraining

8

dietary order that could be formulated and even written down and prescribed by the law.

As we shall see in the next chapter, the earliest attempts at defining dietary systems were unstable because they were still mixed up with the problems of sexuality and marriage, were articulated with the dynamics of meals and did not yet benefit from the detailed codifications of the monotheistic religions to come. I will discuss them briefly here, taking my lead from Mary Douglas's work on Leviticus (Douglas 1970 [1966]) which provides a perfect illustration of the incredibly detailed religious prescriptions that regulated dietary behaviours. The British anthropologist became famous for demonstrating that the link between cleanliness and hygiene is recent, and that its origins are in fact religious: dirt was matter that was in the wrong place and which therefore posed a threat to the sacred. At the level of mentalities, the quest was not for hygienic cleanliness but for purity. And the demand for religious purity was even greater when it came to foodstuffs because they penetrate the body in dangerous ways. Sacrilegious mixtures and impure contacts had to be avoided at all cost by anyone who wished to commune with the divine: 'By rules of avoidance holiness was given a physical expression in every encounter with the animal kingdom and at every meal' (Douglas 1970 [1966]: 72). The Bible can be read as the first great dietary guide, and whole pages are devoted to what is good to eat and what is not. 'All winged insects that go upon all fours are an abomination to you' (Douglas 1970: 56, citing Leviticus) but 'those which have legs above their feet, with which to leap upon the earth' you may eat. 'Of them you may eat: the locust according to its kind, the cricket according to its kind, and the grasshopper.' As for 'the beasts that are of earth',

> Whatever parts the hoof and is cloven-footed and chews the cud, among the animals you may eat. Nevertheless among those that chew the cud or part the hoof you shall not eat these: The camel, because it chews the cud but does not part the hoof, is unclean to you; And the rock badger, because its chews the cud but does not part the hoof, is unclean to you; And the hare, because it chews the cud but does not part the hoof, is unclean to you. And the swine, because it parts the hoof and is cloven-footed but does not chew the cud, is unclean to you. (Douglas 1970 [1966]: 55)

Why eat crickets and not pork? Why are fish without scales unclean, even though their fatty flesh is very nutritious? The explanation is neither dietary nor rational, but the product of a metaphorical imaginary that is governed by it own internal logic (Douglas 1999). The new dietary order is all the more imperative in that we do not know where it comes from. It is coherent because it is divinely ordained. The order is a commandment from God and it is not open to discussion. For centuries and centuries, dietary behaviours were regulated and compulsory. Every little detail of day-to-day life was regulated. The sensation of taste became of secondary importance. What is good to eat was completely determined by what is 'good to think' (Lévi-Strauss 1969 [1962]: 162),[1] as willed by God. The nature of what was good had more to do with intellectual codes than with sensory or personal perceptions: it was religiously correct rather than tasty.

All the great religions, including Hinduism, use dietary prescriptions to formulate a world order. As Christian Boudon (2004: 343) describes in detail, Hinduism remains a powerful force in contemporary India because cooking and eating are 'practices that express the unity of man and the universe'. The very detailed codes that describe the interaction of fire and water determine a dietary order providing day-to-day confirmation that everyone has their place in society. 'A failure to respect that order means a rejection of all the values that found both it and the very idea of the divine.'

The discovery of pleasures

The modern societies of the West are still imbued with these early classifications. Much more so than they think. Although we have forgotten the religious origins of the taboos that shape the likes and dislikes on which our culture is based, they still operate and explain the misunderstandings between frog-eaters and dog-eaters that we mentioned earlier. All modern cultures establish 'categories of what can be eaten' (Poulain 2002a: 176) that channel dietary behaviours. Because they respect those categories in their day-to-day lives, eaters help to reproduce them and thus inscribe themselves in the culture that supports them (Poulain 1997). Other series of medical, scientific,

[1] The famous formula 'for food to be good to eat, it must be good to think' [with] was originally Lévi-Strauss's. To be more accurate, he actually says: 'We can understand . . . that natural species are chosen, not because they are "good to eat", but because they are "good to think"' (1969 [1962]: 162). The author in fact never really develops this idea and he does not use it in his later writings on cooking (Sanitch 1999). It is not unusual for quotations, taken out of context and endlessly reproduced by the rapid interplay of cross-references, to take on a life of their own (whatever the author may think) and to acquire a fame that has nothing to do with the reasons why they were first enunciated. This is because they correspond to something important that has to be said in one way or another.

10

gastronomic and cultural prescriptions have of course replaced the old religious taboos and the result is a relative cacophony that makes the categories less imperative. But they are still part of an overall 'dietary model' that remains coherent and that still has a prescriptive force in any given period and any given culture (Poulain 2002b). As we shall soon see, scientific ideas have been converted into personal beliefs as we all form our own little religions and define what is good and what is evil. It is still the case that what is good to eat cannot be bad to think. What is good to eat must first become part of the categories of what is intellectually acceptable, and those categories are ultimately based upon moral judgements. As Carolina, a young Swedish woman interviewed by Magdalena Jarvin (2002: 352), put it in a graphic phrase that requires no commentary: pizzas, sausages and chips are 'not good for you'.

The problem is that some people – lots of people – like chips. There is a gap between our intellectual and ethical categories and a very different range of perceptions such as desire, pleasure and taste. I have pointed out that taste, in the very rudimentary form of a danger signal, was already an effective mechanism in the higher animals and in the first human beings it developed into an indicator of health and nutritional values. It was then repressed, at least at the official level, by the great religious categories of purity and impurity. Even though religious texts rarely speak of taste as such (except when they are condemning gluttony), the discovery of the pleasures of food was secretly at work.

It is difficult to reconstruct the history of their gradual discovery. Whilst we are fairly familiar with the hedonism of the banquets of Ancient Greece, and even with the rudimentary gastronomy associated with Roman discussions of wine and oysters (Tchernia 2000), what happened next is more problematic. Because pleasures were experienced in secret, they have left few written traces. The great religions sometimes attempted to include them in the 'pure' category. The Koran, for example, establishes a link between what is 'permissible' and what is 'excellent' (Urvoy and Urvoy 2004: 59), or between what tastes good and what is morally good. But an enjoyment of food for its own sake was usually seen as something that was deeply subversive, rather as though it was an expression of uncontrolled and uncontrollable individual passions that posed a threat to the sacred dietary order. The passions helped to bring about a revolution in dietary behaviour that freed individuals from prescriptions and gave free rein to subjective sensations. The history of the Middle Ages is full of condemnations of the gluttony and orgiastic excesses of the wealthy (Verdon 2002). Pleasures gradually emerged from their clandestinity and eventually became enshrined in books on gastronomy. The first guides to gastronomy appeared at a very early stage in China (Boudan 2004) but it was not until the nineteenth century that they became clearly differentiated from dietary treatises in Europe. 'The great cuisine of the nineteenth century, or the art of extreme preparations and transformation, more or less forgot about health and left the doctors to fume about greed' (Fischler 1993a: 237). Both in restaurants and around bourgeois tables, the sensations of the palate and the stomach defied taboos and proved irresistibly attractive to diners (Aron 1975 [1973]).

Pleasures were able to take centre stage because they had come to pose less of a threat to the social order which was losing its overall hold as its component elements became more autonomous (Gauchet 1998 [1985]) and as individuals discovered the world of sensuality (Corbin 1990 [1987]). And yet a new imperative was also becoming more insistent. The individual order was replacing the social order. Even before the psychological equilibrium of the individual became a major social issue in the second half of the twentieth century (Ehrenberg 1998), the subversive nature of pleasure had begun to pose a major threat to the equilibrium of the individual's health. The paradox of modernity is that culture now has to reconstruct natural harmonies (or what are believed to be natural harmonies). Given that neither biology nor religions can regulate behaviours, there is a great danger that the liberation of desires (together with the greater availability of new products, each more delicious than the last) will lead to a normative void that is the harbinger of the disasters to come. Medical and scientific knowledge was mobilized in an attempt to fill that void (Csergo 2004). In 1865, Dr Fonssagrives noted that: 'We have good cause to worry about the very complex chemical problems that greed raises for the stomach every day.'[2] He was unaware that scientific work was about to escape from the confines of the chemistry lab and gradually spread a new way of thinking amongst the entire population. It was to trigger a second behavioural revolution: permanent reflexivity.

Healthy eating

Dietetics is probably one of the oldest forms of human knowledge. It took on a new dimension with the beginnings of agriculture some

---

[2] *Dictionnaire des sciences médicales*, cited in Csergo 2004.

10,000 years ago. Agriculture led to a quantitative increase in food-stuffs but reduced the variety of species that were eaten and thus led to the development of diseases that had to be treated thanks to a new understanding of the therapeutic effects of food. This does not mean that an understanding of its therapeutic effects displayed from the outset what we now understand by the characteristics of scientific thought. Christian Boudan (2004) demonstrates that dietetics origi-nally developed in three places: China, Greece and India. The great traditional dietetics crossed sacred prescriptions with lessons learned from experiences which were passed down from one generation to the next. The latter took the form of closed and imperative bodies of knowledge that were subordinated to the beliefs that held society together and were based upon the links between tastes and sensa-tions. In the Indian system, for example, many illnesses were seen as resulting from the 'weakness of the digestive fire' (Boudan 2004: 302) because the stomach was thought to be a sort of cooking pot – hence the frequent recommendation of spices which increased its combus-tive heat.

Intuitive and metaphoric conceptions were also dominant in Greece. According to Hippocrates' theory, hot, cold, wet and dry were the central givens. The food that went into the human cooking pot had to respect a cosmological harmony. Having been half forgot-ten for centuries, during which time Greek dietetics had migrated to Iran before spreading from Baghdad to the Islamicized East, it reemerged in medieval Europe in translations from the Arabic. Sensations remained central to the construction and prescription of codes of dietary behaviour. Jean-Louis Flandrin (1992) traces the history of the melon. It came to be believed that melon came into the category of 'cold' foods which were useful when virtue required the fires of sexuality to be cooled but which could also dangerously affect digestive combustion. Melon should therefore not be eaten on its own but together with other foods which were believed to contain a lot of heat, such as spices, wine or charcuterie. Hence the practices that still survive today (*melon au porto* in France or *melone e prosciutto* in Italy), even though we have forgotten their origins. Hippocrates' pre-scriptions are (after some long geographical detours and even though they seemed to have been forgotten) still with us.

Whilst this long, subterranean memory was still being transmitted, a decisive break occurred with the Enlightenment. It paved the way for truly scientific thought and for a neglect of both sensuality and the divine. The cult of Reason was to lay the foundations for our modern democratic societies but it also led the sciences astray.

Scientific errors

The new science triumphed in the nineteenth century. Two images quickly became dominant. The success of mechanics generated an image of human beings who functioned like machines. 'Foodstuffs are designed to sustain combustion in the same way that coal keeps the hearth hot.'[3] That image encouraged calorie-counting, which is now the basis of any self-respecting diet. But it was chemistry that radically changed dietetic knowledge. Far from being hot and cold or wet and dry, foodstuffs proved to be composed of specific elements (sodium, iron, carbon, nitrogen, etc.) whose organic functions were continually being discovered. Chemists were easily tempted to become doctors, and dietetics became a branch of chemistry.

The scientists had made a mistake. Given the context of triumphant science, it was a logical mistake but we are still paying the price for it. They thought, because they were right and had been proven by experiments to be right, that their ideas had a general import. Yet their discovery, like all discoveries, belonged within a limited and provisional field of knowledge. Their idea may well have been correct but they did not make it possible to regulate the dietary behaviour of a population that had broken with its ancestral habits which, in many respects, seem to us to be more judicious than the prescriptions of the scientists. Reading a list of the pieces of advice given to people who did not know any better does little to honour the scientists, but our stupefaction or desire to laugh is quickly forgotten when we think of the number of people they sentenced to death. Green vegetables were relegated to the rank of foodstuffs that were 'not enough to sustain life' and fruits had 'real drawbacks'.[4] For a long time, sugar was one of the foodstuffs most frequently prescribed for their medicinal properties.[5] Sugar was soon dethroned by meat whose praises were sung throughout the century, especially if it was very fatty or,

---

[3] Louis Figuier, *L'Année scientifique* (1865), cited in Csergo (2004).

[4] Eugène Lefebvre, *Les Aliments* (1882), Paris: Hachette, cited in Boudan (2004).

[5] The use of sugar as a drug has a long history. According to Sidney Mintz, it was in fact one of the essential drugs used by apothecaries all over Europe from the thirteenth century to the end of the eighteenth. According to Tobias Venner's *Vita recta ad vitam longam* (1620), 'it excellently assuageth and moystneth the asperitie and siccitie of the mouth, throat and wind-pipe; and it is very good for a dry cough and other infirmities of the lungs' (cited in Mintz 1986: 104–5). But nineteenth-century science found new chemical arguments for going on prescribing it, especially for nutritional reasons. At the beginning of the twentieth century, diets that were very high in sugar were recommended for sportsmen and soldiers (some even did away with other foodstuffs). Such exaggerations eventually gave rise to polemics about the side effects of sugar (Fischler 1993a, 1993b).

14

better still, 'concentrated' by using tablets of 'extracts' concocted by chemists (Csergo 2004). 'If it is to be intensified as much as possible, strength must be concentrated. That cannot be done with the fibrous and bulky volume of vegetables' (Vigarello 1993: 151). Rural diets (which were poor, and based on legumes and cereals) came in for special criticism. Drawing up a list of the most outrageous howlers would, however, be both unfair and pointless. The reason why so many mistakes were made is that the scientists were not the only ones responsible. The new science made its contribution at the very time when traditional forms of regulation were breaking down. Society as a whole was looking for norms that could guide dietary behaviours and this was a period of ostentatious gastronomy. Nutrition was 'day by day in a better position to locate the dangers, to prescribe the right choices and to say where dietary good and evil lay' (Fischler 1993a: 10). Science was not so much establishing norms as caught up in a spiralling demand for norms. We have yet to escape that trap.

What the 'Cretan diet' teaches us

It is easy to believe that all this is in the past and that science is now based upon solid knowledge. It is easy to believe that science *knows* and can tell us what is good and what is bad in nutritional terms. It is not and cannot. The scientific approach does not mean simply accumulating positive data in the way that a bricklayer builds a wall by putting one brick on top of another. Science works by deconstructing and reconstructing hypothetical structures. Sometimes a wall of knowledge has to be knocked down, not because it is badly built but because it is no longer in the right place. What is true today may not be true tomorrow or may be true in a different sense. What is more, this approach is less 'scientifically pure' than the general public imagines and has difficulty in getting away from circumstantial representations, even in the so-called hard sciences (Latour 1989). This is especially true of nutritional medicine. It is striking to note the extent to which scientific publications have, in recent years, followed trends within public opinion (Fischler 1993a), which rates foodstuffs on a scale of good and bad. Olive oil, for example, has been at the top of the hit parade for some years now (and will no doubt remain there until such time as it is discovered to have side effects), whereas sugar no longer has anyone to defend it (the very fashionable 'slow sugars' are the exception to the rule). Wine, which used to be at the very bottom, now proves, or so it is said, to have hidden benefits for the heart and the neurons. We are constantly being given new advice and public opinion therefore changes more quickly than it did in the nineteenth century. Today's scientific truths, which claim to govern behaviours, have an even shorter life span than those of the past. The peremptory tone is therefore scarcely appropriate. Christian Boudan (2004) asks us to think about the epistemological implications of the discovery of the nutritional benefits of the 'Cretan diet'. The world's chemists and biologists have been deploying their battalions of researchers for over two hundred years but it now transpires that a local peasant culture is at the cutting edge of innovation simply because it has handed down its traditional knowledge. That should, to say the least, teach us a lesson in modesty.

Does this mean that we must systematically distrust all the nutritional advice that is handed out to us? It does not. Even if it is uncertain and provisional, the scientific knowledge available to us today is greatly superior to that of the past and is highly critical of it. It now has no competitors that might allow us to define our dietary behaviours. It is, for the moment, the best advice available to us. And besides, now that it has replaced both religion and biology, it regulates practices from the centre and is therefore both ubiquitous and inescapable. If we add that the health risks associated with junk food are becoming clearer and point to the possibility of future disasters, we can understand that the need for this knowledge is more imperative than ever before. We simply have to learn how to use it. A few big ideas have gradually become widely accepted truths and they lay down a few essential guidelines. The main point is this: some of us eat too much (and especially too much fat and sugar) and do not eat enough green vegetables and fresh fruit. Where dairy products and cereals are concerned, opinions differ. And quickly become involved in polemics about this or that product. Despite the apparent consensus that would seem to tell us what is dietarily correct, we are in fact being trapped in endless contradictions.

Cacophony

These contradictions arise mainly because the research itself is contradictory, being based upon the criterion of falsifiability. They are made even more acute because of the way the media report scientific discoveries. The media present new knowledge in an 'incantatory way' and give advice in the form of lists of fetishes and taboos (Defrance 1994: 110). Of course sensation sells. But that is not the only reason.

16

At a deeper level, a public that is greedy for information and certainties demands it. Newspaper articles and television programmes readily adopt a moralizing tone and issue behavioural prescriptions with a confidence that is all the more surprising in that their advice is contradictory or contradicts what was said last month. Whilst there are a few ideas on which everyone is agreed (less sugar, less fat), the ambient dietary discourse is truly a cacophony that is made even worse by the fact that a lot of the scientific information has already been filtered by big institutions, such as the state's health services, the consumer movement and industry, all of which have their own interests and their own points of view (Fischler 1993a), not to mention the way our diet is influenced by other social dynamics, such as the ideal model of slimness which is violently forced upon women (Hubert 2004). We do not know which way to turn.

That is not all. The cult of the god of health that leads us to worship grapefruit or brown rice is only one factor. The more beliefs there are, and the more widespread they become, the more they encourage individuals to be reflexive. Whether they want to or not, they therefore think about their changes of attitude and the instability of their beliefs. They think they are simply eating better because they are better informed. But when they change their habits, they disregard the old regulations and base their new modes of behaviour on scraps of information and their ability to think critically. Their actions are, in other words, built on sand, or on the shifting sands of ideas. The media cacophony is nothing compared with the destabilization which results from changes in their action regime.

As their reflexivity becomes more pronounced, individuals have no choice but to believe in several things at once and at the same time to harden their beliefs in order to prevent their day-to-day lives becoming a hell of mental fatigue and disorganization. Claude Fischler (1994) emphasizes the extent to which we go on developing magical ways of thinking, just as we did in the earliest human societies. The present survey confirms that Fischler is right. We all have our own beliefs and rituals, our credos and our lucky charms: all our dietary choices are influenced by magical thinking. And although we may not say so, we still believe in the insane dream of perfect health, even in the face of death, and nourish the unconscious hope that 'food will give us the immortality of the West or the Nirvana of the Far East thanks to virgin olive oil and organic vegetables' (Diasio 2002: 250). There is a direct link between the modern rise of dietary magic and the cacophony. The more our behaviours are based upon reflexivity, the more our points of view diverge, and the greater the need for beliefs that actually work. The magic that now appears in so many different forms is by no means a hangover from older societies which is doomed to fade away. On the contrary, it is a product of the most advanced tendencies within hypermodernity (Kaufmann 2004). The result is inevitable: we cannot live without our fetishes and taboos, and we will be even less able to do without them in the future. Because it has infiltrated critical thinking in the social body, science itself generates dietary magic.

Minor compromises

What is good to eat must first be good to think. And it must be defined as good simply, rapidly and in both analogical and ethical terms (Hubert 2000): chips are bad for us and green vegetables are good for us. Everyone succeeds in establishing their own little categories and they respect, to a greater or lesser extent, the general advice given by society which, despite the cacophony, establishes the central list of deadly sins: fat and sugar. The survey shows that these personal categories are relatively stable and do work (even though they are ambiguous and subject to change, depending on the context). But the survey also shows that the arguments on which they are supposedly based are both weak and confused. One index of the problem was immediately provided by the interviewees' reluctance to explain at greater length the reasons for their dietary choices. Their initial answers to the interviewer's questions were confident. They were sure of their categorizations and their overall ethics, and worked backwards from their actual practices to the theories they thought they had come up with and could express in simple terms. And then they realized, to their embarrassment (which did not last), that there was no theory.

Whilst scientific thought calls the tune at the level of society, the same is not true at the level of the individual consumer. Whilst individuals think about their day-to-day practices in very sophisticated terms, they must first of all establish the self-evident truths that guide and facilitate their behaviour. They do so by appealing to effective beliefs or, better still, by simply reproducing the dietary habits they have acquired. Unless they are being interviewed by a sociologist, they do not really need grand or coherent theories. But they still believe, in their naivety, that they do have a theory. Individuals are the first to believe that their current behaviour is rational.

Paradoxically, the exceptional nature of the interview situation, which encourages individuals to explain their behaviour, does provide elements of an explanation for their day-to-day behaviour. In their everyday lives, they are in fact obliged to work with temporary cognitive constructs. They may not need well-established grand theories but they do need elements of a theory. The use they make of their constructs is so furtive that they forget what they are doing and go on believing that, somewhere in the background, there is a powerful coherent theory. When they have to explain it in detail, they find that it is, on the contrary, approximate, confused, opportunist and manipulative because it is dominated by the art of minor compromises. They are not lying to the researcher. But they have to lie to themselves and hide the fact that there is no real theory, or that their theory is manipulative. Take the example of Prune. Unusually, she has little difficulty in finding arguments and quickly becomes heated as she denounces dietary fashions that go against her way of doing things. 'I'm very traditional because I believe that food has existed since time immemorial and that people have always made their favourite things. All this talk of low-calorie food is just a social phenomenon. And all that talk of olive oil because it's supposedly more natural!' She prefers butter and fat . . . in large quantities. But all the ranting and raving cannot really hide her disquiet: she feels that, if she denounces dietary modernity too loudly, she will be pilloried. So she uses subterfuge: she expresses her traditional loyalties in the language of 'nature' which, just like 'low cal', is the cutting edge of dietary modernity. So she cooks 'natural' food: 'I try to keep things as natural as possible: the sausages are from the butcher's.' An interlocutor who is in a hurry and who feels intimidated by the impassioned tone may well be satisfied with Prune's explanation. The researcher who decodes what she is saying one word at a time owes it to himself, on the other hand, to note that her verbal skills fail her in the end. We can overlook the fact that tradition has been turned into nature. But the fact that nature has been reduced to meaning a sausage on the grounds that the sausage is from the butcher's rather than a supermarket seems, to say the least, disappointing. The famous sausage is supposedly the proof of her earlier abstract demonstrations but a few more questions would probably have undermined Prune's self-confidence. So what is so 'natural' about her sausages? We often use words loosely because we assume they have ethical overtones. Prune is presumably unaware of the fact – or chooses to ignore the fact – that sausages are at the very bottom of the hierarchy. She is convinced that the very mention of the word 'butcher' makes everything right. Buying sausages from her butcher rather than from a supermarket proves that what she cooks is natural and allows her to speak with contempt of 'low-cal food'. Amandine uses precisely the same kind of argument. 'I used to buy my meat from the supermarket, but not any more. I care about quality, so I buy it from my butcher.' Further investigation shows that the 'butcher' in question in fact has a concession inside the supermarket. But it is not just any supermarket: it is 'a small supermarket', on a human scale, and 'it's not the same'. Anyone who is prepared to overlook the flaws in the theory they are referring to can manipulate its categories as they see fit.

The words 'natural' and 'organic' now have such magical powers of attraction that they encourage us all to make conspicuous use of them, even though our actual practices (in the survey, trips to hypermarkets were under-reported, whilst trips to traditional markets were over-reported) take no notice of nutritional norms which place more emphasis on the need to avoid eating too much sugar and fat than on the need to eat organic food. Yet, if we take the example of low-fat products, they are by definition less 'natural' (because the fat has been taken out) and are usually products of chemical processes (Jarvin 2002). We argue in two different registers and, whilst they sometimes intersect (fresh green vegetables), they usually diverge. At a purely theoretical level, we should be able to choose between 'low calorie' and 'natural'. But ordinary consumers, who are influenced by ideas that are fashionable, believe they are invoking a category that is simple, obvious and 'good to think' [with] when they say they are, on the whole, in favour of natural and low-calorie food. They are in fact simply playing with elastic notions and using them opportunistically.

They base their rules on what they do and what they eat. And then come up with some kind of justification when they have to. Prune often cooks sausages. She justifies herself with talk of what is 'natural' and her ultimate argument is the sausages themselves ('I get them from the butcher'). Hortense also uses the word 'natural', and her tone is even more radical and militant than Prune's. She is revolted by 'all the crap you get these days, GM crops and all that muck', cooks fresh vegetables bought from wholefood shops and will go to the other side of town to buy free-range chicken. She hasn't a good word to say about frozen foods . . . but suddenly begins to sing the praises of canned vegetables. 'Canned vegetables. Oh yes. You can get very good green beans in cans. On the whole, canned vegetables are very good. The ones that come in glass jars are very good too.' Then comes the explanation. She used to have a large vegetable patch, grew vast quantities of green beans and bottled them for the winter. Although those days are long gone, she is still fond of canned

20

beans and habitually eats them. 'I bought two jars of green beans this morning.' That is the way she likes them. Because they remind her of her family's garden, it is quite understandable that she should vaguely associate them with 'natural'. On the other hand, she deliberately ignores all the semantic shifts (from garden to jar, from home bottling to industrial canning) that mean there is nothing 'natural' about her beans. She deliberately ignores the contradictory nature of the reference points that take her across town to buy her free-range chicken which she serves with green beans that come from cans. She tries to ignore the flaws in her theory but is vaguely aware that they are there when she is faced with an interviewer. Now that she is less at ease, she no longer dares to be so vehemently critical of frozen foods and falls back on the argument that there is no accounting for tastes. 'But I usually take care to choose good beans; you know, the ones that come in glass jars. As for frozen foods, it's true that there are people who say . . . I don't like them myself. That's all there is to it; I don't like them.'

When we are forced to justify our dietary practices, we quickly find that we are contradicting ourselves. Our day-to-day practices are much less grounded in a coherent theory than we would like to think. We are increasingly drawn to the magical words of the day, regardless of how we actually behave, and find that there is a contradiction between what we say and what we do. And so we buy more and more industrialized products, even though, officially, we go on cursing them and dream of an unlikely golden age of a lost rural existence (Labarre 2001). The Romanian mothers interviewed by Nicoletta Diasio (2002) dream nostalgically of the teas they had when they were little girls (simple things like good bread), complain about the Americanization of food . . . and feed vast quantities of it to their children. When it comes to shops, anything that is 'small' automatically puts the consumer on the Good side (or so she thinks). Anything that is 'big' is Bad. The adjective 'small' is in itself enough to make Hortense (free-range chicken from 'a small stall in the market') and Amandine (a 'small supermarket') feel that they are being evaluated positively. And yet the big supermarkets go on expanding their empire and now take the form of out-of-town sheds and warehouses selling everything at discount prices. What we say and what we do are two different things.

The same is true when it comes to frozen foods, which are regularly criticized . . . and eaten just as regularly. Tony is one of the few people who never buy them. As a keen cook with a real passion for fresh vegetables, he can afford to voice his opinion loud and clear, as

21

it is consistent with what he does. 'For a start, I never go to the frozen foods section. It's a matter of principle.' Even as he is basking in the glory that comes from taking such a radical stance, he cannot hide the fact that his vegetables are not always as fresh as he claims (he does only one shop a week, and salads and radishes begin to wilt badly after a few days). Paule-Dauphine seems to be singing from the same hymn sheet: 'It has to be fresh and healthy. That's what matters.' Her ideology is impeccable and we have heard her conclusions a thousand times before: 'I avoid frozen foods.' But the discussion gradually reveals how difficult day-to-day life can become for someone who refuses to eat convenience food. She feels relieved when she finally admits: 'But I do have a freezer.' We are always trying to construct a coherent identity for ourselves. We try to be coherent but fashionable ideas can induce a sort of schizophrenia. We have heard Hortense singing the praises of canned beans and complaining about frozen foods. She then lets slip that she does eat frozen fish (and often eats it). Is she being contradictory? Have we caught her lying? Not at all! Frozen fish is fine but not frozen vegetables. It's just not the same: 'Because I think the fish is frozen at sea, so in theory it's fine.' The categories get more and more complicated. The free-range chickens she buys from the small stall in the market are, for example, also frozen but she freezes them herself (which tells us that she does have a freezer). Nothing in the world could persuade her to buy a frozen chicken (but she will buy frozen fish). But when she freezes it at home, 'It's very good, as good as if it were fresh.' When it comes to beans, however, the opposite is true: because she can no longer bottle her own, the ones she buys from the shop are excellent. At this point in the conversation, Hortense is beginning to feel a little tired. She would rather talk about something else.

A guilty conscience

Fashionable ideas are manipulated to make them fit in with practices. That is not very complicated when we are dealing with notions as vague as that of what is 'natural'. The sausage comes from the butcher's and that is all it takes to make it natural. Things are very different when we turn to the nutritional advice we are given day by day by the media or by institutions (educational or medical) that speak with the voice of authority. It is not so easy to manipulate science and it is science that sets the tune we have to dance to. Science does not, of course, speak with one voice, though it may seem to. There are a lot of wrong notes and a lot of controversies. Even so, a few central ideas have been solidly established, and they are often unpleasant to hear: eat less, less fat and less sugar.

Nutritionists are regularly surprised to find that there is a discrepancy between the opinions of consumers who claim to be well informed and their actual practices, which take little notice of the advice they have been given (Guilbert and Perrin-Escalon 2004). They jump to the conclusion that they are not as well informed as they say. That is not the case. Consumers are relatively well informed and they listen very carefully to anything new that they are told about nutrition. But believing that the information is correct is not enough to change dietary behaviours. That will be one of the leitmotivs of this book: we shall see – page after page – that the culinary world is incredibly complex and that it does as much to produce social bonds and culture as it does to assuage hunger. No matter how powerful and correct they may be, ideas usually have only a limited power to influence something that is, in anthropological terms, so complex. Ideas come from outside and are stored in a separate mental stratum that may be either active or dormant and which is divorced from our actual practices. They have no immediate effect on the underlying mechanisms that govern our practices which reshape the things that make individuals what they are day by day. The personality splits into two: a concrete, active being on the one hand, and a sort of parallel cognition that takes the form of an ethical consciousness on the other. That consciousness is scientifically informed but it is increasingly unhappy. Anyone who eats a meal knows very well that they are not exactly absorbing what they should be absorbing. When his or her guilty conscience does not trouble him too much, he or she tries to turn a blind eye and simply tries to appease the latent guilt by eating something lighter or saying no to some little treat. Tony reduces the number of rich ingredients that go into his gastronomic creations. Anneth reassures herself by reducing (very slightly) the amount of fat and sugar she uses 'for the good of my health'. Clémentine feels very uncomfortable when she is asked about fat and calories. She takes the view that she is still learning to cook and is proud of the various changes she has introduced (less tinned food): 'Now that I'm using fresh produce, I tell myself that it must be healthy!' It is the fat that is the problem. And she is beginning to be quietly obsessed about this. Butter? 'Yes, I do use a lot of butter, it's true. It's better that way, no doubt about it. It's true: I've still got a long way to go in that department.' The goal is not to define categories that are intellectually perfect. On the contrary, we try to think as little as possible about our basic diet in order to reduce the mental pressure and to make life easier. And when we are talking to someone who is less demanding than a researcher armed with a tape recorder, we are quite prepared to think about what we eat in very vague or even magical terms. Eugénie is very careful: 'I'm going to stop buying fatty things.' But, like Clémentine, she cannot resist butter. 'Yes, I do use butter, but it's fresh butter. On grilled meat, for example.' Given that it comes from a good source (a dairy), that she does not use it for cooking but as a sauce to go with grilled meat, it cannot be as bad for her as common or garden fat. Eugénie feels reassured.

The magical ritual of using fresh butter is, alas, not enough to overcome the doubts that regularly trouble her. She is 62. And the survey shows that we take more interest in nutritional information as we get older. 'Oh, I'm careful! You have to be when you get older.' This is especially important when it comes to health risks. 'We know that today's cardiovascular problems are caused by a poor diet: too much fat, too much sugar. We know that we have to improve our diet if we don't want to have problems' (Anneth). We go one step further when we are given a more direct warning (illness or advice from a doctor). In most cases, what had been no more than an afterthought suddenly becomes an imperative. Science, armed with its directives, becomes a central part of everyday life. Look what happened to Hortense. Having found that her cholesterol level was a little high, her doctor gave her a choice: either take medication or consult a dietitian ('But you really have to do what he tells you to do'). She chose the dietitian. 'I waited for a while before going to see him. And he explained everything to me. He told me I should eat *fromage frais* and fruit between meals. So I've changed my diet. My husband still finds it a little hard', because her husband had to do the same, even though his cholesterol is not high. The truth is that they have not changed their ways. Same meals, same canned beans, same free-range chicken from the little stall in the market. Now that their conscience is quite clear, they have simply introduced 'tea' and eat their fruit and *fromage frais* religiously. As Tony says of his fresh vegetables: 'I know that my body will appreciate it . . . it's pure.' For her part, Olivia thought that she would never have to follow such medical advice. In her world, cooking and eating well are synonymous with pleasure. And the pleasure has to be intense and without any restrictions. 'I take no notice: when I want *crème fraiche*, I want *crème fraiche*.' And then one day, the lashings of *crème fraiche* began to have some undesirable side effects. Her husband had to see a doctor and was put on a strict diet. 'He said, "Otherwise, it's hospital for you!"' With a heavy heart, she set about cutting out the fat. Olivia tried making *pot au feu* [boiled beef with vegetables] with lean meat, and found it was completely tasteless. So she added a piece of fatty meat, just for herself. Despite all the temptations that were on offer, her husband managed to hold out, followed his doctor's advice to the letter, and lost the excess kilos. Having managed that feat, he felt able to come off his diet and a whole world of possibilities opened up. Profound desires that had been repressed for a while reappeared and excited him more than ever, as always happens when we rarely get to eat the things we like. On the day of the interview, he told Olivia what he would really like the next day (an ordinary weekday): her brilliant recipe for prawns in *crème fraîche* . . . flambéed in whisky.

When the terms of the medical advice are too strict, dieters do not have too many problems. On the contrary. Their usual system has been thrown into confusion by their dietary reforms and they need guidelines to channel their new behaviour and to control their desires. That is why they adapt to the new rules they have been given with such docility, even when they are pernickety. They follow them for a while. But coming off a diet may prove dangerous. The old system of dietary habits no longer works and has been criticized. They are now at a loss and are navigating by guesswork on a stormy sea of desires that have been kept in check for too long, and they jump out of the frying pan into the fire. The ambiguity of this relationship with diets (acceptance of their strict or even pernickety requirements, followed by the problems that arise when they come off them) extends beyond diets that are prescribed for medical reasons. This is particularly true of women who are worried about their weight and who try to conform to the 'slimness' model. Going on a diet means following detailed instructions if their behavioural discipline is be kept under permanent reflexive control. It is the brain that calls the tune. Giving up a diet creates the same difficulties because a new system of habits has to be constructed.

Because we do not want to change our habits completely, the 'diets' we follow are often inside our heads (and make us feel guilty). We do not try too hard, and we cheat a little. Paule-Dauphine is convinced that she is sticking to her diet: 'I've always had a tendency to put on weight, so I'm very careful. Low-cal products, not too much starch, free-range chicken, green vegetables.' There is no denying that this is a good list. But the inclusion of free-range chicken (because of its 'natural' qualities rather than its dietary virtues) shows that it is ideological rather than real. The rest of the interview reveals that Paule-Dauphine's diet is actually based upon magical thinking. Before buying eggs, she goes around the whole market to find the stallholder who has fewest because she is convinced that this is the decisive criterion. 'I'm not going to buy eggs from someone who has a whole basketful of them!' And eggs are good for you, are good for your health and they do keep your weight down, no matter how many you eat, and no matter how you cook them. 'Well, they are healthy, if you buy them from a small stall. Healthy cooking is what counts.'

The tastes of pleasure

Can something be 'good to think' before it is 'good to eat'? That is now impossible. Even though we cobble together and manipulate approximations and forms of magical thinking, society constantly exposes our sense of smell and our taste buds to a whole range of products that are indisputably bad to think with (fat, sugar, chemicals) but they are just as indisputably delicious to eat. The cognitive dietary order is constructed with difficulty, precarious and not very coherent, and it is constantly threatened by the assaults of desire. How are we to describe what we desire? There are two possible solutions. We can stick closely to our own theories of what is 'good to think' and relegate our disruptive desires to a different category. Or we can go on trying to subscribe to a general theory that includes our domestic desires. Different individuals make different choices. There are also major cultural variations, even between countries that are, in geographical and cultural terms, as close to one another as France and Germany. Jean-Vincent Pfirsch (1997) makes this point in a comparative study of young people. Whereas the French associate healthy eating with gastronomic pleasure, the Germans refer to two different and potentially contradictory sets of categories. As a result, young Germans have a much more realistic and specific definition of what is natural (they are not embarrassed about explaining that 'natural' products are described as such and marketed by specialist chains), whereas the French have to use a looser definition in order to preserve nature's role as a magical operator. The French have to be able to make all pleasures fit into the categories of what is ethically correct. And so they either fudge their categories and describe everything as 'natural', or work on their desires so as to make them fit in with their intellectual categories.

Not all Germans opt for the dualist explanation and not all French people opt for the 'single theory' explanation. The divergence appears only at the level of statistical averages. But it is interesting in that it

26

indicates that dietary categories can be constructed in two different ways and that we can choose between two alternatives. One is more rational and sticks more closely to the facts and the other implies that we have to work on our tastes and pleasures, or the tastes of pleasure. It is therefore not surprising to find that the second option is very present in the survey which was carried out in France. 'It's good for my body', Tony said throughout his interview. In his view, 'good' was primarily an intellectual and ethical category. But it also explains the extent to which his support for that belief allowed him to discover positive taste-sensations. He acquired a taste for, and derived pleasure from, food that he initially thought of as being simply healthy in dietary terms. It is the same with Hortense. 'To begin with, it was the healthy side that mattered to me. But in the long run, you realize that the food does not taste the same.' Most sensations are the result of individual and interactive constructs: we have to be convinced that caviar and dry Martini are delicious before we can derive any pleasure from them (Becker 1963). We have to be convinced of that before we can internalize a 'taste' which, once acquired, will become an operator that guides our practices. The likes and dislikes that generate pleasure are much more plastic than one might think. Reformulating them can even have surprising results. Very strict diets, for example, can lead to frustration and discomfort but they can also transform negative feelings into a badge of honour because we have achieved the ideal of the slimness we dream of. But when the pain of having to do without becomes the 'intoxication of the first twinges of hunger' (Tonnac 2005: 16) and becomes a real pleasure, there is a danger that our behaviour will become deviant. It can even put us on the road to anorexia which then becomes difficult to recover from (Darmon 2003).

The likes and dislikes that rule us

The political history of taste is quite fascinating. It can be divided into three episodes. In the first, the (religious) dietary order is the only thing that matters. The sensations that everyone experiences must conform strictly to that order and are rarely discussed as such. The second episode, in contrast, is characterized by the sudden and subversive emergence of pleasures which, being crude signals of a modernity to come, free individuals from the weight of institutions, open up new possibilities and transform a social destiny into a trend. This dynamic becomes more pronounced at the end of the Middle

Ages and, at some point in the seventeenth century, leads society to openly raise the question of taste (Flandrin 1986), which becomes 'both a legitimate subject for reflection and discussion and a social issue' (Pfirsch 1997: 30). This broad debate, which is grounded in concrete practices, responds to the anarchic explosion of pleasures by defining codes and hierarchies, and establishes the notion of 'good taste', which becomes a hierarchical marker of social distinction. 'A liking for certain foods therefore comes to be regulated by the general principles that determine both judgemental rules and norms, and the appreciation of achievements and behaviours' (Pfirsch 1997: 31). Pleasures are then channelled, not into the fixed order of the past, but into a flexible order in which we have to make it obvious that we experience them (and at the same time control them) if we are to enjoy their benefits in terms of social distinction. It is by concentrating on this very period that Norbert Elias (2000 [1939]) develops his famous thesis on the emergence of the civilizing process. Good taste is a central operator within that process.

One aspect has, perhaps, not been given enough emphasis: the historical inversion that transforms the very notion of taste. Because it is a product of the broad process of social distinction, taste is not reducible to a system of norms that is imposed upon individuals by external forces. It is transformed into 'a form of individual self-control that is largely unconscious and that results from the incorporation of collective cultural elements and responses to external social constraints' (Pfirsch 1997: 18). Whilst it is socially regulated within a field that defines contrasting positions (Bourdieu 1984 [1979]), taste itself becomes something that regulates individual dietary behaviours when the context no longer supplies any markers. The senses become a guide to the sense or meaning of life.

We are now living through the third episode in this history. Good taste is still determined by social trends, but many other dynamics also intervene and broaden the range of choice. In order to ward off the danger of being unable to make up our minds, we must once more define our likes and dislikes, and convince ourselves that they will not change. Our likes and dislikes are always the same and are therefore self-evident. We can therefore use them as guidelines. This protects and reassures us because we have ourselves to ignore the fact that they are actually products of an arbitrary construct. The more alternatives there are, the more established tastes act as internal regulators. We then witness a huge objectification, naturalization and even essentialization of our likes and dislikes. We all think that we decide what we like but we are in fact defined by our likes and dislikes. Some of the expressions used by those interviewed for the survey are very eloquent in this respect. Charlotte, for example, begins by describing her preferences but is torn between different registers of judgement (pleasure, competence, and so on). 'I'm not so keen on . . . I'm not so good at . . . I don't know how to put it . . . starters are not really my thing.' And then she finds the synthetic phrase that says it all in one word: 'I'm very much a pastry cook.' *I am*. A whole life is crystallized in that existential given: Charlotte *is* a pastry cook.

We try to convince ourselves that we decide the likes and dislikes that determine what we like and dislike. They are like mooring ropes that prevent us from drifting out to sea. Even when we change our dietary habits, we think that we can decide what it is that we like or do not like. But we are deluding ourselves and, at the intuitive level, we know that. Taste is a powerful social regulator that has been internalized but it is not the only thing that is calling the dietary tune. It competes with reflexivity, amongst other things, and reflexivity is a mental stratum that is very free and independent of practice because it is sustained by an increasingly invasive cacophony of nutritional information. We are in reality constantly torn between what our brains tell us and what our likes and dislikes tell us. That duality means that no form of regulation can really have any lasting effect. As we have seen, strictly codified medical advice can, for a while, allow scientific criteria to be the sole regulators of practice. But only for a while. Desires eventually resurface. Our likes and dislikes reassert themselves and come into conflict with the nutritional advice we have been given.

The converse is not really true. Likes and dislikes themselves cannot really regulate behaviours except for very short periods. They can do so when they are articulated with collective habits but it is the habits that have the decisive effect. An inherent failing means that likes and dislikes cannot regulate the social. It will be recalled that they are born of the discovery of pleasures and of the subversive nature of pleasures. And they are still bound up with the idea of pleasure and with the possible subversion of all the orders that strive to constrain practices. Having a liking for something stimulates desire and pleasure. And desire and pleasure are basically uncontrollable. In the dietary domain, as in love, they resist the power of institutions, destroy their prescriptions for the future and open up new worlds. Hence our curiosity about 'things that taste different' and the hunger for them that underpins the growing popularity of culinary exoticism (Régnier 2004): taste is also something that take us out of ourselves. At the individual level, it is not unusual for both these contradictory mechanisms (reassurance as to one's identity, and self-invention) to come into play at once. They can also alternate.

> 'I have a weakness for potatoes. Potatoes, potatoes. Sometimes, it's potatoes on their own, either mashed or boiled. There's no point talking to me about caviar or foie gras; potatoes are the best thing in the world. And then sometimes – you've seen my spice rack . . . it's a real Aladdin's cave . . . I can do anything with my fairy dust. You can be certain you've never eaten that before! You discover things, and you never know what it's going to be. Even my beloved potatoes . . . once I start adding my spices, believe me, they no longer taste like potatoes.'

Cannelle loves being reassured as to who she is (her potatoes always taste the same) but she also likes the way her magical spices allow her to enjoy things she has never tasted before. She constantly goes from one extreme to the other.

Taste is also much more complex than its naturalization might suggest. It is of course based on strictly gustatory sensations, which are tactile and thermal, and upon elementary flavours but they are in fact quite weak. That is why it really comes into being when it is associated with another range of sensations, most of them related to the sense of smell which is richer and subtler. It should also be remembered that sight, hearing and touch converge on the brain via different paths and therefore introduce their own data into a sensory system in which taste in the strict sense plays only a minor role. Now the various cognitive systems that help to shape our likes and dislikes do not all work in the same way and do not all have the same history. What we normally call taste is obviously the sense that is most closely bound up with biological determinations. Sugar, in particular, has become popular in very different civilizations (from the earliest societies to hypermodernity) because we have certain innate predispositions. As Alain Corbin has clearly demonstrated (1986 [1982]), the sense of smell, in contrast, is a social construct that is inscribed in an imaginary: our perception of good and bad smells has changed considerably since the nineteenth century. And there is more to it than that. Leaving aside the sensory system, taste emerges as a category of it is 'good to think' because it has been filtered through certain mental categories, even when we obey the pure logic of pleasure. It is the idea of good and bad, and of delicious and disgusting, that organizes all the stimuli received by the senses and that gives them a meaning (Pfirsch 1997). We are governed by our likes and dislikes, even though we think we govern them. Had her life taken her in a different direction, Charlotte might say that she was 'not a pastry cook'.

The geopolitics of sugar

If her life had taken a different course, Charlotte might have had very different likes and dislikes. It would, however, be a mistake to conclude from that that we can change our likes and dislikes simply because we decide to do so. Liking something is not a question of will-power. Our likes and dislikes are products of a long history that we have internalized. And we do not determine them for ourselves; the way we interact with our friends and family has a decisive influence. More generally, a host of institutions bring pressure to bear on us to change them. We are at the centre of multiple networks of influence.

Individuals try to determine their likes and dislikes to convince themselves that they have done so and to positivize and naturalize them. Charlotte thinks that she *is* (without doubt and by her very essence) a 'pastry cook'. The process of naturalization works in similar ways at the level of institutions which form very clear-cut ideas about 'likes', which are seen as objects that are stable and easily defined (this is a precondition if they are to be able to function effectively). This is a reflex response on the part of all institutions, which need to be able to define their subjects in determinate and reductionist ways (a few criteria from a formulary) because that makes them easier to manage. But in this case, the tendency to do so is accentuated because dietary categories are unstable. The increase in the number of products on offer opens up new possibilities, as do the desire to find something new, the instability of desires and the endless questions raised by the nutritional information we are given.

Like the Roman god Janus, eaters have two faces (and two palates). Someone may say that he *is* 'cakes' or 'potatoes', but has no qualms about doing away with such points of reference and going wherever his desires take him. Institutions are also Janus-faced. Whilst they do essentialize and define likes and dislikes, all their energies in fact go into changing them to fit in with their interests or ideas. Taste wars have been waged throughout human history and they are now being waged on a global scale. Whole empires have been built on the basis of what people like to eat. Indeed, tastes can give rise to a real geopolitics on a world scale (Boudan 2004). I will take the brief example of one product: sugar.

The liking for sugar (which developed in Persia and India before spreading to the Middle East and the Mediterranean) is very old, and its increased popularity was encouraged by the Hippocratic medicine of medieval Europe. England, in particular, had a great fondness for the spice, which gave a contrasting taste to meat and fish dishes (Mintz 1986). But the first truly decisive element in the epic story of sugar was a product of the process of social distinction. Because it was scarce and expensive, it became a marker of 'good taste', especially for the wealthy bourgeoisie in its struggle against the aristocracy. A strange crystallization (if I can be forgiven the pun) occurred amongst England's new ruling classes. Sugar found a sort of 'natural' place in their protestant ethics of asceticism. Max Weber (1992 [1922]) has demonstrated that the the expansion of capitalism was a product of the protestant ethic. Now religious asceticism is suspicious of anything that is fatty or bloody, but is defenceless against things that are sweet (Andlauer 1997). Surprising as it may seem, sugar, which was an eminently acceptable consumer product for anyone who wished to stand out from the crowd, also proved to be the perfect medium for commodity exchanges. In the seventeenth century, England destroyed Portugal's monopoly and became the leading actor in the world trade in sugar which was based upon the horrors of the slave trade (Mintz 1986). Because of the close link between production and consumption – one could not develop without the other – the steps in this process 'followed in so orderly a fashion as to seem almost inevitable. On the one hand, they represent an extension of empire outward, but on the other, they mark an absorption, a kind of swallowing up, of sugar consumption as a national habit. Like tea, sugar came to define the English "character"' (Mintz 1986: 39). I will not describe here how the sugar colonies contributed to the development of English capitalism but will concentrate on certain aspects of the consumption of sugar.

Sidney Mintz provides a convincing analysis of how, as sugar lost its power as a mark of social distinction (when it became cheaper and spread throughout the population, thanks to the expansion of colonial production), every social group that gained access to it was able to justify its taste for it. The process began with big businessmen as they turned against the aristocracy, and then spread to all those businessmen and shopkeepers whose wealth gave them access to the newly fashionable product. Sugar thus became 'a spurious leveller of status' (Mintz 1986: 96). The taste for sugar then spread to the working population of the cities whose diet was inadequate for the heavy work they did and who did not really have the time to cook. Sugar was an effortless way of providing calories and it also opened up a playful and liberating world for individuals. It was this that would give it its irresistible (and devastating) strength when hyper-modernity reached its apotheosis. Sugar became a concentrate of something that is acceptable to everyone and that has had a major influence on the standardization of what we understand by food. It is the smallest common denominator. The demand for sugar is now potentially infinite. It is not just that sweetness is pleasant in its own right; it has a soothing effect that helps us to cope with social aggression, stress and mental fatigue. And, most important of all, it panders to our unspoken desire to be free from what are now very complex calculations, and to indulge in the simplest of pleasures. In a word, it frees us from dietary constraints and restrictions and allows us to live fluidly in a world in which there are no sharp edges. This is a modernity that is light and liquid (Bauman 2003), and this is a world that is both childlike and enchanted.

The sugar-based English dietary model is perfectly suited to the aspirations of the autonomous individual of today's societies – an individual who goes on dreaming of casting off his few remaining chains. It is therefore no accident that the model should have been transmitted to the United States (whereas other dietary traditions introduced by immigrants have been resisted). The United States now aspires to being in the forefront of the battle for individual emancipation (and Americans consume even more sugar than the British). Nor is it a coincidence that it is in these two countries that the propensity to become obese is most pronounced.

Flour and women

Sugar is obviously not the only thing that encourages the propensity to obesity. And, as its history shows, it is not an isolated factor and is part of an ethical, economic and relational environment. The same applies to the geopolitical history that establishes the link between flour and women. It is described in detail by Christian Boudan (2004), and I will do no more than summarize his findings briefly (and very freely).

It begins with the culinary war that broke out between England and France at the end of the Middle Ages. Until then, the two countries had shared a common heritage inherited from eastern cooking, but France now embarked upon the great process of social distinction and an accompanying revolution in table manners analysed by Norbert Elias (2000 [1939]). The court cooks, who had until then not been very different from Europe's other skilled cooks (in Spain, Portugal and Italy), began to discover refinements and all kinds of sophisticated artifices. What was more important, they created a very precious language to talk about it (Poulain 2002a). Cookery became both an art and a spectacle, and food was talked about as much as it was eaten. The English seemed to have been outflanked and great French cooks settled in London. Although apparently discreet, the English counter-attack proved to be formidable and to have an effect at the world level. It was not directed at the cuisine of the wealthy. Ordinary ovens were the battleground.

Initially, English cooks were presumably simply annoyed, on the defensive and critical of French mannerisms and the complexity of French cuisine. They recommended simplicity and elementary ingredients that could be used easily (sugar, and then butter and flour). While books on gastronomy were enjoying an early success on the other side of the Channel, English cooks had to be more modest and fall back on books written for middle-class housewives. It was in this context that they developed a new sauce based on melted butter and boiled flour. It could be made in just a few minutes by any woman who cooked. It became popular so quickly and on such a scale that contemporary cookery writers described it, with only slight exaggeration, as 'England's only sauce'.[6] Social conditions worked in its favour. Those conditions were material – new coal-ovens at a time when the French were still simmering things over embers for hours – and above all ethical. Just like sugar, white sauce could easily be reconciled with the puritan imaginary and puritan morality. 'How could these white sauces, as opposed to luxurious *coulis*, fail to be seen as an expression of an ideal of natural simplicity and discretion?' (Boudan 2004: 381). The fact that they could be made quickly was also important: the dangers of debauched pleasure implied that not too much time should be devoted to meals. The third, and not the least, condition was the emancipation of women. The Protestant ethic did more than encourage the rise of capitalism; it also created conditions that were conducive to equality between the sexes. English women seized upon white sauce as an instrument for their liberation. For want of other means, they emancipated themselves by learning to cook quickly. This did not lead to much conflict within the family. Family members discovered that a simplified cuisine allowed them to autonomize their practices and that was their great ambition as individuals. The best example is the growing popularity of cakes in the nineteenth century. Cakes could be made quickly (before they began to be made on an industrial basis) and they could be eaten as and when the individual wished. 'Cakes based on butter, sugar and

---

[6] Eliza Acton, *Modern Cookery for Private Families* (1845), cited in Boudan (2004).

flour then became an important part of the English dietary regime' (Boudan 2004: 387).

A real dietary model had been invented 'from below and not on high' (Boudan 2004: 388), and it was so powerful that it crossed the Atlantic and was adopted in the United States. Sugar, flour and speed. Once again, the model appealed to women, and a new episode in its history began. In the first half of the twentieth century (during the inter-war period), women in Europe were being forced back into their traditional roles but American women were in the forefront of the fight for modernity (Cott 1992). Being unable to escape from their kitchens, they concluded that their kitchens should be equipped with cutting-edge technologies and should be rationally organized in the light of the most recent scientific information. Domestic science colleges emerged and had links with the emergent food-processing industry. This had three effects. The culinary arts and the pleasures of the table were discredited still further in the name of an ethics of rapid simplicity based solely upon food chemistry. Cookery became less diverse and more standardized, using basic ingredients. The logical outcome was the appearance of new utensils (such as tin-openers) and products that looked forward to the era of ready meals and fast food. The McDonaldization of the world has a long history.

'You've got everything to hand'

A new culinary model is emerging before our very eyes, and it is rapidly and forcefully extending its range all over the world. It is a product of a clean break with a historical past in which individuals were socialized by the family meal, which was a real institution (Herpin 1988). At the same time, home-cooking is being marginalized. Practices are being organized around a new centre, namely the individual consumer who is now free from all social constraints. Some speak of 'junk food' and associate the individual consumer with an 'American model'. It seems more pertinent to describe him or her in terms of an 'eater-consumer' (Fischler 1993a: 220) who is a new structural given. 'The modern eater has, to a large extent, become a "pure consumer"' (Fischler 1993a: 217). Although the United States has, as a result of its economic and cultural dominance, imprinted its own mark on the 'pure consumer', this is in reality a transnational process. It results from a combination of the three forces that lie at the heart of advanced modernity: the emancipation of women, who are trying to lighten their domestic load; the growing autonomy of individuals who are trying to free themselves from commensal disciplines; and the greater availability of new products and services.

We should not make the mistake of interpreting everything in terms of the supply of products and services. There is no such thing as supply without demand. McDonald's does not in itself explain the McDonaldization of the world. Even those who, like Maryse, do not really conform to the model can explain that for us. She loves cooking and makes time to cook. And a passing fancy (such as watching a film on television) is all it takes to take away her desire to cook. She then happily turns to the fridge. 'When you buy frozen food, everything is done for you.' It does not happen very often, but the pleasure lies in knowing that she can, and that allows her to enjoy a wide variety of existential options. Frozen food is just one example of the thousands of new products and services that are on offer. 'Life means that you've got everything to hand these days' (Maryse). The cook, who is usually a woman, can get hold of all sorts of labour-saving devices and foodstuffs and, at best, 'put together or assemble meals, when it is not just a matter of reheating them' (Poulain 2002a: 39). We have been turned into snack-eating consumers who can do without the services of a cook and have easy access to an ever-expanding range of 'ready meals', both at home and in public places. We can now eat anywhere, and with great ease; in the street, at the cinema, in the car . . . Provided that we can pay, we are surrounded by 'abundance within hand's reach' (Vanhoutte 1982). Not to mention the seductive world of the ubiquitous advertising images and the manufacturers' smells that encourage us to give in to our impulses of the moment. Temptation is on offer all over the city, and it is very hard to resist it. How can consumers resist temptation, and how can cooks resist anything that makes their lives easier? Whereas discourses raise high the banner of certain values (by idealizing, say, fresh vegetables or fish), practices have exactly the opposite effect: less vegetable and fresh fruits, more ready meals (cereal bars) and more meals that require little or no preparation (Lehuédé 2004). Foodstuffs (unlike discourses) are becoming further and further removed from their 'natural' form, and are being transformed by packaging techniques. Meat, in particular, is 'reified' and transformed into a banal standard food that has little to do with killing animals (Poulain 2002a). A 'Big Mac' is a brand rather than beef or corn (Badot 2002). The person eating it forgets about the chicken or the pig and tucks into pieces of an imaginary Mexico or Asia. This is not just the pleasure of eating; it is a dream of exoticism. The irresistible desire for snacks suggests that the sector's industrialists have a good future ahead of them.

Products that make the cook's job easier and that satisfy the needs of nomadic individuals who want a snack and who are in a hurry – such is the first aspect of the 'individual-consumer' model. The second is represented by the individualization of practices and the de-structuring of meals. This is a model and, like all models, it schematizes a reality that is much more complex. Individual snacking has long been part of certain cultures, especially in Asia (Poulain 2002a; Sabban 1993) and, as we shall see, meals have not been as de-structured as people say. But it is true to say that, in quantitative terms, the practice of eating alone (meals outside the home) is becoming more common all over the world, and that it is detrimental to family practices. In many European countries, different members of the same family eat breakfast at different times and eat different things. Lunch tends to be eaten outside the home, either alone or with non-family members (whereas dinner and meals at the weekend are still family occasions). The heart of the individualist revolution lies, however, elsewhere or in what we might call the new fridge culture.

The fridge culture

Families used to eat together on a regular basis. They could only do so because the woman of the house, armed with her pots and pans and chained to the stove, devoted herself body and soul to her domestic tasks. One appliance has changed things completely. It is commonly known as 'the fridge'. What was originally an appliance that helped the cook by making it easier to store food has, thanks to the combined effects of the emancipation of women and the availability of ready-to-eat products (and especially individual desserts), brought about a spectacular but discreet change. It has now replaced the stove as the centre around which domestic eating arrangements are organized. Individuals open the fridge door and help themselves to whatever they like, whenever they like, either openly or in secret. Snacking has become as easy (and as tempting) at home as it is in public places.

Other appliances have helped to speed up the simplification of cooking and the individualization of dietary practices, especially the combination of freezers and microwaves. But the fridge has much more radical implications. At one level, such individual consumption is still associated with the family meals that are eaten at the table and can even be a relic of the traditional role of the cook who services the family and mediates between table and fridge. In his fine study of meals, Karim Gacem (1997) gives the example of the Pécheur family.

Pascale, who is the mother, is afraid of forcing meals on her children without paying any attention to what they want. She puts them first, even if it means abandoning any idea of educating them about food. Her son Simon was not slow to assimilate this ethics. 'It's stupid to make someone eat if there's something they don't like. If we don't like it we won't eat it, because it's not what we like. That's the way we like it' (Gacem 1997: 81). For dessert, everyone helps themselves from the fridge. Pascale still makes a main course (often using frozen foods) in the hope that the whole family will eat together. But as soon as anyone raises any objections, she gets up, opens the fridge and lists the alternatives, most of them ready meals, which are on offer.

At the next level, the meal disappears altogether, as does the role of the cook and, in many cases, the dining table itself which is reduced to being an ephemeral support for buttering bread and making snacks. Someone sits down in a hurry, puts together an individual TV dinner, or even eats standing up by the fridge. Some, like Maïté's husband, even do so when it should be time for a family meal. 'When he comes home to eat at lunch time, he never sits down to eat. He takes a slice of bread, some ham or some pâté, but he never sits down to eat. So it's not worth making anything; that's the way we live.' Maïté simply makes sure that there is something there for him: 'I make sure that there's food in the fridge, and that way everyone can eat in shifts.' In what appears to be a less radical version of the individual use of the fridge, a greater variety of things are kept in stock: a combination of food for personal use and food to be eaten as a family. But in reality, nothing is clearly defined and nothing is planned ahead. The individual yoghurts may be eaten together, with the whole family sitting around the table, but the individual picks at what is left of the paella. Because nothing is defined, the fridge de-structures meals even more radically. By leaving all the possibilities open and confusing registers of action (individual or collective), it breaks down established disciplines. Thanks to the fridge, the eater-consumer becomes a law unto himself.

The fridge is the material organizer of personal autonomy within the home. The process works only because individuals want to be individuals, or because they are forced to be individuals by the rhythm of activities that keep them apart. For Maïté the evening meal is scarcely more of a family affair than the midday meal (which is, at best, a plate of pasta). 'In the evening, we eat in shifts. Because we are never together. It's often sandwiches. They make their own. When I get home, I eat what's there. If I'm there, I make something quick, like pasta. I don't bother with making proper meals.' Work and the other constraints of life are often a convenient excuse. In Maïté's case, the lack of synchronization is largely an effect of her family's chosen activities, and especially of her son's enthusiasm for sport. As a general rule, children are the greatest centrifugal force. They begin to want to be autonomous at a very early age, partly because they find certain products very attractive and partly because they dislike the collective discipline of meals (they do not always enjoy being the central topic of conversation, especially when they have just come home from school). The TV dinner (a little tray that they can take anywhere) then becomes the object of endless negotiations and compromises. The cook may serve part of the family meal she has lovingly prepared because that allows her to maintain at least some link with the act of cooking, even though she has given up on the meal itself. But once again, nothing is compulsory and nothing is defined in advance. The negotiations between the individual and the collective are always ongoing. Amandine refuses to give in to the fridge completely. She fought a long, hard battle with her son before giving in. Unfortunately, she is fighting a losing battle. 'If he doesn't want to eat what he's given, he goes to see what's in the fridge, and that's all there is to it.' He has his own little table in front of the telly and always eats the same favourites. 'He always eats the same thing. Breaded fish, burgers, pizzas, chips. And mayonnaise with everything, always with mayonnaise.' With her husband, she refuses to give in and insists that they eat together, despite all the problems that causes. Her husband has sudden fads that never last long, and she refuses to follow suit. Everyone eats what they like. Everyone eats what they like, but she is the only cook, and she has to orchestrate three meals (one for herself and her daughter, one for her son, and one for her husband). After going to Weight Watchers for a while, her husband discovered the benefits of the Cretan diet.

> 'The Cretan diet is all he's interested in, and has been for some time now. It's a new fad, and it won't last. It's based on olive oil, fish, lots of vegetables and usually snails. And the snails have to be fresh. Well. I'm sorry, but I'm not going to go out collecting snails. If I make a potato gratin for my daughter and me, he says, "No, not for me!" so I do some green vegetables for his Cretan diet. But he'll help himself to some of the gratin.'

The low-cal individual

The dietary model of the individual consumer who picks at whatever he or she likes, both at home and outside the home, does more than just de-structure family ties and lead to nutritional aberrations. It also leads to freedom, and that is the explanation for its popularity. And it is also one of the by-products of the rise in individual freedom. The autonomous individual escapes the shackles and rhythms that constrain him and is not restricted by any hierarchies or codifications. Standing beside his fridge or in the centre of the big city, he returns to a sort of state of nature. 'In the "jungle" of the city, you "gather" your bag of chips, your croissant or your sweets. With food available everywhere, you can eat standing up, sitting down, lying down, or as you walk down the street. You munch, nibble, suck or eat with your fingers' (Corbeau 1989: 741). The autonomous individual is on the move and in a hurry, rather as though he was afraid of being caught up in the old disciplines he has just escaped from (Desjeux 2002). He is a perfect illustration of the liquid nature of modernity (Bauman 2003).

That is how it looks from the outside. Within the secret imaginary of the actual individual, rapidity and mobility are less important than the profound feeling of an indefinable lightness. That feeling arises precisely because he has escaped the crushing disciplines of old and can create his own identity: the lightness is the taste of youth and freedom. Feeling light and at the same time eating heavy food, or even overeating, may seem something of a paradox. It is in fact not so much a question of physical lightness as an existential perception. We find it amongst singles (who both cook for themselves and eat alone) who cannot be bothered to spend a lot of time preparing meals. As Joanna puts it, 'A quick trip to the shops to buy food for a dolls' tea party: fruit, yoghurt, ham, cheese and tea' (Kaufmann 2008 [2005]: 85). We also find it amongst mothers who have found a way to lighten their domestic burden: 'In the evening, after a day like today, cooking is the last thing I feel like doing. Coming up with an idea and all the rest of it. Fed up with doing the shopping!' (Melba).

The existential lightness of individuals who are free of domestic and culinary constraints can lead to very different dietary trajectories. The outcome is often bulimia or obesity, and the paradox is no more than a seeming paradox. But it can also intersect with the social processes that encourage individuals to try to achieve a real, physical lightness and to become more and more ethereal. This gives rise to a synergy that, for better or worse, has a powerful effect. The first of these processes is the dominant aesthetic model to which Western societies refer. Over the last few decades, that model has been based upon the need to be slim and has led to the dictatorship of sylph-like beauty (Vigarello 2004). Even though they are 'inaccessible and as

40

palpable as the horizon' (Tonnac 2005: 121), not even top models can really embody that ideal. In an ideal world, the model sublimates her real body, has no buttocks and hips and transcends her normal weight in an attempt to achieve a virtual status that is abstract, ethereal and androgynous (Hubert 2004). She exists in a divine world that lies beyond human contingencies and rediscovers the ecstasy of the mystical saints who fasted in an attempt to leave their bodies behind so as to become closer to God (Maître 2000). The second process revolves around the modern goal of self-control, of managing one's life efficiently (Gaulejac 2005). It gives the individual the illusion of subjective strength, of having the ability to decide his or her goals in life, even in those areas that affect their biological being most closely. There is no denying that diets produce the jubilatory intoxication of self-control. The individual dreams of being able to sculpt her own body which becomes lighter through the sheer strength of her will-power, rationality and self-discipline (Tonnac 2005). She then falls into a trap of her own making and becomes the prisoner of practices which, even though she has instigated them, gradually lead to anorexia (Darmon 2003). Absolute lightness inevitably results in death.

Just as the 'thin' model is basically an abstraction that can never be attained, rational self-control is an illusion. Why do dieters actually succeed in giving up their old dietary habits (at least for a while), lose weight and eat differently? It is not simply because they resolve to do so, but because they find new structures that can define a life discipline. The development of an almost punctilious respect for self-control (weighing, calorie-counting) is, for example, an essential stage in the 'career' of an anorexic (Darmon 2003). She escapes one set of habits and establishes a new one. Her subjective capabilities and will-power are essential if she is to make that transition. But she then retreats into the new system she has established. That is why the individuals can take things too far without realizing it, and that can be fatal. The explanation is that her day-to-day behaviour is something that is beyond her rational control.

The origins of the serious eating disorders that are now becoming such a huge problem in all the developed countries lie in a theoretical issue that is of particular concern to the human sciences. Certain blatant paradoxes should have allowed it to be defined with greater clarity. The first is this: the crisis is most acute in those countries where nutritional information is best. This is especially true of the United States, which has been doing more than any other country to reshape dietary habits on a scientific basis for almost two hundred years (Fischler 2003). Does this mean that we cannot rely on science,

41

and that it only offers us counter-truths? It does not, even though provisional truths have all too often been turned into dogmas and even though mistakes were made in the past. The real problem lies elsewhere, and it is basically a theoretical problem. It lies in our conception of what an individual is and of how individuals function. Over the course of several hundred years, one representative model has become dominant, and it is basic to both capitalist development and democratic politics: the individual who is in rational control of his or her existential choices. This individual is a purely intellectual creature. As rational reflexivity developed over time, the model's role as a model was confirmed. The problem is that a concrete individual is not a model. An individual is not just a brain, especially in dietary terms. To make matters worse, in normal practice, the periods when we do act rationally have very little influence when compared with the ubiquity of our infra-conscious memory, the influence of magical representations, the influence of sensations and the power of the context on which we rely to govern our behaviours (Kaufmann 2001). The mistake is to believe that an isolated individual who is cut off from the history that lives on inside him and the framework that makes him what he is can, if he is well informed, change simply because he wishes to change. It is not only that this idea is false; it encourages individuals to ignore the factors that previously regulated his behaviour. He thus falls prey to fads that can unleash uncontrollable desires. In extreme cases, the outcome is either a potentially fatal weight loss or obesity.

The historical inversion

Anorexia kills fewer people than obesity and that is the most serious aspect of the crisis. A real epidemic of obesity has broken out. People are getting fatter all over the world. Even nations which, like China where opulence is still a novelty, are discovering the fool's paradise in which people's bodies, and especially children's bodies, get bigger, and it is in fact hell. We have already seen the primary reason why this is happening: individualization and the naive rationalization of behaviours. Its effects would not, however, have been on this scale were it not for the intervention of another factor which explains the scale of the epidemic. For, at a time when individuals ignore all dietary rules and are, to a dangerous extent, left to their own devices, a major change is taking place. Thanks to a historical inversion of our relationship with food, we have gone from a problematic of scarcity to a problematic of over-abundance.

Let us begin with a word about biology. Human beings bear with them a long history. Their bodies are, in functional terms, heirs to a distant past and to their animal prehistory. As the gustatory and digestive apparatus has remained unchanged since the human species evolved, modern individuals are still omnivorous primates who are attracted to foods that are fatty and sweet. When food was scarce and, more important, not regularly available, the ability to build up reserves of fat in anticipation of periods of scarcity was essential. The principle of storing fat, however, comes up against permanent over-abundance. After hundreds and hundreds of years of civilization during which, for the majority of the population, the relationship with scarcity and possible shortages still persisted, the biological and the social are diverging and coming into conflict. This encourages us to build up reserves of fat, or at least to prefer food that 'sticks to the ribs', especially if we belong to the poorest groups which are still threatened with penury or which still have painful memories of that threat (Bourdieu 1984 [1979]). 'They do not eat lots of butter or meat because they are greedy, but because they are afraid that, one day, there will be none, and it will not be the first time that has happened' (Pétonnet 1968). Clarisse, who lives in a very underprivileged area on the island of Réunion, locks her supply of rice away in a cupboard by her bed. Her treasure is too precious. She cannot forget the days, and they are not so long ago, when there was not a grain of rice in the house (Wolff 1991). When you have gone without once too often or are afraid that there will be nothing to eat, nothing can prepare you for a reversal of the situation, or for even a slight improvement. 'As soon as they have a little money, the children buy ice creams, sweets, and cakes as well of tins of sardines and pâté, and they eat them straight out of the tin, with a gluttony that matches their frustration.' (Wolff 1991: 71). The transition is very difficult to handle as few people think that abundance might be as problematic as scarcity.

Although it is harder for the poor, the transition is delicate, if not difficult, for all of us. We are now living in a tantalizing society in which everything is 'within reach' and yet we still have an atavistic propensity to hoard. To make matters still worse, the more sedentary and bureaucratized lives that we now lead in heated, motorized worlds mean that we need fewer calories. The result is a radically new situation: in a world of greed and pleasures that are there for the taking (always assuming that we can pay for them), we have to learn to say no, and to go on saying no. 'The central problem has become that of regulating individual appetites in the face of almost unlimited resources' (Fischler 1993a: 390). Individuals now have to fight a very

43

different fight. They have to fight themselves and the most tempting thing of all, namely the promise of pleasure. They have a duty to resist temptation. In order to do so, they develop an ethical shell by establishing firm 'moral lines' (Coveney 2000) to structure their subjective self-discipline (Mennel 1985). In terms of their day-to-day diet they have, especially since the 1980s, inverted their system of values and are now trying to replace 'nourishing' with 'balanced' or even 'low cal' (Fischler 1993a; Poulain 1998). *Small is beautiful* [English in the original].

Ordeal by fat

'Modern societies have become "lipophobic": they hate fat' (Fischler 1993a: 309). Anyone who can adapt to the new era wins respect and admiration; anyone who strays away from the thin model is stared at. And if they do not respect 'low-cal' food, they begin to look suspicious. The fat now have to justify their existence.

The way people stare at them as they put on the kilos tells them that they are contravening a secret code. Officially, society proclaims that individuals enjoy complete freedom: everyone can do what they like. But the way people look at anyone who goes against its codes says something very different: of course everyone can do what they like but the more closely they conform to the model, the happier and the more promising their lives will be. This even applies in the world of work where, despite the legal bans and the assertions to the contrary, more doors are open, and open more easily, to those who are not overweight. As a result, everyone knows that the dietary battle pays off, and that anyone who fails to conform to the model pays a very high social price. And so everyone tries to make an effort, or even goes on a diet. Although they do not know it, this personal tactic is part of a collective mechanism. It strengthens the model's hold and further stigmatizes those we look at disapprovingly.

All this is, however, nothing, compared with the unspoken ideas that hide behind the disapproving looks which convey a terrible silent reproach: the fat have no self-control, and self-control has now become a crucial value. Fat people are people who have no self-control, who cannot resist temptation (which is a venial sin) and have no rational will-power (which is a cardinal sin). The dietary regime was from the outset intrinsically bound up with the idea of rationality. In etymological terms, it is the art of using reason [*raison*] to direct our behaviour [*se diriger*] (hence the use of the word 'ration'

44

to describe doses of calories). Fat people opt for the easy solution but they are also guilty of sinning against the mind's intelligence. The new deal created by the historical reversal condemns everyone to draw the moral lines that structure their self-discipline, and fat people are therefore suspected of understanding nothing and going on eating as they always have done.

Once again, it is a mistake to believe that individuals can be purely rational. Just as there are biographical trajectories that lead to ano-rexia (Darmon 2003), there are biographical trajectories that lead to obesity, and they are to a great extent determined by social, and often biological, factors (Waysfeld 2003). Some people are born fat or very quickly become fat even before they have developed any autonomous subjectivity. And many others are defeated by forces that are quite outside their control (a biological predisposition to build up reserves of fat, a system of incorporated habits, their relational situation, and so on), to say nothing of the global process of dietary deregula-tion. 'The bodies of fat people are beyond their control' (Duret and Roussel 2003: 67). People who are fat are strangers to themselves and are caught up in a system and heirs to a situation over which they have little control, try as they may. Their lives are wretched because they see their bodies as other people see them and frustrating because 'controlling their appetite is an ideal they cannot achieve' (Duret and Roussel 2003: 67). The guilt they feel when they internalize the unspoken criticisms is even worse. 'The obese see themselves as *guilty*, when they are above all *victims*' (Waysfeld 2003: 55, emphasis in original).

The stigmatization reaches new heights when they are doubly handicapped by being both fat and poor. As I have already explained, poor populations are less well protected against the destructive effects of the historical inversion of our relationship with food, which has an even more devastating impact upon them. Food can also be an antidote to a loss of self-esteem: we eat to reassure ourselves and to fill ourselves up because our lives are empty and meaningless. The compensatory effect (heavy food, cigarettes and alcohol) is particu-larly obvious when we lose our jobs. The passer-by who stares is, of course, unaware of the social conditions that lead to obesity. And the accusation of having no self-control and sinning against dietary reason is all the more damning when the fat person is also poor. Non-egalitarian violence has never been as physically based as it is in our society, in which both beauty and slimness have become social discriminants. If we also recall that the techniques used in cosmetic surgery are becoming evermore sophisticated and expensive, we can understand why there is a widening gap between those who can afford to be biologically beautiful and those whose natural ugliness indicates their social position. Being thin and good looking is not a luxury that everyone can afford. Being fat becomes even more unacceptable and shameful.

The void within

History will record that, at the end of the second millennium and in a world of super-abundance, individuals were left to their own devices: they were drunk on freedom and unable to stop putting on weight. History will also record that, at the same time, individuals became emancipated in many other domains and demanded the right to become autonomous subjects (Kaufmann 2004). Once again, they discovered both the intoxication of freedom and the dark side of the same process, namely the 'yearning for infinity' (Durkheim 2006 [1897]: 317). They were weary of being who they were (Ehrenberg 1998) and in desperate need of recognition (Todorov 2001 [1995]. As more and more possibilities opened up, the certainties on which the self was based collapsed. When we take a critical look at our own lives, inner cracks open up and threaten to sap our energy for action. The feeling that our bodies are becoming weaker and that we are empty inside is the result of a vast social dynamic that sweeps individuals away despite themselves. We have to find a new impetus and fill the gaps in one way or another. This explains the addictions that have become the modern individual's existential crutches (Ehrenberg 1998; Valleur and Matysiak 2002). The best known – drugs and alcohol – are typical of the way individuals are being reconstructed by trends they cannot resist; the more they escape from their own lives, the more real they feel. Other addictive mechanisms are much gentler and work simply because they fill individuals up in an attempt to fill an inner void. Curiously enough, they work in similar ways. Eating is a response to a very concrete lack which we experience as a form of emptiness: we have an 'empty stomach' or 'feel peckish'. Clémentine, who in fact does eat a lot, derives a strange pleasure from family parties at which there is almost too much to eat: 'You're full.' How can we fill the indefinable emptiness that lies at the heart of the lives we lead today? The eating reflex represents an attempt to fill the void by magic. It is all we can do, but the attempt is, unfortunately, doomed to fail. 'I can never be filled with pleasures (or recognition) in the way one pours liquid into a goatskin' (Todorov 2001 [1995]:

55). The demand for happiness and love is infinite, and it can never be satisfied in the way that mere hunger can be satisfied. And the real lack is not a lack of food.

Using food-as-a-drug (Waysfeld 2003: 117) is often a prelude to more serious complications, firstly because it fills lives to the point of obsession. Bernard Waysfeld (2003: 117) describes the case of a woman patient who is both bulimic and obese, and who describes herself as 'a walking stomach'. Her whole life is just one big stomach. She then intensifies the analogical reflex to an extreme degree in a desperate attempt to gulp down her inner suffering. 'I know that the scream is there, and that I'm going to eat even more to silence it' (Waysfeld 2003: 61). She is even prepared to accept the possibility of social death: 'I can lead a completely independent life with my bed, my sofa and my fridge. I've created a perfect world, just for my own pleasure. I don't need to go out any more. I've been annihilated, smothered, destroyed.'

The bulimic trajectory does not always coincide with the anorexic trajectory I described earlier. The origins of the bulimic's tragedy lies, rather, in the inner void created by individualist modernity and by the perverse role food plays in our lives. Hence the other paradox (and dietary issues abound in paradoxes): bulimic crises often begin during or after periods of strict dieting. When we suddenly go on a diet in order to change our lives completely, there is a danger that our dietary behaviours will take on an addictive existential dimension' (Valleur and Matysiak 2002: 135).

Diets and regression

Dieting can have terribly perverse effects, especially when it is a technique that is used on its own (Waysfeld 2003). It can trigger addictive mechanisms and can destabilize the dieter who, when he or she comes off the diet, no longer has any points of reference and goes from one extreme to the other. I have already explained why this happens. Dieting is not usually enough to establish a pattern of behaviour; human behaviours are not based upon rationality alone. Dieting, which is an inevitable response to obesity, is something to be undertaken with caution. There is no miracle solution to the serious dietary problems of our period but some things could be considerably improved. As Claude Fischler and Jean-Paul Poulain have been saying for a long time, it is vital not to think of people who eat as individual atoms, and still less as atoms of rationality. That conception has led to incalculable disasters over the last two hundred years and changing it is now a matter of urgency.

We need support, and we need to stabilize our choices. Our freedom sometimes makes us tired and anxious. Self-service, which Europeans were delighted to discover in the 1970s (Poulain 2002a), is no longer really an ideal. 'Everything on hand' is a perspective that can open onto a mental hell. Regressive (and sometimes vaguely addictive behaviours) and repetitive fixations on a few fetish-foods reassure us that we are who we think we are and therefore represent an attempt to get out of that hell. Life becomes as simple as chips or Coke. Or ham, in the case of Maïté. 'At home, it's ham . . . lots of ham . . . lots of it.' The repetition is protective. Always eating the same thing becomes a source of reassurance, and the Maïtés of this world are sometimes tempted to restrict their diets still further and to concentrate on primary sensations that combine the intensity of instant stimulation (things that are sweet, salty or spicy) and foods that are easy to chew, or even that can be just swallowed as they are and without any need for mastication (Badot 2002). Alternatively, they may revert to childhood habits and opt for things that are sweet, liquid and runny (Corbeau 2002). It is, in this context, striking to note that, in China, children are currently in the forefront of the revolution in dietary behaviours (snacks and fizzy drinks). Children are the perfect incarnation of the general trend (in China and elsewhere) that encourages a regressive infantilization of the eater-consumer, who feels quite helpless. Children are the trendsetters and they are much more creative than adults because they are so familiar, albeit uncritically, with brands and new products. For them, greed is not so much a sin as a sweet wrapped in brightly coloured paper. Similarly, in Italy, the traditional word for 'tea' (*la merenda*) has been reduced to the diminutive *merendina* and has come to mean an industrial product that has replaced a meal rather than a real meal (Diasio 2002). Faced with this supply of products, adults find it very difficult to resist. Their children are leading them, not into the enchanted world of childhood, but into the guilty conscience of regressive infantilization.

The calm assurance of nutritional policies, which are confident about their scientific certainties, is in stark contrast with the gravity of the dietary crisis and the lack of publicity given to more complete remedies rather than mere diets. The 'French paradox'[7] has drawn attention to the fact that it is probably more helpful to stop seeing

---

[7] The 'French paradox' arises because a tradition of good eating and the institutionalization of meals coincide with a lower incidence of obesity.

eaters as isolated individuals and to look at what happens between meals (Rozin et al. 2003). Meals are not in themselves, or not in all circumstances, the only solution to the crisis: a liking for good food can result in plates being heaped dangerously high. But they are obviously a partial solution because they prove, if proof be needed, that the context in which we eat is the best regulator of all.

The goal of this book is not to save the planet from the dietary aberrations that are lying in wait for it. This analysis of meals is not designed to provide practical answers or to give behavioural advice. It is simply an attempt to understand. To understand what is going on in the world of family cooking and family meals (which is much less familiar than the world of 'dietary behaviours'). In order to do that, I must once more begin by going back to the past and relate a second historical chronicle, which is very different from the first. It does not deal with orders and classificatory systems. It begins with tales of fury, fervour and blood but ends, strangely enough, by talking about the most ordinary and peaceful affection. Here, then, is the tumultuous history of meals.

— 2 —

MEALS: FROM SACRIFICE TO COMMUNION

The individual-consumer model is extending its hold inexorably. It is not, however, the only model to structure dietary practices. A countervailing tendency based upon the group rather than the individual, and on sensuality and identity rather than rationality, encourages us to use very different criteria to regulate our behaviour. It seems to me that it is essential, if not a matter of urgency, to study this tendency, which is why most of this book about cooking and meals is devoted to it.

The history of meals is so different from that of dietary behaviours that it is dangerous to confuse the two. If we make a distinction between them we are in a position to understand the extent to which the way we now eat is the result of two sets of factors that often differ in every respect. Even the sequence of events is different. My first story was about the almost linear evolution from religion to science that allowed nutritional good and evil to be defined and classified in detailed ways. The second, in contrast, is an endless series of new beginnings. Most of them concern the meaning that we try to give the social form in which we are inscribed when we eat. It is as though society could never establish, and still less stabilize, the specific function of meals.

A clanship of porridge

The history of meals is usually passed over in silence. When that is not the case, it is confused with the linear evolution of dietary behaviours, precisely because we do not know enough about it. There is also another reason why the two things are confused. Certain aspects of meals may well suggest that they have no real history. They suggest that meals are something functional and very simple, and that they scarcely change over the course of history, except in the sense that they gradually get better. The image that immediately comes to mind is that of primitive groups that meet to share meat that is grilled over the embers, and we assume that they have existed ever since human beings discovered fire. The fire cooked food, supplied light and warmth, and was for centuries both the centre and the symbol of domesticity. A second image then comes to mind. It is one of ordinary meals in modest rural milieus, with the family coming together to consume the wretched contents of their platters. The final image is that of the carefully laid tables and highly refined fare of bourgeois families and then, in the nineteenth centuries, of working-class families. The images are not in themselves inaccurate. They do correspond to one aspect of the reality. Soup, especially, has played an astonishingly constant role in the history of rural societies (Touvenot 1997). There are two sides to soup. Because it is more elaborate than grilled meat and presupposes a degree of domestic organization, it 'civilized men allowing them to leave behind the infantilizing barbarism of living on meat obtained by hunting and milk from the herd' (Rowley 1997: 14). Soup (together with bread and various forms of porridge) was their main defence against hunger. In periods of famine or amongst the very poor, it was reduced to a thin gruel around which rudimentary 'meals' were organized (Lambert 1998; Shorter 1984).

The great and tumultuous history of meals that we are concerned with takes, however, a different direction. It has more to do with a dialogue with the gods and with festive occasions than with ordinary food and is more influenced by the extravagances of the rich than by the diet of common cottagers. Although the diet of the wealthy was that of a minority, it is its history that traces the contours of what we now know as meals. And yet the story does begin with something resembling a banal story about soup. Sharing food has always set the seal on friendship and peace and forges social bonds in all societies. Some anthropologists, and especially William Robertson Smith, therefore speculate that the first forms of alliance may have been elaborated by sharing food. This is what the Ba-Ila of Africa call 'a clanship of porridge' (Richards 2003 [1932]). It is probable that, in the earliest societies, 'the act of eating together acquired the meaning of consanguinity' (Makarius and Lévi-Makarius 1974 [1961]). The primordial forms of kinship did not fall from heaven and were concretely constructed by the sense of family that emerged from sharing meals.

It is undeniably obvious that kinship has something to do with sex: there can be no descendants without copulation. And that is the starting point of our second story, and it is a tumultuous story. My description of its beginnings draws heavily on Raoul Makarius and Laura Lévi-Makarius's *L'Origine de l'exogamie et du totémisme* (1974), a book which is now overlooked despite its subtle pertinence.

Dietary incest

The origins of human societies lie in kinship structures organized around the incest taboo: blood relations cannot marry. The literature of anthropology has elaborated impressive tables that synthesize and schematize with an almost mathematical rigour the rules that govern association between the sexes in different cultures. Everyday reality, however, has often been much less clear-cut, not least because populations found themselves faced with the insoluble contradiction generated by the recurrent but discreet ways in which 'porridge' was used to construct families. The idea of committing incest by sharing a meal was just as unacceptable as copulatory incest. These early societies therefore had two main concerns: 'keeping blood relations apart so as to prevent them from marrying' and 'distributing food in such a way that those who had sex together did not share food' (Makarius and Lévi-Makarius 1974: 68). The former preoccupation was theoretical, abstract and based upon a principle that was 'passive, negative, and in a sense inert', but it was stable and enduring. The latter, on the other hand, was from the outset 'active, positive and dynamic'. It was a constant day-to-day preoccupation and was 'acutely concerned with details' (Makarius and Makarius-Lévi 1974: 77).

As the two principles were almost contradictory, attempts to articulate them at the practical level gave rise to unheard of complications. Raoul Makarius and Laura Lévi-Makarius describe in detail the wealth of theories – many of them astonishing – that people all over the world dreamed up. Most centred on a principle of division and attempted to prevent the development of incestuous 'dietary communion' (Makarius and Lévi-Makarius 1974: 69). The most simplistic tried to introduce a radical division between men and women, with each sex providing its own food and inhabiting different territories. Such attempts rarely got beyond the outline stage (as the Amazon myth reminds us) because it was very difficult to reconcile this radical division with procreative unions. Physical separation could not in itself resolve the problem. The idea of a territorial division was untenable. It survived, at best, in the form of gender-specific positions during meals (in some societies, women still eat slightly apart from the men). Dietary classification was the only viable solution. Given that men and women could not eat in different places, the idea was that they should not eat the same things. The Winnebago Indians had already made some progress in that direction by dividing their villages into two. Those in the 'upper village' ate birds, and those in the 'lower village' ate animals that lived on land or in water. Two cosmogonies and two dietary modes coexisted in the same village. Attempts to organize society by concentrating on different classifications of food-stuffs also ended in failure. It proved impossible to implement them on a concrete or lasting basis, and they proved to be anti-functional and anti-economic. Minor compromises with the official theories were common and they undermined their organizational principles. And they gradually demonstrated that sexual exogamy was the only way to structure kinship.

Fears and magic

This development was made possible by the discovery of the shrewd idea of totemic symbolism. Symbolism meant that, when classified as part of a broader category, a particular food could 'absorb the taboo on forbidden foods' and thus make it possible to eat them without breaking the taboo. This idea could only emerge because the contradictory complexity of the two exogamic principles which triggered an outburst of imaginative creativity. Human intelligence and human culture are probably products of the existence of insoluble social contradictions (Kaufmann 2001). Human beings were forced to think. And they did so in ways that were far from being coldly rational. The discovery of the symbolization of dietary taboos was a matter of trial and error, and it was both exciting and terrifying.[1] There had to be

---

[1] In the depths of our emotions, contemporary dietary fears carry echoes of this distant past. They are, however, relatively minor compared with the panic generated by the fear of ingesting taboos, which explains why the gesture of absorbing food was often hidden from the gaze, either by the hand or, better still, a piece of cloth. This is, as it happens, the origin of the veil, which then became widespread in the East, although its meaning changed and came to focus on women in the context of a patriarchal society. 'Thanks to patriarchy, women become commodities exclusively reserved for their owners: no one else could look at them. The veil was a ready-made symbol of that exclusive right. Women were veiled for reasons that no longer had anything to do with dietary exogamy' (Makarius and Lévi-Makarius 1974: 164). In our societies, a further slippage of meaning then occurs. The veil acquires a religious meaning, and it is the hair rather than the mouth that is concealed.

visionaries and breakers of taboos before taboos could be displaced and reduced to a smaller number of foods. And someone had to be bold enough to eat parts of the taboo itself. The totem of the Oraons of the Paddy clan, for example, is a cereal-based porridge. They refuse to eat the scum that forms on the surface but eat the rest because they regard it as inoffensive.

Magical thinking was born of the excitement of violating taboos. And it has a lot to do with dietary practices. Michael Symons (2004) is right to say that the origins of civilization lie in cooking. Those who violate taboos feel a power within them and are carried away by the strange force known as *mana*. They are tormented by dreams and hallucinations that are sent from another world or that come from deep within themselves. Their thoughts 'subjectivize the world around them in terms of their experience and in their own image' (Makarius and Lévi-Makarius 1974: 230). This inventive subjectivity can find expression because it is not experienced as pure subjectivity. It creates a world of explanations, most of them relating to the symbolism of food. And in practice, sharing meals becomes a way of warding off the threat of incest.

Had it at last become safe to eat together? Is the idealized image of meals that has survived unchanged for centuries an accurate image? One event was soon to lead to new and bloody upheavals.

Bargaining with the gods

There is nothing anecdotal about this episode: we are talking about the great transformation of magic into the sacred. Magic 'is practised by individuals . . . mysterious, furtive, scattered and broken up and, finally . . . arbitrary and voluntary in nature' (Hubert and Mauss 1964 [1904]: 39). It is characterized by its ambivalence, dangerousness and effectiveness (Lévi-Makarius 1974). Although it cannot be defined, *mana* is discussed in terms of the very concrete results that are expected from it. The sorcerer is not afraid of getting his hands dirty, operates at the limits of what is permissible and is a past master at the art of inverting meanings. He uses, for example, large amounts of blood, even though blood is often seen as the source of the greatest of dangers. Religion, in contrast, emerges gradually[2] and in the

---

[2] This reconsideration of the origins of humanity in the light of the history of cooking and meals leads me to correct a point I made in *Ego* (Kaufmann 2001), as I now think that I was mistaken. In *Ego*, I explained that society is born of religion, thanks to a sudden break that occurs before the emergence of the social fact, and is forced upon individuals.

form of a process of institutionalization that clarifies and establishes categories and makes a clear distinction between pure and impure, and Good and Evil. The sacred then becomes divorced from creative subjectivity and dominates society in transcendental fashion. 'It will be seen as having no beginning and no end, as something that is as increate, immutable and eternal as the gods it brings to life with its creative breath' (Lévi-Makarius 1974: 128).

In the earliest forms of religion, human beings' dealings with the gods are very similar to the magical compromises they reached with spirits. The gods are not above the fray; they are rather like strange partners who make it possible to hope for certain gains, especially where food is concerned. Even before the emergence of blood sacrifices, offerings of food appear to have been widely used in a form of magical bargaining. Even after the emergence of sacrifice, the earliest religions 'were still overwhelmingly prosaic and materialist. Sacrifices were made to obtain very specific favours from the gods' (Caillé 1995: 278). Whereas the symbolism of taboos helped to expand the range of things that could be eaten, offerings and sacrifices made it possible to obtain an abundance of food.

A major transformation came about when religions were institutionalized, and this profoundly changed the nature of sacrificial meals. Alain Caillé (1995) emphasizes the real change that came about when the horizontality of exchange gave way to a verticality that implied a social hierarchy. The origins of society do not lie in sacrificial acts; the bloodiest sacrifices appeared later, when human beings began to turn their eyes to the heavens. And because human beings began to turn their eyes to the heavens.

Sacrifices and banquets

These few pages were necessary because magic, religion and sacrifices are of great interest to the historian of meals. Ritual sacrifices made communications with the gods possible, but they were also a way of sharing food and eating meals together. Emile Durkheim's (2001 [1912]: 249) comment on Robertson Smith makes this quite clear: 'First of all, [the sacrifice] is a meal, consisting of foodstuffs. Moreover, it is a meal in which the faithful who offer it take part

---

I still hold that view, but I mistakenly overlooked the long period that went before it. I overlooked the gradual emergence that established the preconditions for that break and which is so well described by Raoul Makarius and Laura Lévi-Makarius.

along with the god to whom it is offered . . . Its essence [was] above all an act of dietary communion.' In his analysis of Brazil's *candomblé*, Roberto Motta (1998) emphasizes the almost banal alimentary nature of the sacrificial rites. The sacrifice is not just 'good for praying'; it is also 'good to eat'.

The act is very strictly regulated and centres on the figure of the 'priest-butcher'. For the Greeks, there was no distinct dividing line between the domain of religion and that of butchery. 'Normally, meat cannot be eaten except on the occasion of a sacrifice and by following its rules . . . from Homer to the end of the classical age, Ancient Greek has no other terms to convey the idea of slaughtering an animal to butcher it than those referring to sacrifice or killing for the gods' (Vernant 1982 [1979]: 25). As in many other societies, 'the Greeks combine [butchery, religion and cooking] into what . . . we call sacrifice' (Durand 1982 [1979]: 133). As religion comes to be organized around a vertical axis, a subtle distinction (which is already present in Greece) begins, however, to be made between the strictly sacred work of butchery and the rather more human task of cooking. The cooks, who have been given responsibility for a practical task on which the quality of the feast depended, gradually become butchers rather than priests. The butcher not only performs the crucial act of slaughter; he also – and this may be more important – divides the meat out and gives each participant a carefully calculated portion.

One share for the gods and one share for men. There are often many more subtle subdivisions. A distinction is, for instance, made between bloody offal and ordinary meat: 'The viscera are roasted on a skewer in the first phase of the sacrifice and are eaten on the spot near the altar by the inner circle of those taking full part in the sacrifice, while the quarters of meat, put to boil in a cauldron, are intended for a large feast or for distribution, sometimes over a distance' (Vernant 1982 [1979]: 10). It was believed that the gods really did eat the meat and that they sometimes even sat at the table in the shape of statues perched on chairs (Witherington 2003). The shared meal had to be eaten within a sacred enclosure. In many cultures, however, minor compromises began to be made. Pieces of meat could be taken home for ordinary consumption, even by the priest himself (Hubert and Mauss 1964 [1898]). Various symbolic tricks ensured that men were no longer denied the best morsels. 'To men the meat and the entrails laden with fat, everything that can be eaten, and to the gods the bare bones consumed in the sacrificial fire with some fat and aromatics' (Vernant 1982 [1979]): 21). The symbolism could go even further: given that they were celestial beings, the gods fed only on the smoke from the cooking fire.

Parties with the gods?

Sacrificial meals were anything but stilted rituals. Before they began to speak through the *logos* of theology, sacrificial religions were characterized by their physical exuberance (Motta 1998). The gods actually manifested themselves through the physical excitement of the dancing and the trances. The images transmitted by Greek banquets are not images of sadness or sobriety. And yet it was believed that the gods really did share the meal, like the Hindu gods who 'enjoyed banquets in the company of men. The guests joyfully shared the same pleasures of the table' (Gardaz 1998).

The same pleasures? But was it pleasure or religious fervour? How can we distinguish between sacred physical exuberance and the profane pleasure of dancing? How can we codify what the privileged butcher-priest feels as he enjoys the best pieces of meat? Are they the gods' pieces, or do they taste divine? The societies of the day could not grasp the difference. But with hindsight, we can see the extent to which the subversion of pleasure took sacrificial meals in a different direction that was more festive, sensual and hedonistic. Banquets, from the Roman Saturnalia (Guittard 2003) to China, were becoming civilized all over the world. And as Plato's famous *Symposium* shows, banquets were an expression of intellectual and literary creativity. They gave rise to monumental events, like the banquet of Kalah in Assyria (Boudan 2004), which brought together 70,000 guests over a period of ten days. No fewer than ten thousand skinfuls of wine were drunk. And wine was a different problem.

Wine was initially seen as the elixir of the gods, mainly because it could be metaphorically likened to blood which is central to all sacrificial rites. Over three thousand years ago in ancient Iran, it was believed that the gods were nourished by the blood of the animal that had been sacrificed. The liquid contained the soul of the animal and it was poured into a hole dug in the ground. The participants absorbed the same liquid in order to commune with the gods. Because it was impossible to obtain sufficient quantities of blood, wine was seen as an acceptable substitute. The ritual banquet known as the *bazm* still existed much later in the ninth century, and it was washed down with lots of wine. 'Wine was clearly designated as a substitute for sacrificial blood in a rite that was explicitly bound up with the religious tradition of the Zoroastrians' (Boudan 2004: 143).

Wine is divine in two senses. It is not simply a substitute for blood; it has its own effects. In Egypt, Harthor, the daughter of the god Râ, was transformed into a bloodthirsty lion and went on the rampage. Râ himself took fright. He therefore mixed the blood that had been spilled with wine. Harthor drank the mixture, fell asleep and had calmed down when she woke up (Nourrisson 1998). But wine's main effect is intoxication, and that makes it easier to commune with the gods. It was only later that drunkenness became reprehensible. For the moment, it represented the heights of rapture. This explains why they got the animal drunk before it was sacrificed, as in Mexico or on the island of Rhodes: 'The drunkenness was a sign of possession. The divine spirit was already pervading the victim' (Hubert and Mauss 1964 [1898]: 30). Other alcoholic liquids could produce this sacred communion just as easily. Beer, saké, pulque and palm wine were all means of communicating with the gods in animist, polytheistic and Buddhist societies (Pitte 2004). So too were various drugs which were often taken in combination with alcohol. 'In the early stages in their history, all religions' used 'psychoactive substances to establish a link between the profane world and the sacred, between men and higher powers'. Magicians and shamans had 'an extensive knowledge of the sacred plants that allowed them to travel' to the world of the gods (Valleur and Matysiak 2002: 160). Alcohol and hallucinogenic plants produce ecstasy in the etymological sense of the word, *exstasis:* 'being outside or beside oneself'. There were by no means marginal practices; they were essential ways of communing with the gods (Furst 1974).

Wine, like other forms of alcohol, was central to communing with the gods, and it has left long-lasting traces in the cultural memory. It is not by coincidence that Rabelais applies the adjective 'divine' to the bottle. He was an intellectual master of the pleasures of the table. And that is where the problem lies: in the pleasures of the table and drunkenness. Surely they lead to reprehensible excesses, especially when getting drunk has obviously become an individual act (Fehr 2003)? Socrates himself comes close to that conclusion at the end of the *Symposium*, when a gang of drunks interrupts the philosophical debates. As religion became more vertical and as the gods became less familiar, a more important question arose: could the devout join in these festivities? Wine, especially, is a 'telluric aliment' (Roche 1997: 255) and, as it became more ambiguous, it signified both 'the path to salvation and the path that led to sin, drunkenness and everything that implied' (Roche 1997: 254). Christianity was to make wine's duality explicit by referring to it in two contrary acceptances.

Towards profane meals?

Islam condemned the same excesses in even harsher terms and forbade alcohol, even in the many wine-producing regions from the Middle East to Afghanistan and Georgia. The ban met with stubborn resistance, even in the courts of the caliphs.

> And yet, more austere life-models did spread, and the consumption of wine and drunkenness were widely condemned. A different conception of the oriental banquet began to emerge. The more frugal sociability of an Islamicized Orient required people to eat quickly and then linger over sweets for the simple pleasure of conversation between friends or being honoured by the company of the powerful. (Boudan 2004: 162–3

Christianity, for its part, was not just concerned about drunken excesses. Something else bothered it: the sacred status of meals. Could the fruits of the earth provide the experience of faith in the same way as sacrificial rites and the 'abject practice of devouring bloody flesh' (Detienne 1982 [1979]: 18)? Could faith coexist alongside the most prosaic physical pleasures? When religion becomes vertical, dietary practices must be sublimated through the use of sacred euphemisms. The path that led to symbolization had already been opened up by early sacrificial rituals, and especially by those who broke taboos and thus expanded the range of acceptable foodstuffs. The entire history of sacrificial banquets is characterized by a gradual move towards symbolization as human beings bargained and reached minor compromises with the gods. Georges Gusdorf (1948: 101, cited in Caillé 1995: 279) gives a picturesque example taken from Plutarch. The pious King Numa was trying to persuade Jupiter to stop hurling bolts of lightning without demanding human sacrifices in exchange.

> Jupiter demands heads. 'Of garlic', Numa immediately promised. 'No, human heads', insisted the god. 'You can have the hair too', said the king in an attempt to reach a compromise. 'No: living things', insisted Jupiter. 'Then you can have small fishes too', concluded Numa. Having lost the argument, the terrible lord of the heavens accepted the bargain and, ever since then men have been spared from lightning at little cost to themselves. (Caillé 1995: 279)

Christianity was not happy with such minor compromises and tried to introduce a radical divorce between places of worship and eating places, times of worship and meal times, and the fruits of the earth and spiritual nourishment. 'Meat commendeth us not to God', proclaims St Paul (I Corinthians VIII: 8). 'As concerning therefore things offered unto idols, we know that an idol is nothing in the world, and that there is no other God but one' (VIII: 4). He rejects Jewish law, speaks as a real propagandist for nutritional value, and his conclusions brook no argument: 'Whatever is sold in the shambles, eat that . . . If any of them that believe not bid you to a feast, and ye be disposed to go, whatsoever is set before you, eat, asking no question for conscience sake' (X: 25–7). As a result of this secularization of dietary practices, a transference occurs; in the symbolic ritual of the Eucharist, the bread and wine that are blessed sublimate the body and blood of Christ. 'Thanks to this symbolic displacement, the consumption of meat and blood became divorced from religious taboos and became widespread in the West. The obligation to fast went hand in hand with a sort of secularization of cooking' (Boudan 2004: 348).

It was, however, no more than a 'sort of secularization', as the divorce was never made complete. The nature of the Eucharist itself remained uncertain, and it was for a long time a euphemism. During the Reformation, red wine was abandoned in favour of white, and leavened bread in favour of communion wafers that 'melt in the mouth and can be swallowed whole. Chewing a communion wafer would profane it and reduce it to the status of human food' (Poulain 2002a: 217). But it was what were now in theory profane meals that posed the real problem: centuries of commensal worship are not easily forgotten. Monks were not the last to have to deal with this concrete difficulty. Some contemplative orders of nuns, for example, would like to do away with the biological need to eat altogether. 'If there were no readings, meals would be a waste of time', said Sister Dominique when she was interviewed by Jeanne Andlauer (Andlauer 1997: 46). And yet dietary rituals, including fasting, punctuate the religious life in extraordinarily detailed ways. They can also become metaphors. The refectory functioned as a 'second chapel' (Andlauer 1997: 39). As popular iconography reveals, some monastic brotherhoods did less to euphemize the fruits of the earth, and thus raised the delicate issue of pleasure. The secularization of dietary practices obviously could not mean licentiousness, especially for monks.

And nor was it obvious to ordinary mortals that meals had been completely secularized. This was because of a new development in the history of meals, which really is full of surprises. The element of transference in the Christian Eucharist both liberated and secularized dietary practices. But, thanks to a strange reversal, the change was announced during a meal, and the image of the Last Supper became decisive, or even foundational. An image of a meal! How could Christians forget that image as they sat at a table to share bread and wine? They could not, and ordinary meals came to be surrounded by rituals. Prayers were said to bless the food, and the sign of the cross was made over the bread before it was cut, and so on.[3] There was still something sacred about eating together but now one knew exactly what it was.

A short history of tables (Part I)

Although we do not always realize it, elements of the sacred rituals of the past live on in the objects we use in our ordinary day-to-day lives. Nothing, it would seem, could be more materially obvious or more purely functional than a dining table. We scarcely trouble to ask ourselves why it is that, in many parts of the world, people eat much closer to the floor, sitting on carpets, cushions or low chairs. Why is it so important to sit up (and to sit up straight) in the Judaeo-Christian West? Because of the symbolic transference that occurred in certain religions.

A table was originally just a sacrificial altar. As the spirits or gods lived in a celestial world, the offerings had to be placed high up. Most rituals contain survivals of the custom of placing food at a height. During the feast of the dead, the Nahua Indians of Mexico, for instance, take a table and decorate it so as to turn it into an altar. Once the dead have eaten the aroma of the meat and the scent of the fruit, the living can help themselves and eat, either standing up or squatting around the altar-table (Chamoux 1997). The verticalization of religion inevitably encouraged the existing trend to raise the height of the altar-table, which began to reach closer and closer to heaven. The symbolic relationship with the table is especially strong in the Jewish religion which did not adopt transference rituals such as the

---

[3] Bread had a particularly strong influence of the symbolism of ordinary Christian meals. Just as Jesus presided over the Last Supper, it was, for centuries, the father sitting at the head of the table who distributed the bread. 'Breaking bread is a commitment that unites the family and regular visitors to the house' (Roche 1997: 253). Whilst we no longer make the sign of the cross over bread, many discrete traces of its symbolism still remain (we avoid placing it upside down, for example) and thus demonstrate that it is not just any form of food (Kaplan 1996).

Eucharist. A real cult of *la table dressée* [the expression means both 'a table that is elevated' and 'a table that has been laid'], to use the title of Joëlle Bahloul's fine book (1983), still survives today. The choice of foods and the way they are laid out, especially for celebratory meals, still recall their religious origins. The table is *dressée* in both senses of the word.

Early Christianity did not elevate tables in quite this way, as the reference to Greco-Latin culture and its familiar gods confused things somewhat. Banqueting tables were low and placed at right-angles to the guests (who were semi-recumbent); they were not the structural centre of the meal. In Greek culture, they were often removed before the main part of the banquet – a symposium at which the wine flowed – began. Paradoxically, the seated position tended to be reserved for women and slaves (Schmitt 1990). It took time for the modern dining table to develop. Tables certainly grew higher but a table on solid legs and surrounded by chairs arranged in a set order was by no means the rule. It was only in the seventeenth century that people stopped improvising tables by placing planks on trestles and covering them with a cloth for banquets. At this point, Christian civilization once more began to attach great importance to tables and gave them a new meaning (or rather a series of different meanings) that has a profound influence on commensal practices all over the world. And as we shall see when we look at the second episode of their short history, it is not only at mealtimes that they are important.

Meals without a compass

For the moment, let us go back to the secularization of everyday meals. Was all the fuss over? Could the history of meals begin again, and did it finally conform to the idealized image of a family gathered around a simple bowl of soup? Were the banquets anything more than an epiphenomenon that was noisy but devoid of any real meaning? Even in the Ancient World, they were of concern to only a minority. The ordinary fare of those living in rural Greece consisted of a few onions and olives, a little goat's cheese and porridge made from barley. The Roman plebs obtained their modest rations of chickpeas, and sometimes a few sausages, from hawkers. It is in fact as though the history of meals were woven from two different threads. One thread tells the basic history of what the common people ate and retraces the epic story of the battle between soup and the 'snacks' of bread and cheese that quietly laid the foundations for today's family meal. The other thread is coloured, whimsical and luxurious. Meals come to be surrounded by a deafening cacophony of contradictory definitions. The meals we eat today are of course products of these parallel histories. One gradually shapes their framework and works bottom up, whilst the other supplies their meaning and works top down. But the peculiar thing about the history of meals is that their social meaning has never stabilized in any lasting sense. That is why everything that helps to define them is of decisive importance. The extravagance of banquets tells us more than soup.

Sacrificial meals are a rare example of how the meaning of a meal can really be established, with fervent intensity, as the participants commune with both the gods and the group. And yet the subversive effect of pleasures undermined that meaningful unity from within, even before Christian secularization dealt it the death blow. In the Middle Ages, the nobility of the West slipped the last mooring rope of meaning and set sail without a compass. This was initially the result of the liberation of pleasures, especially in the fourteenth century, when the nobility, now that they were less involved in the government of the kingdom, were looking for ways to ward off boredom. 'The melancholy that stemmed from the feeling that they were useless encouraged hedonism. They thought that they had the right to more entertainments than the peasantry because that was how God had created social categories' (Verdon 2002: 125). How could banquets, where there was drinking and dancing, be prevented from descending into debauchery? At the court of Charles VI, they frequently did so. 'At the great feast organized in Saint-Denis in May 1389, for example, the guests drank so much that the supper on the last day ended with an orgy of adultery and fornication' (Verdon 2002: 124). And it should not be forgotten that, at this time, religion provided the moral framework for all social practices, including meals. Various forms of licentiousness therefore coexisted with demonstrations of piety. In 1454, Philippe le Bon, Duke of Burgundy, gave a sumptuous meal that stands out as a milestone and is recorded in the annals as the 'banquet of the pheasant'. The festivities were punctuated by tableaux inspired by the rituals of the mass. As was the custom of the day, the guests sat along one side of the table so that they had a better view of the show (the *entremets* [literally, the 'between courses']) that was put on between the different courses. One depicted a marvellous forest, with strange animals. Another featured a huge pâté, with twenty-eight people playing various instruments, and the last depicted a church surmounted by a cross. A bell was rung to mark the start of the festivities, and everything came to life. 'The organ was played in the church, and the musicians in the pâté acted out a hunting scene' (Verdon 2002: 117). In came a giant armed with an axe, and threatening a Beguine. This was Holy Church being subdued by a Saracen. And then in came a white lady – 'The Grace of God' – accompanied by twelve beautiful girls representing the twelve Virtues. Wine and spices were brought, and 'the Virtues stayed for the entertainment' (Verdon 2002: 119). The Virtues joined in the party.

We find the combination surprising but we should not use our modern categories to interpret it, as the intellectual framework was quite different. Just as the secularization of meals was never really complete, the Eucharist was never purely euphemistic. Memories of the old sacrificial rites, in which eating was a way of communing with the gods, lingered on in some minds. Hadewijch of Antwerp, a Beguine and mystical woman poet of the thirteen century, makes the point in passionate terms: 'the lovers really savour one another, eat one another, drink one another and greedily gobble each other up' (cited in Verdon 2002: 182). It was the same with God in mystical forms of love: to feel hunger was to feel a desire for the physical union of two bodies. 'Eating means becoming as one with your food; God is food, and food is flesh; and the flesh is suffering, and therefore salvation' (Verdon 2002: 178). The confusion was becoming extreme, and no one knew where meals were heading.

Disciplina

As I said earlier, the subversive effect of the pleasures set free by the secularization of meals could have led to an epicurean civilization of banqueting. Regrettable as it may be, history took a different direction, especially in the Christian West. Long before Hadewijch wrote those inflamed words, a very different current of opinion had begun to make itself felt. It rapidly became influential, eventually to triumph and define the meaning of meals in new terms.

The initial principle was very simple: frugal asceticism led to religious fervour. Union with God implied that we had to distrust the pleasures of the table just as we had to learn to control the pleasures of the flesh. This rule, which has been passed on for hundreds of years, found its perfect expression much later in a manual for young seminarians published in 1823.[4] It has been analysed by Pascal Dibie

---

[4] Louis Tronson, *Manuel du séminariste ou Entretiens sur la manière de sanctifier ses principales actions*, Paris: Librairie Mequignon Junior.

(1999). The author, Abbé Tronson, warns against the dangers of food which he likens to 'a stormy sea full of reefs and precipices'. Eating is a base action; there is something animal about it, but it can also invite the devil into our lives. We should therefore not seek out 'exquisite foods, tasty morsels and delicate meats'. On the contrary, we should avoid 'big meals' and feasts, and rejoice at having 'the opportunity to deny ourselves'. Saint Louis is the real model for this asceticism. He in fact enjoyed good food but made an effort to eat very little. He ate the most ordinary foods, did without all the things he liked and often fasted. All this was far removed from the groaning tables of other royal courts.

Although it influenced the dietary practices of the religious congregations, the principle of asceticism and frugality was not the decisive factor. Profane meals were revolutionized for other reasons, and the revolution began very quietly. The ethics of asceticism in fact proved to have little effect on the subversive effects of the pleasures and delights of banquets. A frontal attack was impossible. Some began to think that it would be more effective to work on gestures that could be seen by all rather than on the subjective dimensions of emotions and thoughts. They concluded that a few behavioural rules should be established, and most of them were designed to prevent lapses into quasi-animal behaviour and to establish a modicum of self-control at mealtimes. In the twelfth century, Hugues de Saint-Victor outlined such a programme in his *De Institutione novitiorum*, which focuses mainly on the notion of *disciplina* and attempts to ensure the religious salvation of the soul. Discipline, which was applied to every aspect of behaviour, is 'a good and honest way of living in society' and implies 'the coordinated movement of all the limbs and the adoption of all the appropriate attitudes and actions' (cited in Schmitt 1990: 175). Most of the examples given have to do with table manners. Hugues de Saint-Victor is especially critical of those who 'rinse their fingers in the cup from which they are drinking', who 'wipe their hands on their clothes', who 'use their bare fingers as spoons to fish vegetables out of the soup', or who 'put pieces of half-eaten food, the cakes they have bitten into, what is stuck between their teeth or what they have dipped into their drinks, back on to the plate' (cited in Schmitt 1990: 197).

Many other treatises followed. The way the same advice is tirelessly repeated obviously shows that it was difficult to adapt behaviours to this discipline. The salvation of the soul could not in itself domesticate either the spontaneity of manners or the anarchy of pleasures. In 1530, Erasmus published his treatise *On the Civility of Children's Behaviour*. Although the practical advice was slow to change, something had changed: the key-notion was no longer *disciplina*, which was designed to structure an order. The goal was now good manners, or 'an ideal for of social behaviour' rather than 'an individual programme for salvation' (Schmitt 1990: 225). This behavioural ideal inspired a trend (a product of the will to distinction) rather than a new order. The dynamic of change was under way.

Fork to the left, knife to the right

What happened next is more familiar because it has been wonderfully described by Norbert Elias. By disciplining the body, the civilizing process leads to a self-control that lays the foundations for the emergence of modern subjectivity. Elias, who is especially interested in table manners, identifies three periods. The first (pre-fifteenth century), which has just been mentioned, is only evoked in passing. Order was the main preoccupation, and order was characterized by restraint and tinged with disgust at man's animal nature. The important thing was to do away with every indication that banquets had not completely replaced the sacrificial meals of old. Game, pork and beef, for example, were roasted on a spit and brought to the table whole. Carving them was one of the most noble and coveted tasks, and it was the preserve of the privileged. The carver had to know how to distribute the meat according to the social rank of the guests. The priest-butcher was not far away. Most of the instructions given (in very imperative ways) by the earliest treatises revolve around the idea of keeping food at a distance: eating with one's hands was ill-mannered (even though most people did so) and soup should not be drunk straight from the shared bowl. A text from the thirteenth century proclaims: 'You should not drink from the dish, but with a spoon as is proper. Those who stand up and snort disgustingly over the dishes like swine belong with other farmyard animals' (cited in Elias 2000 [1939]: 73. 'Do not put back on your plate what has been in your mouth' (cited in Elias 2000 [1939]: 76). 'Do not pick your teeth with your knife' (cited in Elias 2000 [1939]: 104). 'May refined people be preserved from those who gnaw their bones and put them back in the dish' (cited in Elias 2000 (1939]: 73). 'A man . . . who blows his nose on the tablecloth [is] ill-bred' (cited in Elias 2000 [1939]: 74). The tablecloth was used for other purposes, such as wiping greasy fingers. 'Do not spit over or on the table' (cited in Elias 2000 [1939]: 129). In retrospect, we can conclude that all this talk of 'disciplining bodies' really meant what it said.

Few people listened to this advice, and things were very slow to change during this first period. Elias concentrates on the second (which lasted from the sixteenth to the eighteenth century), when the trend accelerated and began to affect the whole of court society. Everything had changed. The goal was now not so much to establish an ethical order as to win social status thanks to a conspicuous display of good manners. The reason for this competitiveness was that the codes were constantly changing and becoming more and more detailed. A high level of competence was required on the part of anyone who wished to be admitted to society. It was ill-mannered to touch food with one's hands. Before long, it would be essential to know how to peel an apple or orange with a fork and knife, and without touching it. Conversely, using a knife to cut leaves of salad or a loaf of bread was strictly taboo. Salad had to be carefully folded, and bread has to be delicately broken with the fingertips.[5] The banqueting table had become a huge battlefield. What was at stake no longer had much to with the preoccupations of *disciplina*. As Elias demonstrates, the civilizing process had a huge impact on the formation of the state, the emergence of the modern individual, and so on. Even pleasures were of secondary importance: 'Civility recognizes neither likes nor dislikes' (Roche 1997: 256). The passion was now invested elsewhere: good manners were the key to upward social mobility. Meals appeared to have acquired a new meaning and that is quite in keeping with the way they were changing. They were in fact being instrumentalized by social conflicts that went far beyond mealtimes. The great period during which table manners were codified tells us nothing about actual meals.

A strange encounter

Norbert Elias simply mentions the third phase without going into too much detail, which is quite logical from his point of view. The social issues at stake in the definition of table manners are now much less clear. The civilizing process, which is now proceeding calmly, gradually begins to influence the lower classes but it remains within the

---

[5] Many of these rules are arbitrary, and it is precisely because they are arbitrary, and because the discordant rules are so cacophonous, that social distinction demands such sophisticated skills. The case of bread is different, for several reasons. The fact that country people used their own knives to cut bread was an example of how not to do things. At a deeper level still, there is also a reference to the Christian image of the last supper: one does not use a knife to cut the body of Christ.

framework of accepted norms. It appears to become lost in increasingly punctilious details and to accommodate itself to bourgeois comfort as the number of people sitting around the table decreases. Good manners now seem to exist for their own sake and to have become a sort of framework with no content. They are reproduced but do not change. And yet this framework without content plays a decisive role because the attempt to achieve social distinction which characterized fashionable dining for centuries has, paradoxically and unintentionally, produced a tightly regulated order. It was a *habitus* based upon good manners and restraint and was influenced by a bourgeois culture that required us to eat 'with all due form' (Bourdieu 1984 [1979]: 196).

Manners are a social form that, like other forms, has a strange ability to live on through the ages independently of its content. There is a striking contrast between the precise definitions of the gestural codes, which gradually stabilize, and the social landscape within which they evolve. During the second phase of the civilizing process, it was a weapon to be used in the social struggle that was being waged against the public and spectacular world of meals at court. During the third phase, it quietly goes on in domestic interiors and is far removed from the old conflicts. A form inherited from a flamboyant past could now acquire a new content. And it would no doubt have quietly disappeared, had not the accidents of history caused it to interact with another social process.

At the same point in the nineteenth century, there was a great intellectual turmoil in what appeared to be a very different domain. The emergence of urban modernity was beginning to completely undermine the social bond which was becoming divorced from the hierarchies characteristic of the old world. The fathers of the newly emergent discipline of sociology were all concerned with this problem. Comte, Le Play, Tocqueville and then Durkheim attempted to analyse a 'deep crisis that was gnawing away at a society that had been destabilized' (Cicchelli-Pugeault and Cicchelli 1998: 5). The question that preoccupied them was as follows: 'How can the social order be preserved in a context of changes that were so rapid as to alarm contemporaries?' (Cicchelli-Pugeault and Cicchelli 1998: 6). The whole of active society (politicians, hygienists and other social engineers, and philanthropists) gave the same answer: by redefining and consolidating the family. Whilst opinions as methods and goals differed, a broad consensus agreed that the family was the basis for a disciplined socialization. It was as though, given that socialization was a failure at the highest levels of society, we had to fall back on intermediate structures. And as though the most 'natural' of those structures, namely the family, provided a solid basis on which to reconstruct socialization. The nineteenth century abounded in discourses that idealized the family. The fight for family values was won without difficulty, but order had yet to be restored. That proved to be difficult in the nineteenth century, especially in working-class milieus suffering the effects of uncontrolled industrialization. Finding a way to construct the social order was a matter of urgency.

History is sometimes the product of strange encounters that allow what should have been no more than minor details to play a vital role. Table manners are one example, as they intersected with a new attempt to promote family values that had mobilized the whole of society. The gestural order was still tentative and formal, but that was precisely why it was the ideal instrument: it was based upon the most concrete gestures and objects, and was concerned solely with regulation. The modern project of using meals to structure the family was about to begin.

The rigid family

The bourgeois society of the nineteenth century obviously did not invent the family meal. The whole family had gathered around the table at meal times in earlier centuries, in all milieus and in both town and countryside. What was new was that the shared meal now escaped the category of day to day practices of which there is nothing to be said and for which there is no model, and was explicitly given a central role in the domestic sphere and in the workings of the family. It became emblematic of the family as pivot of the social order (Marenco 1992: 113).

Table manners crystallized a real 'model for manners', as Claudine Marenco so nicely puts it. They were at once punctilious because they were so strictly defined, and they foreshadowed a broader pedagogy that implied a complete ethics.

The unavoidable starting point was the disciplining of bodies. Discipline was the starting point for everything: behavioural rhythms, postures and codes had to be learned. Mealtimes were respected to the minute. Everyone gathered around the dining table and sat on their chairs without moving. Where they sat was not left to chance. Departing from the custom of medieval banquets, people sat facing one another, though that did not mean that families were deep in conversation. Children had to ask for permission before speaking. Good behaviour and restraint were de rigueur at all times, and especially when it came to expressions of pleasure. The goal was primarily normative and organizational: social pressures meant that meals were a way of institutionalizing the family and establishing order.

As I have said, the use of table manners to structure the group went hand in hand with a rampant celebration of family values which centred on the idea of genteel domesticity (seen as an antidote to popular violence). This campaign to influence public opinion inevitably influenced bourgeois families themselves. The inculcation of certain gestures, which remained as rigid as ever, was therefore part of a broader moralizing problematic. According to a text published in 1916, the 'happiness of the family' depended upon good table manners which 'guaranteed the morality of the family'.[6] The appropriate method consisted in creating 'a gentle, calming moral atmosphere; disputes and even over-lively discussions should be avoided', according to a treatise from 1914 (cited in Marenco 1992: 111). The model therefore propagated not just an order but also an atmosphere, and it was more than a moral atmosphere. If it is restricted to ethical principles, 'gentility' is nothing more than a word; if it is to be truly meaningful, it has to strike an emotional chord. Order, ethics and gentle affection: it seemed that these different strata could be superimposed quite unproblematically, rather as though the model naturally enriched its content.

Towards a new communion?

At this point in history – the first half of the twentieth century – the situation suggested that, after so many changes of direction, meals had at last found their true meaning and that it would remain the same for a long time to come. The model appeared to be coherent, and it would be implemented by one central actress. The mistress of the house who gathered 'her family around the table at set times' was 'the best agent of happiness'. The new religion was based upon respect for rituals. 'Within bourgeois space, repetition does not mean routine. It ritualizes, and rites reinforce trends.' The mistress of the house both 'controls the rhythm of private time, regulates it and turns it into a performance' (Martin-Fugier 1987, p. 194) She was all the more concerned about these rituals in that she did not do the cooking

---

[6] Marguerite de Saint-Genes, *Traité de savoir-vivre*, Maison de la Bonne Presse, cited in Marenco 1992: 112.

herself; the way meals were organized was all-important. And for some women, the introduction of a gentle affection softened the cold rigidity.

Once it was well established in bourgeois homes, the model was adapted for use in more modest milieus and became a reference point for a broad trend in domestic education. The role of the working-class 'mistress of the house' was expanded to include the role of cook. It took a while for the theories taught by the handbooks to become a reality. This was primarily for material reasons. It was, for instance, only in the nineteenth century that the use of plates became common-place in the countryside (Roche 1997). The soup was poor, and eaten without ceremony. 'In modern times, both peasants and townspeople spent as little time as possible inside their homes, which were often cold, dark and uncomfortable' (Muchembled 1988: 205). Even at the beginning of the twentieth century, men still preferred to linger in the convivial warmth of their taverns. The wives who propagated the new model (and who were therefore referred to as *la bourgeoise* by their husbands) therefore had to drag them out of the taverns and lure them to the family table by cooking something tasty. The trend towards domestic acculturation reached its apotheosis in the 1950s. Improved living conditions and better domestic appliances then allowed meals to become the architect of richer and orderly family relations in all social strata. The function of meals had never been so clear, obvious and consensual since the long-gone era of sacrificial meals.

In ancient times, the purpose of meals was to commune with the gods. Although they had been plunged into confusion by so many events, they now centred, for a second time, on a strong meaning and a new form of communion based upon family fervour. The paradox was that this outcome was the result of a certain emotional cooling. Structuring the desired order meant distancing ourselves from both people and food. But once its basis had been established, bourgeois morality could add a (moderate) dose of affect, and thus establish the preconditions for a more intense communion.

Part II of this book will look in detail at how that happened. As we shall see, a more relaxed order helped to promote the expression of sensuality, a quest for pleasure and more relaxed conversations. In a word, all the ingredients were therefore conducive to a real group communion, which was in keeping with the contemporary expecta-tions of the relational and affective family (Singly 1996). But we will also see the de-structuring power of the individual-consumer model examined in chapter 1. That model demonstrates that the stabilization

71

was illusory, or no more than a provisional moment of tranquillity. The tumultuous history of meals goes on and alternates between a quest for a more intense communion and a purely defensive function in which meals are 'the last bulwark against the break up of the family' (Marenco 1992: 197).

Part II

'Food's Ready!'

— 3 —

MEALS MAKE A FAMILY

When a loud 'Food's ready!' rings through the house, everyone knows that their personal rhythms are about to be interrupted by family time and that they are about to board 'the frail skiff known as the harmony of a meal' (Muxel 1996: 66). Eating together as a family is no small matter and no one emerges unscathed because 'whole personalities are constructed as we eat' (Rivière 1995: 191). Everyone is part of a 'network of very different values' (Pezeu-Massabuau 1983) and we are the social products of the collective order in which we are inscribed. These networks also help to produce our domestic reality precisely because we are inscribed within that order. Meals, which are warm moments and nourishing gatherings, also institutionalize the family group by structuring the way people and things are arranged (Douglas 1972). Meals are the 'architects of family life' (Sjögren 1986: 54): day after day, they tell everyone what their place is and what their role is. 'In a sense, meals shape the life of a family' (Muxel 1996: 64).

That was especially obvious when table manners imposed a specific discipline that was both strict and regular. Many traces of that discipline still survive. Although families try to relax the rules, it is in fact impossible to socialize without some minimal constraints, which implies that we have to reproduce many of the conventions we learned in the nineteenth century. Which rules should we retain and which rules should we abolish? That is one of the questions that everyone, or almost everyone, is faced with. The few families that function on a traditional basis do not need to raise this question because they cling to the old disciplines. Like the last of the Mohicans, they are representatives of an endangered species. Whilst they are not representative of the new developments we will be looking at, they are still

75

of interest and worth looking at because they indirectly tell us about the mutations that are taking place.

Pure discipline

Karim Gacem's detailed survey of the Lacroix family provides a good example. On the basis of a rapid description, it might be said that the Lacroix family is 'Catholic'. The religious dimension is very important to them in intellectual terms, even though they rarely go to mass these days. They are a perfect illustration of the partial secularization of meals, and they attempt to cling to their faith in minimalist fashion through the daily repetition of ordinary rituals with a symbolic import. As Martine, who is the mother, explains, this is especially true of mealtimes. 'I attach great importance to meals because a meal is the Last Supper with Jesus Christ. Meals have a huge importance throughout the Bible' (cited in Gacem 1997: 14). Meals are sacred. Prayers are a thing of the past, and the family no longer respects the custom of eating fish on Fridays and has fallen back on a deification of the family order itself. This is order for the sake of order, and the tiniest details have to be respected. The system is not really based on civility but the rules are certainly respected: 'Serve the girls first, don't start until everyone has been served and mother has sat down. No singing at table. Finish your plate. Eat nicely and discreetly. Fold your napkin on your lap. Ask permission before leaving the table, and so on' (Gacem 1997: 15). It is, however, because the smallest details never change that the family's meals have their structural effect. Napkin rings, for example, 'must not be placed any old where. You always place them to the left of your glass' (Rodolphe, who is (in his modest way) the family rebel; cited in Gacem 1997: 15). Violette, who is one of the girls, can describe where everything goes so readily that it is obvious that she has internalized the whole system:

'Everything has its proper place on the table. The big table mat goes in the centre, and the small ones we use for the water jugs go on either side of it. The salt and pepper go to the left on the small table mat, with the big serving plates in the middle and the plate for the bread on the right. The cheese dish goes to the left on the side where no one sits, the fruit bowl on the right or in the middle, along with the coffee cups. When you pick something up, you have to put it back where it was, or you'll be told off, but if my father picks something up we put it back to set him an example.' (Cited in Gacem 1997: 15)

76

The mother, who organizes every moment of the meal, hides behind the somewhat enigmatic figure of a father who says nothing but who is a stickler for discipline. Obviously out of step with the times in which he lives and undermined by a society that no longer supplies the values that once structured his subjectivity, he has retreated into a silent world of his own but clings to table manners as though they were a guard rail and uncompromisingly insists that everyone behaves properly. So much so that his children sometimes dread mealtimes. They cannot, on the other hand, imagine any other way of doing things and are as good as their parents at reproducing the system. Elisabeth is horrified when her father takes the liberty of breaking a rule, but says nothing. Violette has completely internalized this life discipline which she regards as perfectly normal. 'I'm a great stickler for the rules. I'm perfectly happy to accept the rules my parents have laid down because having a normal meal means a lot to me' (cited in Gacem 1997: 16). Even Rodolphe, who is regarded as something of a rebel, accepts the rules: 'Well, yes, it looks like an imposition to begin with, but it's part of our life now.' He cannot imagine a family living any other way: 'I obviously want things to be like that with my own children, the way it is at home on a good day. I want us all to eat together, and to respect each other.'

On a good day . . . because there are also some very bad days (lots of them). Mealtimes are rarely pleasant. The atmosphere is frosty, and no one says a word. Being at close quarters is not easy, and makes for difficult relations, particularly between father and children. Elisabeth admits: 'I try to avoid looking at him, because he can't stand being looked at. So when I'm at the table, I try to look at him no more than I look at the others, and when I think I can't do, it makes my flesh creep' (cited in Gacem 1997: 17). Although every gesture is controlled, the shared intimacy can be embarrassing. 'I find it very hard when he passes the food because it means being in really close contact, and I don't like it when our hands touch, so even taking the plate he is passing me makes me feel uncomfortable. So I make sure I wait until he's set it down on the table' (cited in Gacem 1997: 26). It would be a mistake to interpret these episodes in the life of the Lacroix family as an indication that they have succeeded in going back in time, or that they exemplify what the 'table manners' model was in its heyday. Even though the older children are served water in the sort of metal goblets that are used for communion, the Lacroix are thoroughly modern. And it is precisely because their attempts to express their feelings and to relate to one another (which are a sign of modernity) are frustrated by the rigidity of their system that mealtimes are so intolerable. 'Clinging to the form of the meal unites the group and preserves its family image, but does not allow it to experience the sort of cohesion that comes from emotional closeness and sharing happy moments' (Gacem 1997: 29). They express their emotions in outbursts of anger and a refusal to conform rather than in a tender closeness.

And the irritation can sometimes lead to shouting and tears, and to doors being slammed. 'Things like table mats sometimes get flung across the room, and plates or glasses sometimes get broken' (Gacem 1997: 29). According to Jean-Paul Aron (1975 [1973]: 214), 'The dining room is a theatre wherein the kitchen serves as the wings and the table as the stage.' In the Lacroix household, the plays have both the pathos of a Greek tragedy and the sparkle of a light comedy.

> 'Walking away from the table in anger during a meal really does mean that things are getting out of hand. It means things will be very tense for the rest of the evening and the next day. Things settle down at the start of the week, and we forget about it as everything gets back to normal. And we pretend a bit, and make an effort.' (Violette, cited in Gacem 1997: 57)

Unfortunately, the tension builds up until the explosion everyone was secretly dreading occurs: Saturday night. 'Saturday nights really are the worst. You hold your breath and your heart is pounding when we have to sit down to eat' (Gacem 1997: 56).

Discipline in pieces

Whilst the example of the Lacroix family is scarcely typical, it does show that paternal authority is crucial if the disciplinary model is to be maintained. The very presence of a 'traditional' father imposes a certain rigidity. Sophie, who is 28, explains that everything is more relaxed and even playful when her father is not there. 'My father was never there for lunch. We could chat and mess around over lunch. Evenings were reserved for the news. There was no talking; my father was listening to the news' (cited in Garabuau-Moussaoui 2002a: 89). As a rule, and as in the Lacroix family, it is the mother who actually organizes things and who holds the system together by taking care of all the details. She will be even more intent on reproducing the system when the father expresses himself in purely abstract terms. This is especially true when table manners are used as a way of educating the children. Prune cannot stop herself from taking a harsh line: 'We must not lose these traditions.' Meal times are strictly adhered to and everyone's posture has to be perfect. 'It's the only time when we're all together, and when we all sit still. If your plate isn't empty, you can't leave the table, so you stay where you are.' We have already learned something about Prune and her liking for 'natural' sausages. When it comes to food, she really would like to turn back the clock. When asked to describe her dream kitchen, she said that she did not need any modern appliances, but would like to have a big kitchen garden, with rabbits and chickens, so that they would be able to eat nothing but fresh produce. When it comes to meals, however, she is less of a traditionalist. She certainly rules her family (including her husband) with a rod of iron. But the discipline has a purpose and is designed to create a family occasion that allows her to talk to her two young children. 'Meals are very, very important in this household. There's no question of this one or that one eating as they please. We are a family, and mealtimes are when we talk to each other.' Her husband would like to watch television from time to time. 'No! I won't have it! I'll switch it off. I'm getting angry now!' Mealtimes are for family conversations. Prune is 33. She dreams of having a thoroughly modern family in which everyone talks to everyone else. The very strict discipline she demands at mealtimes is in fact no more than a means to that end: an element of constraint designed to promote the easygoing relationships she would like to enjoy. In defensive terms, it is a way of preventing the bond breaking down still further (and she is probably trying to do both things at once). 'If there isn't a moment in the day when we can all get together, we'll never see each other, and that would be the end of everything.'

The discipline of old often survives only in the form of isolated fragments that still survive in a relational world that has become more relaxed. Families try to cling to some point of reference or other (mealtimes, mealtime conventions, where various objects go on the table, dietary choices) but they are always open to negotiation. Take the example of Hortense. She brought up her children to be on their best behaviour at mealtimes: 'Leaving the table before the meal was over was out of the question!' She is very disappointed when she goes to see her daughter, who now has children of her own. The children do just as they please and, horror of horrors, make their own TV dinners of Coke and crisps. Although she does not dare to say that she disapproves, the silent message has got through. When she is invited to her mother's, her daughter is very strict with her children. 'When we're at Nana's, we behave ourselves!' They obey without too many protests, rather as though they were acting out a part. They presumably think that they have gone back in time when they are at Nana's.

A domestic revolt

The Lacroix family have (with some difficulty) succeeded in maintaining an overall disciplinary framework, and not just fragments of it. To that extent, they are the exception to the rule. And yet, even here, some things are changing. There are hints that their lives are gradually changing. It all started with Mathilde, who had suddenly had enough of being the mother who gave her all and got nothing but abuse in return. She wanted a little more freedom – just a little – and to have a life of her own: 'When you give a lot, there comes a point where you feel you have nothing left to give. Your self-image is very poor, and that's not nice. When I feel completely lost, I try to stop.' In an attempt to find a life outside the home, she has become involved in various kinds of charity work. After all the dreadful Saturday nights and having spent so much time making Sunday lunches, she has actually gone on strike (though she does not actually use the word) on Sunday evenings. 'One day, I thought to myself, "I've had enough of this." All week long, it's always me . . . so now I have my Sunday evenings to myself' (cited in Gacem 1997: 31). The father did not dare to object and acted like a traitor inside the gate. So everyone manages as best they can. They can help themselves to whatever is in the fridge. 'It's not a proper meal. Just a snack.' Although he has no option but to accept the new arrangement, he is actually enjoying this difficult patch, but says nothing to Mathilde.

> 'Well, I'm not sure. Let me put it this way. There are rules in this family, but not on Sunday night. I'm not convinced I would like it if it was like this every day, but I think it does everyone good. It means we can take our time on Sundays. Everyone feels a bit more relaxed, a bit less . . . It's a breath of fresh air.' (Cited in Gacem 1997: 31)

Their new-found freedom comes as a surprise, as it opens up a whole new world of relationships that is very different from that of the disciplined meals of old. In a putsch that no one really planned, the children have taken over and turned the world upside down in the carnival spirit. Violette describes what has changed:

> 'For us, Sunday night is like playtime. We might not spend long on the meal, but we get to have a laugh for half an hour. We just act silly, and when we think about it afterwards, we say to ourselves that it's stupid, carrying on like that. But it's just between us, brothers and sisters. And in fact it makes other mealtimes more relaxed.' (Cited in Gacem 1997: 34).

Rodolphe backs her up: 'We have a good laugh, we laugh in our parents' faces, and that's all there is to it. It's a real moment of complicity, and we like it, all four of us' (cited in Gacem 1997: 37). Their parents are in fact just a few feet away, relaxing on the sofa, watching television and eating nibbles over a drink. Or, according to the children – who are probably trying to stir things – several drinks. 'My parents really knock it back on the sofa,' jokes Rodolphe. The set of silver goblets that usually contain just water are used for a very different purpose on Sunday evenings. The most fascinating thing about all this is that, whatever the father might think, this breath of fresh air is not in fact anarchic. The interaction between the two groups is governed by strict rules. They may be new, but they are precise and strictly defined. In the beginning, all the food had to be cold. And then reforms were introduced, and hot meals became the order of the day (so long as it was not Mathilde who made them). What started as a confused rebellion was obviously going to become a counter-model that would not go away. It has given rise to a new discipline, and that is changing the way they act, think and feel. From Saturday to Sunday night, the Lacroix use meals to construct two very different lives.

Women are not what they used to be

Mathilde's rebellion is in tune with the times, and so are its effects. The changes in dietary behaviours that we are now experiencing are largely the effect of changes in the social position of women (and the rise of individual autonomy). Women are no longer willing to accept a role that means they do not exist in their own right and that reduces their existential horizon to the four walls of the kitchen. But once again, the influence of a past that associated women with nutrition still makes itself felt.

The long story that began in the earliest stages of the late Paleolithic era, when the imaginary was dominated by the primordial mythical figure of the earth mother who was both fertile and catered for everyone's needs, was still alive and well when agriculture began (Bucher 1998). 'A woman was a breast. The breast was the embodiment of the nourishing, bodily essence of woman' (Perrot 2000b: 109). Although this powerful image had a profound historical influence, it must not lead us to hasty or simplistic conclusions. Just as the history of meals is not just a sequence of new beginnings, the association between women and food is not part of a linear history. Women were certainly almost always associated with food in their little domestic worlds or, on a broader scale, in village communities (the woman who presided over the cooking pots and who radiated relational and gastronomic warmth) (Verdier 1979). But women were, as we have seen, rarely the heroines of the culinary and commensal epic. Very few of the taboo-breakers and priest-butchers who helped to prepare the great banquets were women. Coming closer to home, and as we have already seen, women played a major role in establishing the bourgeois model for 'good manners'. Their role as the enforcers of discipline (and sometimes as the creators of a gentle domesticity) was much more important than their nourishing function. At a time when the whole of society was being mobilized to create a female identity that was essentially defined by women's maternal role, the virtues of the earth mother became less obvious. Ideally, women were expected to 'shut themselves away in their little homes, to be servants to their children and husbands, and to be housewives in the new sense of the word. Their domestic roles became more restricted, and tended to be concentrated on or to merge with their roles as mothers' (Knibielher and Fouquet 1982: 249). But not with their role as providers, which did not figure in the discussion. That was quite simply because the bourgeois model did not acknowledge the existence of gloomy kitchens; what went on below stairs was a matter for the servants. Behavioural models do not always percolate down from the top of the social hierarchy, and the earth-mother function is a case in point as it played no part in the bourgeois meal that was becoming the dominant model. In terms of food, the influence therefore came from the working-class milieus in which women did play that role, and were fully identified with that function. Olivier Schwartz has demonstrated (1990: 252) why they played such a decisive role: because they were so closely identified with food, working-class mothers became the centre of a protective microcosm in which they both 'fed on a full system' and fed others.

The situation was as follows: on the one hand, a (bourgeois) model that had forgotten all about kitchens and, on the other, a (popular) desire to nourish others that could not really find the material conditions for its expression. It took a long time for the nourishment function to become fully associated with table manners. When it was, the maternal implications of culinary activities became more pronounced. A descriptive analysis of the kitchen's place in the home (which is a good indicator of the activities that went on there) allows us to conclude that, for most of the population, that mutation did not come about until the 1950s (Collignon and Staszak 2004). Kitchens changed more in the first half of the twentieth century than they had done in the previous three hundred years. The change occurred in the 1950s, or shortly before take-off of the revolution in women's emancipation that destroyed the exclusive link between women and the domestic world. No sooner had women become the centre of the new model than they began to want to escape from it. In the past, women had of course long been associated with keeping an eye on the pans that slowly simmered by the hearth; and, closer to home, they were so closely associated with that role that the word *cuisinière* was applied to both the woman who cooked and the kitchen range where the cooking was done (Vanhoutte 1982). The association with pots and pans was not, however, enough to create the 'woman-as-cook' function in all its mythical dimensions. The nostalgic images that idealize the past overlook the fact that things were not so clear-cut and that women found themselves at the point where two contradictory trends intersected. Culinary activity was, in historical terms, becoming more important (and would eventually lead to the modern passion for cooking) but women were escaping from the kitchen. Or at least trying to escape.

There are still a lot of women who appear to have scarcely emerged from this mythologized past, and who are still fully identified with the role of the devoted cook. Mrs Thomson (as described by her husband)[1] is, like the Lacroix, an exception who is slightly out of step with the times. Mr Thomson describes her as everything he would have liked his first wife to be. She understands him and all his eccentricities. She is a real housewife. The house is always neat and tidy. There is always food in the fridge and something to drink: a bottle of cider or beer, whisky . . . there is always a drink in the house . . . his meals are always ready on time . . . she concocts tasty little dishes for him because she enjoys it. She always does the washing up straight away, and refuses to let him help (Burgoyne and Clarke 1983). Most women are more like Prune, and want to achieve the impossible but reject the hierarchical way roles are defined in the Thomson family. She dreams of having a warm family and her attempts to create one are sustained by the childhood images that keep coming back to her. 'I can remember huge family meals. Everyone joking and talking. Making a *pot au feu* [boiled beef with vegetables] brings it all back.' That is her obsession: trying to recapture 'it' by making stews and tasty meals. She does not

---

[1] This information is drawn from a survey carried out in England in 1981. It would now be much more difficult to find a similar case. It would also be difficult to find a man who would calmly describe his wife in these terms.

spare herself and moves the culinary equivalent of mountains, but the results never quite live up to her expectations. Hence the outburst of anger when her husband wants to turn the television on. And hence her ideological rejection of modernity and idealization of the good old days, which fits in with her enchanting memories. 'I'm not really in favour of modernity when it comes to cooking. I don't even own a pressure cooker. I use an old cast iron casserole. It's a pain in the arse, but too bad. It suits me.' She never finds cooking a pain at all.

Feeding the family and slimming at the same time

Prune is too uncompromising (and too obsessed with the past) to be really typical. The current situation is complex because, although there is a growing passion for cooking, we devote less and less time to it. Women no longer want to be confined to the kitchen. They have their own lives to lead as autonomous individuals within the public sphere. Cooking is now just one of a wide range of activities. Thanks to the mechanization of the home and the development of new products such as 'ready meals',[2] they have been liberated from the domestic tasks that used to take up so much of their time. In less than fifty years, the amount of time spent on cooking meals has fallen considerably and is now down to less than twenty minutes a day in more than half of all households (Guilbert and Perrin-Escalon 2004; Vanhoutte 1982). Suzette used to be very familiar with the feeling of duty that made her do everything without even thinking about it: 'That's the way I was brought up. My mother had her principles, and we were brought up to please other people. You make an effort. It's all to do with the way you were brought up.' When she looks back, she does not recognize her old self, even though she can understand her. And she is now looking for new ways to go on being the cook. Maïté (who also says that she used to be a dutiful housewife) has no such scruples; she has almost stopped cooking altogether: 'I've had enough of being the cook. You make a meal, they turn up and they've already been to McDonalds. I made you a meal . . . and you didn't even touch it. No, I now take the view . . . they can all fend for themselves.' The household now lives on ham sandwiches. How can anyone strike a balance between the loss of any sense of identity that comes from being the only cook and the extreme modernity of

---

[2] As we shall see in Part III, this is a more important factor than the sexual division of labour: men still do little of the cooking.

84

the fridge-sandwich system? Before we go into more detail in Part III, we can make three brief points here. First, it is possible to provide different types of meals (individualized snacks, quick meals, cooking for someone we love, family love-feasts) involving different levels of commitment and time. It is also possible to develop new and quicker ways of doing things, whilst still adding a personal touch. 'If I have no time, I do something quick, but the way I like it. I have my own way of doing things.' Marjolaine is proud of her ability to improvise something at the last moment: 'I'm not very organized. That's one of my failings. But it's also one of my strengths. I do things on the spur of the moment, and I don't make a mountain out of a molehill if things don't turn out the way I expected.' She is always juggling with two contradictory injunctions: something quick, something good. Why does it have to be good? Not out of a sense of duty, as it used to be in the past, but because she is cooking for love. Successful meals are a way of promoting family values. 'I'm not prepared to be their slave, but I do like to do things properly. I'm all for more status for women, but eating as a family means a lot to me.' To that extent, she is a perfect illustration of contemporary family life, with all its contra-dictions and its difficult juggling acts. 'It's something I need to do. If I don't put a lot of effort into it, I have the impression that I'm doing nothing for the rest of the family. I know I'm wrong, so I try to strike a balance.' The strange thing is that things become difficult when she feels that she is giving too much of herself. That is when things begin to get on top of her. 'It's always when I'm peeling potatoes that it all gets too much for me. I say to myself: "Careful! You're creating problems for yourself again!"'

The new emphasis on quick meals is a further manifestation of the existentialist lightness we described earlier. For women, who were, historically, overburdened by the weight of their domestic tasks, this has been a revolutionary breakthrough. As we said earlier when we were discussing the individual consumer, this relationship with the world can lead to a very different kind of lightness. This lightness is physical and it is largely a side effect of the new ideal that requires women to be slim. In the world of food preparation, the combination of the two leads to another contradiction, and it is very difficult to resolve. How can a woman succeed in feeding the family she loves without eating too much herself? This is a conflict between two iden-tities. On one level, she is the earth mother who has the responsibility for creating a family home that is warm and welcoming; on another level, she is an individual woman who is autonomous and reflexive, who is in control of her diet and who looks after herself (Charles and

Kerr 1988). It is not easy to reconcile these two identities. The gap is, of course, not altogether new. The contrasting male–female roles produced by history (the hard-working male breadwinner was entitled to the best food and the most copious helpings) introduced women to the habit of eating snacks centuries ago (Perrot 2000b), but they still fed their families. What is new is that they now have to reconcile two different identities. They are so contradictory that every domestic decision implies an existential choice. We are now in a better position to understand Marjolaine's attempts to strike a delicate balance. She is not afraid of doing too much in terms of housework. What she is really afraid of is that she will commit her life and personality to something that does not appear to be in her best interest. The stakes are higher than the apparent banality of the domestic context might suggest. Hence the many ingenious tactics that are used in the attempt to resolve the contradiction in one way or another. Maïté opts for the radical solution we are beginning to know so well. It helps that, in her case, the sense of duty was not associated with any real sense of pleasure derived from either cooking or eating. It was therefore much easier for her to drop the commitment to cooking. Amandine, in contrast, would happily define herself as a woman with a passion for cooking who wants to create a sociable atmosphere at mealtimes. She would like to have a dream kitchen and to make magical meals. Unfortunately, her family (and especially her two boys) are not prepared to sign up to her dream scenario. She makes up for that by cooking meals for friends. Biscotte, finally, has come up with a very common strategy: she makes meals but does not eat a lot of them herself. She hates rabbit, but the rest of the family loved it (when they ate together on a regular basis). So rabbit was often on the menu and everyone tucked in while Biscotte picked at the vegetables that came with it. Given that she hated rabbit, no one had any reason to complain. Doing without did not stop her from enjoying feeding other people. 'I like it when they have second helpings, even though I can't', says Marie (cited in Duret 2005: 53), who is a keen bodybuilder. 'I love cooking, I love making them something nice to eat.'

Different stages

Women have not deserted their kitchens en masse. Given that the division of labour is slow to change (though rather more progress is being made in the kitchen than in the domains of doing the laundry or the housework), they have found ways to prepare meals more quickly and to find some quality time for themselves. This is especially true at weekends when they can give free rein to their wish to create a family through an altruistic act of self-sacrifice. They do so because they enjoy it and because their families like it. This development has been greatly encouraged by the upheavals brought about by the rise of dietary individualism, both at home and outside the home. Some meals, and especially lunch, are eaten away from home. Others, like breakfast, are a matter for the individuals concerned. The maternal presence in the kitchen has become less pronounced. Individual family members come and go, and use the kitchen primarily as a larder (Corbeau 1992; Diasio 2002). The emergence of the fridge as a central organizing principle is part of a trend that has nothing to do with women's reluctance to cook.

Meals are now acted out on different stages. The old sense of order has given way to mobility and uncertainties. The process begins at a very material level: the number of tables in the home has risen. In most households, the kitchen table is still the most important, even when the room is no more than a few metres square. Over the last fifty years, interior designers who have rather too much trust in the triumph of scientific reason have tried to make surfaces smaller and to drive meals out of the kitchen in the name of an 'American' modernity of a 'laboratory' space that is dedicated solely to the work of cooking. Families have squeezed up, but continue to resist so long as there is some kind of table there (Léger 1990). Fashionable interior designers have now come up with the trendy idea of the convivial kitchen but the trend is quietly resisted in council houses and suburban homes, and tables refuse to go away. The kitchen table is important because it lends itself to all sorts of purposes. It can be a work table, or a table for improvised snacks, more substantial individual meals or proper family meals. It can be used for conversations over a drink or a coffee, or even without a drink. We do not have to adopt any particular physical posture (we can sit for a long time, perch on the edge of a chair or remain standing up). The fridge is to hand, and individual sequences can overlap with family sequences. In some cases, the kitchen is so small that the table has to be used for everything. But for most of the time it serves a specific function. It is the guardian of memory and a symbol of what remains of the disciplinary order of table manners and of the time when everyone had to sit up straight. Its formality marks a break with ordinary life. Its rigidity has all the dated charms of a solemn grandeur. It also has its disadvantages; it is tiring to sit at the table for any length of time and we now tend to prefer more relaxed postures. The lounge no longer serves its official purpose, and has become the setting for informal meals that have neither the chilly formality of a proper dining table nor the banality of everyday meals. Some families try to introduce more variety into their lives by adopting a more playful attitude. On fine days, a fourth table is added for similar reasons; it might be in the garden, on the veranda or the balcony, or by the barbecue. There are many other varieties of table, some more discrete, more individualized. There are TV dinners (which may or may not be eaten in front of the television) that are eaten at a sort of tiny table that is both portable and personalized. Plates are even more portable. Plates and trays can be put on beds. Snacks can be eaten anywhere. The whole house has become a flexible environment for meals that can be improvised in all sorts of ways.

The increase in the number of tables is simply the most visible aspect of the even greater increase in the number of modes of dietary sociability. Practices are becoming more individualized but we also want to enjoy the experience of being part of a group. Freedom coexists alongside discipline. We celebrate important occasions but for the most part we lead a routine existence. The amount of time spent on meals varies enormously. We spend a long time making special meals but we also rely upon the fridge system, and so on. We eat in lots of different places. Ways of preparing meals and ways of eating together vary enormously. We constantly reconcile all these things and alter our arrangements accordingly (Gacem 2001). The availability of new ready-made products and meals that require little preparation has had a major influence on this diversification of modes of action, as has the availability of new services (institutional catering, home deliveries).

Fast food (and especially the McDonald's brand, which has become the emblem of junk food) is a response to a growing demand stimulated by the individualization of practices, but it also allows us to be flexible about how we eat. Parents, for instance, often use fast food restaurants as a way of promoting a different kind of family interaction with their children. Detailed studies (Badot 2002) show that all the bustle and background noise mean that the content of their conversations is poor. That, however, is not the important point; for a short while, certain codes are inverted, and both parents and children enter a regressive, child-centred world (Gacem 1999; Singly 2000).

A child-centred world

There is still a close link between what goes on outside the home and the ways in which families are constructed: even the most individualized practices tell us something about the family, especially when we make domestic use of the service industries. François de Singly (2000) and Julie Janet Chauffier cite the very interesting example of Sophie, who is the mother of three young children. Her husband's work commitments mean that the whole family can eat together only twice a week. Sophie does not take advantage of this situation to cook proper meals for her children. She does not really have the time to do so and, what is more important, does not want to. And when she does make an effort, no one is very keen on the results. So she has found a solution. 'For Sunday lunch, we have McDonald's at home.' They eat at home rather than going out because it is easier to talk to each other at home. McDonald's is Sophie's 'treat' (not that McDonald's is usually described in those terms). 'McDonald's is my treat because I don't have to do anything. And not having to do anything at the weekend is much nicer than spending the whole morning making a *pot au feu*.' She does not have a guilty conscience because her children, and even her husband, love McDonald's. 'So I enjoy not having to do anything, and I know they'll eat well because that's what they like' (cited in Singly 2000: 122).

As we shall see in Part III, burgers from McDonald's have not in fact replaced *pot au feu*, and Sophie's dietary choices are representative of only an extreme minority tendency. But leaving aside dietary and culinary issues, she is the perfect symbol of the way we are trying to find new ways of eating. Three central issues emerge: the child-centred family, new forms of ritual and, most important of all, family conversations.

In only a few decades the role of children at mealtimes has undergone a spectacular change if we compare it with the disciplinary model of old. They obviously used to have 'a subaltern status' and were not considered to have 'either the same needs or the same rights as adults' (Marenco 1992: 222). They were given less sophisticated food and smaller portions and were forbidden to talk at the table unless they were specifically invited to do so. They were small, and they were therefore second-class citizens. And they were presumably more affected than adults by the rigidity that was demanded of everyone. Suzette now regrets having been so harsh on her children and she remembers the constant floods of tears which she now interprets very differently. Trapped in her role and by her principles, she could not understand why they cried: 'I stupidly expected them not to leave the table before they had finished eating. I was being ridiculous, because there are some things you can't expect children to like at that age.' All that has changed and everything now centres on the child (Fischler

1996). This does not mean that children rule the roost in every aspect of family life but it does mean that they are learning to become autonomous (Queiroz 2004; Singly 2004a). It is, however, undeniable that mealtime conversations now centre on the child. Their parents encourage them to express themselves by asking them questions (children, on the other hand, are not very keen to answer them, especially when, as happens so often, their performance at school has not lived up to expectations).This may lead the group to relax its discipline even further, or even to revert to regressive modes of dietary behaviour. Children have inverted the old pattern and are less influenced by their parents' example. They now dictate much of what the family eats because they understand adverts and are manipulated by brands (Heilbrunn 2004). They often dictate what their parents eat, undermine the principles of dietary education and threaten to overturn the 'frail skiff' (Muxel 1996: 66). Even though the discipline has been relaxed, what does remain of it looks intolerable compared with their individual freedom to eat what they like. This is especially true with teenagers: the fact that family members are physically close to one another at mealtimes, sitting opposite each other and looking each other in the eye makes the constraints of family life much more obvious. More relaxed discipline is therefore not enough and cannot in itself guarantee that the family that eats together will stay together. Families have to give meals a more attractive content and cobble together new rituals to persuade their individual members to go on sharing meals.

New rituals

Many traces of the old disciplinary model still survive, and they exist in fragmentary forms, drifting like pieces of flotsam in a sea of informality. These are by no means mere survivals from the past. Families deliberately cling to them and they are the object of constant compromises and negotiations. They provide the minimal points of reference without which socialization is quite impossible. Like Suzette, Babette remembers her old principles, and they appear to have been very strict. 'In our house, my husband said that lunch is at 12.30 and dinner is at 7.30. "If you aren't there, we'll start without you." The children found it hard, but we are not the kind of people who eat at any old time.' Mealtimes were always scrupulously respected to the minute, giving the impression of a discipline worthy of the good old days. But it was in fact only the parents who respected these strict mealtimes. As they grew older, the children took more and more liberties, turning up after the meal had officially begun, or not turning up at all. This did not lead to any major crises. 'They helped themselves to whatever was in the fridge.' Parents are always trying to strike a balance between the autonomy of their children and the transmission of educational principles, which usually take the concrete form of bodily discipline. They are torn between their desire to let the children do as they please and their desire to educate them, which means imposing constraints. And children now find it much more difficult to accept those constraints than they used to. Chloé, who is 25, recalls what she saw as a terribly retrograde litany: 'Hands on the table, sit up straight, knife in your right hand and fork in the left, don't eat with you fingers. Those were the rules that were drummed into me and my brothers at mealtimes' (cited in Garabuau-Moussaoui 2002: 87). Yet all families have to have minimal rules, even though they may not have the same importance and may be neither explicit nor rigid. What is more important, they vary from family to family. Some demand punctuality whilst others demand good manners or specific things to eat.

François Dubet (2002) has analysed how, over the space of two hundred years, French society developed a vast programme designed to promote a republican order that was based upon great institutions such as schools. Its institutions were stable and based upon a system of established values, and they gave rise to disciplines that structured how individuals behaved in public. The 'table manners' model appeared to be the perfect domestic equivalent of that 'institutional programme'. And it was at roughly the same time, or in the 1960s, that the opposite trend towards greater individual autonomy and greater organizational flexibility began to emerge in both domains. The paradox is that, in historical terms, the disciplinary model established the preconditions for the emergence of something very different, more relaxed and sensual: family conversations, the expression of emotion and displays of pleasure. The custom of sitting up straight at the table, for instance, made it possible for family members to sit facing each other for long periods, and that gradually made conversations easier. The fragments of discipline that still survive are often not so much obstacles to innovation as supports for innovation.

This is especially true when they take off the hair shirts of the old discipline and slip into new clothes or new rituals. The new clothes are bright and cheerful, and that prevents the actors from seeing that they are still institutional. Nothing, it would seem, could be more free and easy than the *fondue* evenings David recalls (cited in Garabuau-Moussaoui 2002: 90). 'Happy times. We had them when we wanted

91

a treat.' And yet many of the details specific to this particular context represented structural markers for those involved. 'We had special plates, almost the colour of wood, dark beige. And the skewers we used each had different-coloured handles. Mine was the green one.' Sophie has her own ideas about table manners, and they are far removed from the McDonald's style, even though she does take her children to McDonald's. She explains that she does not really like eating with her children in fast food places because she feels that her authoritarianism is not in keeping with the setting (Singly 2000). But given that 'McDonald's at home' for Sunday lunch cannot be just another meal, she has found a compromise solution. The ritual is very strictly defined (the children have to behave properly but are allowed to eat with their fingers) and the ritual element is all the more striking in that it is inevitably full of contradictions. The packaging is removed and everyone eats from a plate, but no one uses a knife and fork. They use paper napkins but they are folded properly. There is Coca-Cola instead of water but the conventions are respected.

> 'It makes a change because we eat with our fingers; that's not allowed otherwise. And it makes a change because we have paper napkins, instead of using the linen ones. Otherwise, it's the same as usual. You do not get up and leave the table without asking permission. The young-est is not allowed to pour his own drinks. That's very important too.' (Cited in Singly 2000: 123)

Sunday lunch is really not just a meal like any other. Ordinary meals at Sophie's, and elsewhere, eventually make the rituals less obvious because they become almost unconscious habits that are repeated day after day: the family does not realize that it is creating the institution that is creating it. Where everyone sits at the table is one of the simplest examples. For official purposes, no one has any particular place, and the interviewees all start by saying that they sit just any-where . . . and then have to admit that they always sit in the same place; everyone knows where they are because they sit in 'their' place. Mathilde Perrot (2000a) reaches the same conclusion. When she was interviewing one couple, the woman had to raise her voice to bring her husband down to earth and get him to admit the inadmissible: they always sat in the same places. 'If you think about it, we always sit in the same places. Oh yes, we do! You sit at the head of the table. You're at the head of the table, and I'm almost in the kitchen. Yes, that's the way it is.'[3] The realization that they inevitably followed the

---

[3] Cited in Mathilde Perrot (2000a: 44). Their respective positions (the man at the head of the table and the woman near the kitchen) have a very long history.

same routine day after day was the source of some annoyance to the Pécheur family (Gacem 1997; 2002). They hate anything resembling a routine. 'We really don't want to get into a rut like some bunch of nerds', says Pascale (cited in Gacem 1997: 91). So they refuse to get into a routine. 'At least we try not to. We deliberately change places at meal times, mix things up.' It has become a sort of game. Without any warning, someone shouts 'Right, change places', even before everyone has sat down. 'It can be a laugh in the mornings when someone comes down for breakfast still half asleep and then realizes he's not sitting where he usually sits.' A new system is introduced but it only lasts for a few meals. The game that is in theory a form of deconstruction has in fact become a major ritual in its own right.

A dream family

Sophie prefers 'McDonalds at home' because it makes it easier to talk to her family. The conversations she normally has with her husband and children are a source of disappointment to her. We all dream of being able to talk freely and openly, of being able to confide in other members of the family and to listen to what they have to say. The media popularize that idea and give the impression that it has something to do with contemporary reality. It is in fact nothing more than an ideal and if we mistake it for a universal reality, we become even unhappier because we cannot live up to it. We find it difficult to talk to our partners and children, and that is only natural. A family consists of individuals who are, to varying degrees, autonomous. They are subjects who want to be happy but who are also torn between the need to compromise (and put up with things as they are) and the desire to express themselves (and turn everything upside down). There is always a danger that conversations will open a Pandora's box of unspoken frustrations. So we talk, but are very careful about what we say in an attempt to go on talking without saying too much. Not in quantitative terms: families never stop talking. And talking is useful as it helps us to build a world we can share by talking about what has happened in the news and, better still, criticizing friends and our extended family (a frequent topic of conversation). Being critical of others means that we have to develop a shared point of view and that unites the group around its values and ideas. It is not the quantitative aspect that creates problems. The problems have to do with the content of the conversation because there is a whole range of topics that irritate us or hurt us in ways we do not want to talk about. There is a structural discrepancy between what we would like to say and what we actually say.

Because there is always something missing in our lives, meals are special moments. Their long and surprising history has led to the establishment of a bodily discipline: individual members of the family sit around the table facing each other, and in a sense that means that they have to talk to one another for a determined amount of time. Meals institutionalize family conversations, with everyone sitting close together and in set positions. As a result, they may not look like a unique opportunity to make up for a latent deficit but they do represent a precious opportunity to make the dream of the perfect family come true: the family is together, warm and communicative. So much so that its members are expected to give something they cannot give. We can, however, lower our expectations in the light of experience. All it takes is to avoid being just 'mouths that eat', as Madeleine puts it, and to ensure that we are also mouths that talk, but without setting the bar too high.

> 'Being able to talk to one another is what matters. We belong to a generation that had to keep quiet at the table. Mum and dad talked, and the children kept quiet. When we had children of our own, meals were a special moment when we could talk about what we'd been doing at work and at school. Meals are moments of conviviality, not times when you eat quickly, get up from the table and it's all over and done with. And we didn't want to just sit there in front of the telly and stuff ourselves.'

The ideal of the happy family that is calm and pleasant to be with actually encourages us to keep an eye on what we say and to avoid getting involved in overheated discussions that might degenerate into rows. Pandora's box is, at best, only half open, and meals cannot solve all the problems. 'It gives us a chance to talk, to tell each other what kind of day we've had. It's a chance to relax.' Anneth has limited ambitions. Making up for a lack of conversation is not the only function of meals. They also have the less obvious, but equally important, function of gently wrapping the individual up inside the group. Everything has to go smoothly and there must be no upsets. The conversation must not go too far and certain codes have to be respected so as to allow the whole family to achieve that psychological equilibrium. And conflict must be avoided at all cost. 'Doing someone's head in over a meal is just not allowed.' Prune is categorical. A survey carried out in Switzerland led Benoît Bastard and Laura Cardia-Vonèche (1986: 47) to the same conclusion: 'Families hate to

94

have rows at mealtimes.' But how can there be any real discussion if all the difficult topics are avoided? Every family gradually identifies its favourite topics of conversation. As a rule, politics are only discussed when there is already a consensus within the family. If the disagreements are too serious, we avoid talking about them and speak freely outside the family (Stevens 1996). Family meals are not always the best times to speak our minds. Discussions of what was on the news are less problematic. And so is sport, a topic that is always raised by male sub-groups. Whatever the topic of conversation may be, the ideal schema is a clash of micro-differences of opinion against the background of a consensus. This makes the conversation lively without leading to rows. 'There's a state of mind and a set of values, and we are quite a close family, even though we rarely agree about everything', says one the Pécheur boys (cited in Gacem 1997: 71). A basic agreement means minor differences of opinion will not lead to major rows because they can all become part of a game. 'Besides, we like arguing for the sake of it, so even when we are almost all agreed we squabble over little things as though they really, really mattered' (cited in Gacem 1997: 71). Having lively conversations requires certain skills and a willingness to join in that not everyone finds easy. The Pécheurs take it in turns to make an effort. Quentin's brother confirms this: 'It's unusual for no one to have anything interesting to say. We're quite good at picking up where someone else left off' (Gacem 1997: 71).

Disjointed conversations

Mealtimes are well suited to these conversational games because they encourage a particular style of conversation that is freer, more concrete and more direct than in other areas of family life (Frain 2004; Serfaty-Garzon 2003). The term 'conversation' is in fact somewhat deceptive in that it suggests that those involved speak in sentences and use polished turns of phrase. When it comes to oral style, we are a long way from the disciplinary model of the past. The phrases we use are disjointed and lead nowhere. They are full of digressive or allusive formulae and everyone interrupts everyone else in an attempt to pursue a monologue that is constantly interrupted, especially when a large number of children are present. The observer who tries to understand what is being said during a lively family conversation over a meal finds it very difficult to reconstruct its meaning, which often has more to do with what is being insinuated or even acted out than with what is explicitly said. Marianne Modak (1986), who attempted to do just that, found that many themes are picked up and then immediately dropped and that others are impossible to identify because they are so brief or drowned out by the background noise. Despite all the sound and fury, she notes that attempts are made to introduce more structured arguments and that these often centre on issues the family is trying to resolve. Table talk can lead to real negotiations. But when the questions raised are neither too serious nor too urgent, family members are not slow to use jokes and mockery to liven up conversations that might otherwise turn nasty. 'The serious tone obviously bothers people, who become sarcastic, make jokes or change the subject to avoid what looks, to an outside observer, like a development that might spoil the mood of complicity' (Modak 1986: 65). The jokes and calls to order in fact represent a stylistic battle which will decide whether the meal leads to a proper conversation or whether everyone concentrates on what is on their plate.

Every family has its own preferences, or settles into its own habits, ranging from open negotiations or a theatrical liveliness to a calmer atmosphere. There is no common pattern to mealtime conversations. For Charlotte, a relaxed atmosphere is what matters most, and the main function of what is said is to create that atmosphere. 'Mealtimes are good. We sit down to eat, relax, talk to each other and listen to each other. We exchange ideas and respond to what has just been said.' For Clémentine, too, being together is much more important that the content of the conversation, which must not be allowed to disturb the serene tranquillity of the family meal. 'It's a pleasant moment. We're all together, and we talk about this, that and everything. But we don't have the kind of discussion in which everyone tries to set the world to rights. Things like that do not get discussed over a meal in this house.' The Pécheurs, in contrast, really enjoy setting the world to rights over a meal (Gacem 1997). This is usually just for fun, and a great deal of fuss is made over very minor differences of opinion. But the discussions do sometimes focus on serious issues that have implications for the future, as when Quentin started his first year at university in a half-hearted way because he was more interested in playing music with his friends rather than settling down to work. This came up so often that it was beginning to poison the atmosphere. And then Quentin stopped coming home to eat so often in order to spend more time with his friends. Negotiations become delicate when they are pushed too far. They can easily destroy the pleasant atmosphere, or force individuals to stay away. And yet the irrepressible desire to say what we want to say often encourages us to go too far despite ourselves because the ability to speak freely and sitting opposite one another is conducive to self-expression. There are no explicit rules stating that certain types of conversation are unacceptable and it is unusual for the person at the head of the table to lay down the law. Discussions over meals are self-regulating and we have to interrupt the conversation when we think that the discussion is becoming too heated or when the banality of the conversation indicates that no one is really saying anything. In his comparative analysis, Jean-Vincent Pfirsch (1997: 177) finds once more that there is a clear difference between young Germans, who prefer meals to be 'calm', and young French people, who like them to be 'lively'. The difference is particularly obvious from the way they relate to food which the Germans see as a form of sensual pleasure, whilst the French tend to see it as a pretext for loud conversations.

Table talk

My survey confirms that food itself is a major topic of conversation. Families discuss what they are eating (the cook receives compliments if it is good, and diplomatic criticisms if it is not), ask each what they like, describe what they can taste, and so on. Every remark can trigger a lively discussion in the form of a family micro-event that suddenly makes the conversation more animated. Such discussions can become family memories and can acquire an almost mythical status. Babette provides an example: 'Oh, he'll eat anything . . . Except the other day, he wouldn't! I'd made something with anchovies in it . . . And it has to be said . . . It really wasn't very nice. And he said so.' 'So what happened next?' asks the interviewer. 'Oh, we had a good laugh about it . . . a good laugh! And then he ate it all up anyway!'

Discussing what they are doing encourages people to talk about food and as the discussion becomes more general, the conversation may turn to dieting. 'He often criticizes me. So we talk about fat, sugar, diets . . . things like that' (Amandine). Or, and this is more common, the next meal. As we shall see in Part III, 'coming up with an idea' for the next meal is always a problem. Mealtime conversations are therefore a precious opportunity that allows whoever is in charge of the cooking (and it is usually the woman) to find out what people want to eat. 'I often discuss what I should make with my husband. During the week, we talk about what we're going to have on Sunday and exchange views. If my husband says "No, I don't fancy that", I do something else' (Charlotte). Babette plans even further ahead and talks about Christmas a month in advance.

'Over lunch, we were talking about Christmas and what we are going to have. As it happens, we'd been looking at some leaflets that came through the door, and we said to ourselves: perhaps we should have something else for a change. And it's true that it's always the same: foie gras, smoked salmon, turkey . . . So we thought about it, but we didn't come up with any ideas.'

Babette's example illustrates another common theme, and talking about plans for the future does a lot to structure the group. Families obviously plan meals but they also talks about trips out and holidays, about what they should buy and about DIY projects and redecorating the house. All this turns a group of people sitting around a table into a small business that is developing strategies. The important thing is that for a moment the group fuses into something that might have a different future, and that shows that it is alive and creative. Such flights of fancy cannot be allowed to become too frequent, however, as there is a danger that people will tire of them and that the dream will lose its attractions. The return to ordinary chatter therefore does not represent a failure (provided that the silence does not go on too long). Especially as conversations over meals have many other more specific functions. They also include descriptions of how the day has been, which are so common as to look like real rituals. Everyone comes out with their tales of woe and describes their minor disappointments. These things are very important. We are now forced to construct our identities and to give them a narrative form. Minor incidents feed into a broader self-portrait, which the family group validates over a meal, and it then becomes part of the family's collective story. Tales of woe are also very important. When we are the object of aggression or when our self-esteem takes a few knocks in the outside world, we need to recover our psychological balance and the sympathetic audience around the table helps us to do so. The 'bad' or 'nasty' figure that poisons the atmosphere at work often features in these narratives in a recurrent, even obsessional way. Once again, meals can only play their regulatory function if we stay within certain limits; if we go beyond those limits, we lose the attention of our audience, which loses its ability to empathize. Mealtime conversations have to remain pleasant and must not involve too much effort. They can only repair minor psychological damage. This does not mean that they are always superficial. On the contrary, the freedom to say what we like and the spontaneity encourage the sudden emergence of more intense fragments, and the idealized dream of intimate communication becomes a reality over lunch.

> 'The other day, he was telling us about a friend who had burst into tears because his mate was going away, moving house. And then he said to us: "You know, I've never seen a mate of mine in tears." So we began to talk about feelings. My husband finds it easier to open up over a meal than when we're sitting on the sofa in front of the telly.'

Prune gets very emotional as she tells her story. It is very unusual indeed for her husband to let his feelings show in this way. An ordinary meal produces a minor romantic miracle.

What the children say

Children are not interlocutors like any others. Even today some families are still under the influence of the old model, which was both disciplinary and hierarchical, and the children are not allowed to talk at mealtimes (Fischler 1996). In most families, however, conversations centre on the children. They are either the subject of the discussion (their parents talk about them but do not necessarily allow them to say anything) or the object of various jokes and are teased by their parents, which makes for lively meals.[4] Children are often expected to describe 'how things went at school' (Candy). And their parents are often disappointed because the answers are so brief, and are upset because they have to become interrogators in order to find out more. The transition from conversation to questioning places even more pressure on the children who already feel constrained by the discipline of table manners. As a result, they cannot repress their desire to leave the table. When that happens, the parents have to become skilled orators and learn not to ask too many questions, especially if their children are getting into the habit of leaving the table. That is what happened with Amandine's eldest boy. She does not find making meals easy, given that her husband is very faddish (he is on his 'Cretan diet' at the moment) and that her son will eat nothing but pizza and mayonnaise. And yet mealtimes are still important to her and to her idea of what a happy family should be like. 'We all sit around the table, all of us together, with everyone looking at everyone else. So everything happens over meals. It's inevitable.' Candy lives

---

[4] I cannot resist citing the blog of the novelist Virginie Despentes (27 September 2004): 'It's nice having kids at the table. You can ask them questions and laugh about them. A bit like having a kitten really. A kitten at the table.'

alone with her two children and eating together is very important to her, as it is a very good way of strengthening their relationship and of reminding themselves that they are a real family. 'It's the only time the three of us are together. We talk about what kind of day we've had. They talk about school, and I talk about work.' The problem is that her daughter won't 'stay at the table'. Although they never come to blows, negotiations are difficult. 'It's not as though I expected her to sit at the table for half an hour. Fifteen minutes is not a lot to ask.' But it is too much. 'They give me the impression that meals are something they have to put up with. Get it over with in five minutes, and off upstairs.' Candy would sometimes like to leave the table too. And yet the discipline she tries to impose on her children is not so terrible. For a long time, she fought to ban television for the duration of their short meals, but now she gives in more and more. When she does impose her ban, the fact that the children have got into the habit of watching television makes it difficult to pick up the thread of the conversation. 'There are times when no one says a word. Too bad.'

Fortunately, meals with the children are not always so problematic in other families. A more playful atmosphere may keep them at the table and encourage them to join in the conversation, which can become very lively as a result (though they may introduce a note of humour that is not always to their parents' liking). Asking fewer questions can also help because it allows them to feel that they are playing the starring role without being judged. François de Singly (2000: 128) gives the example of Etienne, who has four children:

> 'I let them talk because I don't see much of them during the week, and that makes weekends special. My wife and I try not to monopolize the conversation so as to let them say whatever comes into their heads. So, it can range from "What I did at school yesterday" to the eldest, who's obsessed with museums, asking me when I'm going to take him to the science museum at La Villette, to one of the others asking me to look at the tyre on his bike. It's all very disjointed, but we let them talk.'

This kind of conversation encourages the emergence of family 'characters' (the clown, the cheat, the chaotic one . . .) who are not afraid to exaggerate so as to be better at playing the role in which they are cast by other members of the family. Etienne describes how the members of his family are cast in different roles. 'One of the girls says almost nothing because she really is very quiet and eats nicely.' Her brother is the clumsy one who makes everyone laugh with his antics, which are to some extent deliberate. 'He can't touch anything without knocking it over or breaking it. So the other two monopolize the conversation' (cited in Singly 2000: 128). Such games allow children to discover 'the signs that give them a social and family identity' (Muxel 1996: 77). But when it goes beyond a joke, the game can turn cruel, especially when it becomes a staged confrontation between the quiet one and the 'child star'. A meal is a 'stage and the way we act depends on the way others see us, what they expect of us and how they judge us. Some find it easier than others to stand being put on show like this' (Muxel 1996: 77). Being told in playful terms not to say something can be an ordeal for a quiet child and being compared with brothers and sisters who are more talkative can have a profoundly unsettling effect. Especially, paradoxically, when the conversation is rich, free-flowing and cheerful. Another line may have been crossed. Individuals may begin to compete with each other, whereas being wrapped up in a blanket of mutual reassurance should be the order of the day. Even the liveliest and funniest meals are not immune to that danger.

Television

Conversations over meals can be very free and easy but that cannot alter the fact that table talk is a very delicate exercise that is fraught with dangers and that everyone is always very careful about what they say. Everyone has to say just enough to keep the conversation flowing and at the same time be careful not to open Pandora's box and let out something unpleasant. Sitting opposite one another for the whole duration of the meal is inevitably conducive to intimate conversations. Every meal is therefore a sort of test that tells us whether or not the family members have anything to say to each other. If they do, the family is alive and well in relational and not just institutional terms. Conversely, silences send out a negative message. Nothing could be worse for a family than a meal at which the only thing that can be heard is the clatter of forks when no one has anything to say.

> 'Ten seconds is fine; you have to eat, after all. But after a minute you begin to feel very uncomfortable, and you have to find something to say. And sometimes, it really is anything you can come up with! You know the old cliché "Cat got your tongue"? You make a joke of it, but that really isn't very clever, because once you've said that, the silence becomes even more uncomfortable. That's the last thing you want.' (Cannelle)

There are a lot of cats in the Lacroix household. 'The problem at home is finding something to talk about,' says Rodolphe (cited in

101

Gacem 1997: 25). This is where television comes in; it fills the silence and makes the family atmosphere more relaxed. 'It gives us something of an alternative' (cited in Gacem 1997: 41). The TV is like a third party who has been invited to share the family meal and families use it to regulate their conversations. Depending on the circumstance and who is there, it can be either background noise (to mask the sound of the forks) or an excuse for comments that stimulate debates. The extent to which it is used is constantly being adjusted. The Lacroix family are especially fond of quiz shows and both answer the questions themselves and make comments on the participants. It is the father, who finds conversation difficult, who is really glued to the telly. Mathilde, in contrast, is careful to ensure that it is nothing more than a tool, even a secondary tool, and tries to make sure that no one becomes really caught up in it:

> 'Actually, everyone watches it to some extent because I think that, once the telly is on, you become hypnotized by it, but if you really want to say something, it doesn't stand in your way and you say it anyway. In fact you're expected to say something. It all depends on what mood everyone is in and, when you really want to say something, you ignore the telly. And we do have meals when the telly is on but no one looks at it or listens to it. Sometimes it gives us something to talk about, or to argue about. You see something and everyone gives their opinion, for or against, but it's not something that gets our full attention.' (Cited in Gacem 1997: 42)

There is nothing anecdotal about watching television over the family meal. The television plays an important role and tells us a lot about what is at stake at mealtimes. Meals are part of the architecture of family life, not least because they involve us in conversations that can be about anything. But a lot of families find it difficult to talk to each other and therefore have to use television as a prosthetic to fill the awkward silence and to get people talking again. That explains why it is used so often. In France, one in two people watch television over dinner, which is when most families eat together, and the figure is constantly rising (Guilbert and Perrin-Escalon 2004). The figures for meals that are often eaten separately, such as breakfast, are lower, which clearly indicates that the telly is, not strictly speaking, an attraction in its own right. The primary function of watching television at mealtimes has to do with the family.

The problem is, as Mathilde puts it so well, that 'once the television is on, you become hypnotized by it.' We get sucked into it. Television is a two-edged sword: we use it to get people talking but it soon begins to have the opposite effect, as they slip into the comfortable role of being viewers and forget about the need to talk to each other as a family. That eventuality really is dangerous because it looks like a blessing, or something that makes life easier. But there is a price to be paid: it is very difficult to turn back the clock and family conversations really can become a thing of the past. The family settles into a routine but no longer has a voice of its own. For a long time, Suzette tried to balance the complex relationship between meals and the television. At first, she tried to stop her children from leaving the table one by one. 'There were times when they were little when they did eat in front of the telly. But I think it's nicer to sit around the table.' The television does preside over the kitchen table. But the sound is turned down and does not drown out the conversation. 'It feels good when we are all together. Even when the telly is on in the background, and it often is when we eat in the kitchen. That doesn't stop us talking to each other.' Except 'when there's football on. There's no talking when the football is on.' So the family moves into the lounge and eats at the table, in front of the wide-screen satellite TV. In Suzette's view, things have gone too far and television is destroying their family life. Her husband and her sons take a different view: they are having a good time together and combining the pleasures of eating with those of watching the football. It does not mean that they cannot talk to each other or exchange their points of view. Even if football is the only thing they talk about, the family (or at least the men in the family) is still a family. Being caught up in whatever is on television does not necessarily mean that meals are no longer an important family occasion. Eugénie takes the view that everyday meals in the kitchen (where there is no television) are not particularly sociable occasions. 'When there's just the two of us, meals are not complicated affairs. We don't make much of an effort.' But sometimes 'when there's a good film on', they eat later and in the lounge: 'a little snack in front of the telly.' The meal is very simple and eaten in silence but, because it makes a change, it encourages a feeling of togetherness. In their modest way, they simply enjoy the pleasure of being together. 'If it's a good film, we're perfectly happy eating like that . . . just the two of us.' It is not always easy to determine just which role television plays. Vincent Caradec (2004) emphasizes that it becomes more important as we get older because it helps to fill the gaps in conversations between husband and wife. As we grow old, what happens next is much worse; when we lose interest in what is on television, it is a sign that we are losing interest in life in general. When we watch it together, television is in its own way an indication that we are still curious about things and still have a certain energy.

The telly does not always mean that we no longer talk to each other as a family and, even when it does, it does not make more implicit forms of communication impossible. But as we have seen from the examples of Prune and Candy (who worry about the inroads it is making) it is often seen as a threat to meals, which should be a central part of family life. When eating in front of the television becomes a matter of routine rather than something out of the ordinary, the group's institutionalizing effect is undermined. And once we get into the habit of staring at the screen rather than talking to each other, it becomes very difficult to learn to start talking again. Certain material indicators reveal that this will eventually destroy the architecture of the family. The first indicator is where we sit at the table. When we cease to sit facing each other and (in an astonishing reversion to the medieval custom) sit side by side so that we get a better view of what is on television, the telly becomes a major distraction. Volume is another indicator. When what was a discreet background noise becomes deafening, it simply becomes impossible to talk to each other. 'Even if I did want to ask something, I never did so over a meal. You couldn't get away from the telly. Even when I go home now, the telly is always on loud. It's impossible to talk. They're just not interested', said the daughter of a farming couple (cited in Muxel 1996: 81–2).

Eating together

Modern meals are the product of disciplined gestures and table manners, and that discipline is articulated around the idea of reconstructing the family institution. That discipline has now become more relaxed, just as family lifestyles are no longer defined by rigid frameworks to the same extent. Despite all these formal changes, the ideal of building families still remains intact and the rigid discipline that once governed table manners has given way to the goal of communication: the fact that we talk to each other is living proof that we are indeed a family. Prune and Candy dream of having real conversations and that is why they dislike television so much. But reality often has little in common with the 'family conversation' model. It is not that the reality of family life is poorer but simply that it is out of step with the model. The way we speak to each other is one indication of the discrepancy between the two: our conversations are cheerful chaos rather than a series of well-turned phrases. And as we shall see, conversation is not everything but part of a whole range of different sensations, many of them discreet.

To begin with the simplest and the most basic: when we get together to eat, we feel that we are sharing something important, that we are creating something resembling the 'clanship of porridge' of old. Simply being physically close to people we are familiar with in itself gives rise to an unspoken intimacy, as does the friendship analysed by Todorov (2001 [1995]: 69): 'The simple presence of one, of whom one demands nothing, for the other is the source of a quiet joy.' Eating together adds a further dimension. 'It's because there's something to eat that we get together. If there wasn't, we would never be together' (Babette). Prune is well aware that her dream of reconstructing the intense, warm conversations of her childhood (or what she remembers of it) is just a dream. As soon as she met her future husband, she could picture herself with children, a happy family gathered around a table. 'The first thing I saw when I met my husband was that I could make a family.' She has now learned to lower her expectations and to adapt a more modest reality and the pleasures of simple togetherness. 'It's relaxing, puts you in a better mood, and makes it easier to talk.' Meals represent a moment of peace and they help to calm things down. 'Even when things are going badly and when I'm angry with my son, we sit down at the table and it's all forgotten. We quickly move on to something else.' Extreme situations clearly reveal one of the basic functions of meals. Clémentine, for example, does not eat at lunchtime. When her daughter was old enough to eat at the table, she intuitively realized that there would be problems if she did not do the same. So she decided to pretend and now she just nibbles at her food, when she isn't actually pretending. 'I just pretend to eat with her. Pretend to be someone who is eating with her. She likes that.' 'Pretend to be someone who is eating with her' . . . eating together is what counts. That is what brings them together and that is the basis of their relationship. 'Eating and talking is nice. Being together to eat, that's what counts' (Maryse).

Eating gives us pleasure. There is the simple pleasure of having had enough to eat and the more refined pleasures of experimenting with our senses. It is therefore unusual for meals to be restricted to their basic symbolic function or to being moments of peace. The survey turned up only one counter-example: Maïté's Sunday lunches. Even though the whole family sits together around the table (and for once ham sandwiches are not on the menu), that does nothing to change their habits which are purely functional: they eat because they have to eat. They eat whatever she puts in front of them. 'They never object, not a word. They eat whatever is in front of them.'

The syncretism of minor pleasures

Most of the time, something else is going on, too, and it has to do with shared pleasures. There is no obligation to actually say anything. 'Yes, you do begin to resent it when people eat without making it clear that they get some satisfaction out of eating' (Suzette). Even when nothing is said, everyone enjoys the pleasure others are experiencing: the pleasure of assuaging hunger and discovering new tastes. At certain moments, silence is no longer a problem and turns into a positive message: the clatter of forks becomes a sign of satisfaction. Sensations that appear to be imperceptible circulate and bring everyone closer together by wrapping them up in a world of quiet contentedness that can be shared. 'First, there's the pleasure of eating, and then the pleasure of enjoying it together. That's important' (Marjolaine). The degree of pleasure varies a lot. 'When it's good . . . oh, I almost said something rude . . .' Maryse pauses, and then bursts out laughing: 'It's . . . like an orgasm! When that happens, you really do appreciate being alive! The pleasure really is orgasmic. When I feel like that, I don't want anyone talking to me, I feel so good.' Maryse doesn't want anyone talking to her at such moments of intense pleasure. As a general rule, however, talking makes everything more intense. What is more important, everyone enjoys the fact that the others are having a good time and that heightens the shared pleasure. Assuming that it is said with enough conviction, a brief comment or an 'Oh . . . that's delicious' is often all it takes to allow a group of people who are sharing a meal to experience the same pleasure. Once again, the break with the codes that once governed table manners is very obvious. It was once thought seemly to 'repress direct or "crude" expressions of sensual pleasure' (Picard 1995: 137). The opposite is now true and the whole art of being a family consists in knowing how to express pleasure. The sin of gluttony has been turned into a virtue. Melba is delighted when her daughter gurgles with pleasure. 'She likes her food! I love it when she comes to see what's cooking for supper. She really enjoys that.' She derives pleasure from her daughter's pleasure.

Meals afford a delicate mixture of pleasures. All the senses are involved but so are certain ethical, intellectual and affective categories. Prune and Melba really enjoy it when a successful meal brings their families to life. They also derive a personal pleasure from eating nice things. It is, however, difficult to divorce those sensations from the family symbolism: they are part of a whole, and every part enriches all the others. The pleasures merge into one. Smells are a good example.

The sense of smell, like the other senses, plays an important role in the overall experience, even though a sense of smell is obviously an individual matter. Smells give us an appetite and arouse desires. But they are also an important part of the group experience and help to create an atmosphere that encourages a feeling of togetherness. There is no contradiction between these two aspects. On the contrary. The way individuals communicate their pleasure heightens others' pleasure, and that collective experience encourages those who enjoy their food to say so out loud. Olivia manages the smells that come from her kitchen very cleverly. She knows that they are an important part of the experience of eating together as a group and that they can help to create an atmosphere long before the family sits down to eat. She has set up a 'back up' kitchen in the garage for 'bad smells' (meaning cabbage and cod). Some meals that are left to simmer for a long time give off strong smells that have, in contrast, pleasant connotations. She makes a point of cooking them – and cakes – in the main kitchen. 'As soon as you go into a house that smells good, you feel good, and that's very nice.' The sense of smell, like sight, the sense of touch, and of course taste and hearing, all help meals to create families. 'If it smells good, it usually tastes good too. The two things go together. A successful meal is a meal that gives pleasure to everyone there. I really do think that it all helps to create an atmosphere' (Mathilde Lacroix, cited in Gacem 1997: 50).

The sense of hearing has less than the sense of taste or smell to do with the pleasure of eating a meal. It is, on the other hand, very much involved in the art of conversation, which is closely bound up with other pleasures. 'It brings us together, and we don't get too many opportunities to get together. And is a moment for shared pleasures. And we can talk to each other, and that has to be a pleasure too' (Marjolaine). There is no separating the two things. That is why the purely conversational model does not really fit in with today's idea of what a family should be. The conversation itself is often free flowing and disjointed, and it is no more than a means to an end. It is one of many tools and it coexists with other forms of sense-perception that are much more diffuse but just as important. We dream of course, of a fusion of pleasures, words and family symbolism. We dream of communing and that takes us back to the sacred dimension of sacrificial meals. We no longer look to heavenly spirits or god: our new religion is syncretic, and it uses micro-rituals, and especially the feeling of well-being, to sanctify the family. We just want to be happy together.

As in the sacrificial banquets of old, substances that help to elevate our souls facilitate the holy communion that we experience at our most intense festive moments. Being slightly drunk binds the group together and adds to the range of pleasures on offer. It can sometimes be combined with refined experiments with taste. Tasting a great wine can, for example, be an event that is both artistic and voluptuous. Amandine recently discovered this world. Given that her meals are a failure (thanks to her son with his pizza and mayonnaise on the one hand and her husband's insistence on his Cretan diet on the other), the new ritual of wine-tasting has, unexpectedly, the effect of bringing them closer together. As the family begins to crystallize, they can at last enjoy the togetherness they have always dreamed of. They eat separately but drink wine together, and they both enjoy it. 'My husband and I began to drink wine at a very late stage. But good wine is delicious, fantastic! We quickly acquired a taste for it.' Carried away by her enthusiasm, she has no qualms about introducing her thirteen-year-old daughter to the delights of wine. 'Oh, she loves it!' She hopes that she will eventually succeed in convincing her sons to join them on their family micro-adventure.

Minor adventures

As François Dubet (1994) has demonstrated, we are no longer defined purely by our social roles and have become subjects. We are involved in an experiment but do not know how it will turn out. Meals are currently bringing about a transition from order to more open forms of experimentation that are at once sensual and many-sided, and which involve us both as individuals and as members of a group. They involve both gastronomic and emotional pleasures. Because they involve conversation and negotiations, they also help to regulate relationships and encourage both analyses of the present and discussions about the future. Even within the same family, no two meals are exactly alike, nor do they serve the same function.

Every time we pick up a fork, we are faced with alternatives. Meals play, for instance, a prime role in the identity problematic but their role is always contradictory. Self-doubts grow as individuals cease to be defined by their social roles and become involved in an open-ended process of experimentation (Kaufmann 2004). The unfortunate modern individual is therefore faced with an ordeal that is difficult to understand and always has to fight two battles at the same time. She must seek reassurance by proving to herself that she really is the person she thinks she is by reproducing the same behavioural patterns.

At the same time, she must not be afraid to reinvent herself so as to ensure that she is not defined solely by her social role. And every time she picks up a fork, she opts for one or other of those solutions.

Someone who is eating a meal can opt for reassurance during those special moments when, by satisfying his hunger, he gets rid of the tensions he feels and regains his biological equilibrium. The feeling of soothing harmony that comes from having a full stomach is then heightened by the reproduction of routines and a subjective rediscovery of the likes and dislikes that make him what he is. This does not mean that he literally repeats the same gestures day after day (that is now quite unusual) but it does mean that he settles into a rhythm of regular rituals and limited variations on his diet. The encounter with the unexpected takes, at best, the form of the discovery of some forgotten family treat (conventionally symbolized by Proust's madeleine). 'I made proper mashed potatoes the other day. My daughter said to me "Ooh, that's good. It's been a long time since you made that." She really enjoyed it' (Babette). Meals mean something because they are such obvious points of reference. They allow individuals to overcome their doubts and uncertainties by 'preserving the things that tell them they are still the same' (Sauvageot 2003: 278) because they are wrapped up inside a body that is involved in a 'sensory experience' and inside a group that is held together by its regular habits.

We can also choose to be more adventurous. Like the Pêcheur family, we can disrupt the routine of always sitting in the same place at the table, give improvised parties (big or small) or be bold enough to try new products and discover new tastes. The current fashion for exotic products is a perfect illustration of this trend (Régnier 2004). When taken to extremes (at a dinner party, for instance), the experiment may encourage one to invite 'guests into a world that is completely unfamiliar to them' (Garabuau-Moussaoui 2002b: 303). In most cases, however, the break from routine eventually becomes a reassuring habit in its own right even though it is slightly out of the ordinary. 'It is something of an event, but it is also highly ritualized and very much a matter of habit' (Garabuau-Moussaoui 2002b: 302). The feeling of reassurance outweighs the taste for adventure. It is much more difficult to channel the very free-ranging conversations that take place over meals into a routine than it is to make novelties become a habit. Even when we do not want them to, they can have surprising results, as an expression of annoyance or some chance remark can start a chain reaction. The Lacroix, for example, know that sparks will fly on Saturday nights but cannot predict exactly what will happen. They would happily do without that unpredictability.

The interplay between I and We

We dream of using the syncretism of meals and of communing through the words and pleasures we share to crystallize the reality of the family. The paradox is, as Georg Simmel pointed out long ago (Simmel 1997 [1910]), that one of the things that does most to bind families together, namely the enjoyment of food, is profoundly individual and personal. Even when we eat with others, we still remain what we are, and the fusion of pleasures does not mean that we dissolve into the group. And that is, as it happens, the principle behind communion. 'In the communion, one is not ignorant of the fact that the other is other; one remains inside a coexistence, but there is at the same time a continuity between the two partners. This experience is absolute certainty, allowing for no doubt that one is accepted by the others' (Todorov 2001 [1995]: 69).

This ability to remain what we are as we commune with the group may give rise to the impression that the individual and the family have no difficulty in reconciling their respective expectations and, more broadly, that the contradictory logics of contemporary eating habits (the individual who eats alone and the communal meal) can coexist without any difficulty. An initial analysis appears to confirm that this is indeed the case, as individuals constantly adapt their behaviour in an attempt to articulate the two modalities. Delphine, a 22-year-old shop assistant, for example, has problems with her mother's desserts because she finds them too rich. She tried to use the 'personal taste' argument (and claimed to prefer low-calorie yoghurt) and then realized that the squabbles died down if she left the family table and ate her yoghurt (which was her alternative to the family's dessert) in front of the television (Corbeau 2002: 34). Paradoxically, the fact that she kept her distance helped to avoid conflict. Marjolaine sums up how contradictory dietary logics can coexist peacefully. 'We've always eaten together. Of course they have snacks between meals. But we sit down together for meals.' It is as though, once they had agreed to spend time together as a family, individuals had the right to eat as they wished when they were alone, either at home or outside the home. How much time families spend together varies from one household to the next, and they probably exaggerate the amount of time they spend together. A closer description of her family's practices would probably prove that Marjolaine is mistaken when she says 'We've always eaten together.' But the important point for our purposes is that, in her mind, the idea of a family meal remains intact. The fact that individual family members make their own breakfast can therefore be overlooked, as can the fact that they have lunch with work colleagues. Idealizing the group also means that we can overlook the fact that the practices of the people sitting around the same table have become highly individualized, that they come and go as they please, take what they like from the fridge, help themselves to different desserts, and so on. The things that do bring the family together as a group are enough to create the image of a family that regularly communes over a meal. This initial analysis is, however, very deceptive. Although it captures one aspect of reality, it conceals another, much more conflicted aspect: families and individuals are constantly at war with one another over meals. That they are at war is not always obvious, as family members make a considerable effort to avoid problems and to make their dealings with one another easier, and thus conceal the real nature of the underlying conflict. The war goes on quietly, but it goes on all the same. The two great logics that determine the way we now eat collide within every family, at every meal and over the slightest details.

This is not an abstract war between the individual and the group, and the question that arises here is especially interesting from the theoretical point of view. The conflict arises only to the extent that there is an emotional commitment to the family and its identity. Anthony Giddens (1984) notes that reflexivity is a central factor in the changes that are occurring in modern societies. Individuals position themselves in relation to their own lives and ask themselves lots of questions. As this reflexivity intensifies, the more they have to do precisely the opposite if they are to establish the self-evident meaning on which their lives are based (Kaufmann 2004). They must stop having doubts as to who they are in order to feel that they really are who they are. Whereas reflexivity is an intellectual activity, the closure of the meaning of their personal lives is primarily sensory and affective. It enfolds them in a collective dimension. Love, relationships and the family are prime examples, but there is nothing compulsory about them. Every individual and every culture has a choice to make. Let us look briefly at the example of Japanese society which tells us a lot about the role the family and meals play in modernity.

Anyone who observes contemporary Japanese society cannot fail to be struck by how loose conjugal and family ties appear to have become in a culture in which so many traditions have been preserved. Its most striking feature is the declining fertility rate which is now becoming a major economic and political problem. There is an obvious connection here; the frequency of sexual relations is now one of the lowest in the world. And if we take meals as an indicator of the

intensity of family life, we immediately draw an irrefutable conclusion: the Japanese family is in a very poor state.

> Women no longer even respect the formalities. When a man goes off
> to work in the morning, his wife does not use the standard formula
> to wish him a good day. She barely turns her head to say: 'No need to
> make dinner for you tonight?' And if he gets home a little earlier than
> usual, she greets him by saying 'What brings you back so early?' (Jolivet
> 2002: 92)

Very few families eat together (thanks in part to the efficient distribution of ready meals) and they do not really talk to each other. It seems
a long time since 'father was always there'. 'We always used to wait
for him to get back for dinner. Fathers used to educate their children
at the table, telling them off when they spoke, teaching them to speak
properly, and showing them how to use chopsticks and how to eat'
(Jolivet 2002: 172). For today's children, a father 'is a guy who comes
home every night to sleep, who eats at home from time to time but
never says a word' (Jolivet 2002: 189). The Japanese are somewhat
unhappy about this development and feel vaguely guilty because
they are convinced they are paying a high price for their spectacular
economic success, and feel that their private lives are suffering as a
result. It seems that they have, unwittingly and despite the fact that
they describe themselves as 'not very individualistic', developed a new
and paradoxical model based upon a mild pragmatism. Individuals
(and especially men; women devote most of their energies to bringing
up their children and bear a heavy and unequal share of the domestic
burden) enjoy a great deal of freedom and have become purely autonomous atoms within a contractual modernity (Rawls 1973). There is
an institutional framework for love but it is now so liquid (Bauman
2003) as to be impalpable. European societies, in contrast, have
promoted emotional and family commitments as an antidote to the
cold logics of advanced modernity. Passion has to compete with self-
control and even tends to take priority in their scale of values. And it
is the individual who aspires to greater autonomy who has to pay the
price: commitment to the family group is compulsory, the discipline
of meals has to be respected, and regular participation in the collective fervour is expected. Individuals cannot have too many nights out
with friends, or eat too many meals on trays in front of the telly.

As identification comes to focus on the family, the conflict between
the individual and the group at mealtimes becomes more problematic.
Snacks that are eaten outside the context of the family are no longer
fully acceptable; they look like an alternative, or even a threat, to the

very existence of the family. There are more and more potential flash-points: a failure to respect mealtimes, leaving the table too quickly and taking phone calls that interrupt meals have all become things no one will put up with. For Amandine, these minor breakdowns in collective discipline are more than a cause for annoyance. In her view, the situation really has deteriorated: three different meals, her son in front of the telly with his pizza and mayonnaise . . . 'Actually, no two people in this house eat the same thing.' She could have downed tools and, like Maïté with her ham sandwiches, adopted the principle of individual meals. But, with the support of her daughter, she still hopes that meals will bring her family back to life. That is why the war between the individual and the collective never ends. And some-times she does win a battle. Witness the new ritual of wine-tasting.

Children at the table

The family ideal now sustains the dream of an all-consuming shared intimacy. At the same time, it is obvious that we are seeing a growing individualization of concrete practices (likes and dislikes, where and when we eat, even when we are at home). It is therefore increasingly impossible to deny that there is a contradiction between these two logics. The contradiction is particularly acute when children are involved. Should parents be transmitting a heritage and educating their children (regular mealtimes, table manners, family meals, an appreci-ation of different tastes, a healthy diet and so on) or should they give them what they want (snacks, sweets and meals in front of the telly)? There is no right answer and there is no universally accepted set of values. Taking what children want into account is not the same thing as just giving in over the question of the soft drinks and sweets that are bad for their health. It means seeing them as individuals who have the right to enjoy a degree of autonomy (Singly 2004a). The trend towards greater personal autonomy is turning all our societies upside down, and there is no way of reversing the trend. Even those parents who are completely unconvinced have no choice but to accept it. And even those who are convinced have to limit their children's autonomy to some extent and impose some minimal collective principles. In the Pécheur family, it is the very lively conversations that take place over meals that bind the group together. But not everyone is interested in the same things. Simon, who is the youngest, has no real interest in politics, which often comes up in these conversations. According to his mother Pascale, he sits on the edge of his seat so that he can make

113

a quick getaway as soon as he becomes bored (cited in Gacem 1997: 73). Is Simon really involved in the group, or is he just pretending to be involved? The situation is constantly changing. And everyone interprets it in different ways. For those who believe in family life, the very fact that he is there is enough to prove he is involved, even if he is sitting on the edge of his seat. For Simon, in contrast, all this is just for show. It is for his parents' benefit, and his mind is elsewhere. The conflict is not just between parents and children who have very different views about these educational principles. It also represents a generation gap between children and parents who were brought up in the days when table manners and meals had a very different meaning. With the best will in the world, grandparents find it difficult not to see the younger generation's increased independence as proof that their children's attitude to education is too relaxed and that they are incapable of imposing even a minimal discipline on their offspring. The issue of what and how children eat is one the most conflicted problems that arise between grandparents and parents (Attias-Donfut and Segalen 1998).

Even though all family members try to avoid friction and to promote peaceful coexistence, and even though real outbursts are unusual, an undeclared war is going on between the two models for dietary practices (individual freedom and family communion). In the case of the parents, it usually takes the form of a clear distinction between strategy and tactics. Whatever the current state of play, the strategy is still there in the back of their minds and it is still focused on the family ideal. Because they are caught up in the turmoil of everyday life, they find it much easier to reach various compromises at the tactical level. Although she still dreams of a family that eats together, Candy has no option but to accept it when her adolescent children tell her at the last minute that they are going to eat at their friends' place. 'I really hate it when that happens. It's understandable at their age, but it really is a pain.' Given the circumstances, she has no choice but she immediately begins to hatch plans for a counter-offensive (a nice pudding to keep them at home, a new rule that they must not tell her at the last moment). Marjolaine has put her foot down: 'I'm not giving in to his whims. I'm not his slave!' But she secretly adds a few potatoes to the vegetables. 'But I'm not going to make something especially for him, and that's that.' Madeleine, too, has a strategic fist of iron in a tactical velvet glove. She was always laying down very firm educational principles. 'I used to say "It's either that or nothing. Everyone has to eat the same thing." I wasn't going to change my plans because they didn't like what was on offer.' But when she cooked a piece of meat or a vegetable dish that her daughters did not really like, she actually also took the precaution of making a starter she knew they liked. With some negotiations and a bit of cheating, they all got what they wanted. For a while, the girls used to complain about their school dinners. Madeleine immediately reduced her educational demands to ensure that they had enough to eat and enjoyed their evening meal. The family strategy remains the same but the tactics are adapted to the context and to fit in with what individuals want. Amandine is well aware of this. She also knows that if she makes too many tactical concessions, dietary individualism will eventually prevail. Her family wants to live in peace and not to declare war at every possible opportunity. 'When the children were younger, we used to get a bit worked up. But not now, not after all this time.' After so many pointless battles over such a long period, everyone grows tired, and parents want some peace. 'If he doesn't want to eat what is on his plate, he goes to see what's in the fridge, and that's all there is to it.' She says she will not make something especially for him (pizza or fish and chips), and that he can fend for himself. And then she breaks her own rules and goes back to the stove. To make matters worse, her second son has learned from the bad example set by his big brother. 'In any case, they will hardly ever eat what I put in front of them. Hardly ever. Last night, I made omelette and salad, and they refused to eat it. I had to make them fish and chips.' The ritual wine-tasting makes up for that, as do the parties she holds for friends. That allows her to give her passion for cooking a free rein. On party night, her eldest 'fends for himself and eats out.' And her youngest 'sits in his corner in front of the telly, and eats off a tray. Breaded fish . . . a burger . . . pizza . . . always the same things'. As during family meals, the role of the combination of television and individual dietary practices varies, depending on the context. It can destroy the collective dimension of family life but it can also be a trap for those who eat alone if the flow of addictive images (Ehrenberg 1995) comes to be closely associated with snacking. Watching television wraps us up in a blanket, whilst snacking fills our stomachs. Both practices obey the same logic of a regressive reassurance as to who we are and that, as we know, encourages obesity.

The strategy (lofty family ambitions) and the tactics (compromise) often evolve in parallel. The strategy may be no more than an idea, but the tactics have a real impact. And the two can sometimes converge to define arrangements in which displays of individuality become part of a broader family strategy that can either tolerate them or transcend them. If they are well supervised (not too much and not

115

too little), little meals at which children eat whatever they like can become real 'autonomy laboratories' (Diasio 2002: 258). Freedom does not always mean anarchy. Allowing children to have tea when they want 'by mutual agreement' and keeping 'family meals' separate helps children to 'learn to adapt meals to the social context, and to adjust their dietary behaviour to different situations' (Diasio 2002: 253). The ability to articulate time and space, and the individual and the family, implies that the children of advanced modernity can acquire very sophisticated skills and can adapt their dietary codes in terms of 'when, what, where, how, and who with' (Diasio 2002: 253). Those skills teach them to live 'freely together' (Singly 2000) within a collective structure that controls and negotiates its margins of freedom.

— 4 —

FAMILY TRAJECTORIES AND CONTEXTS

The sweet jar, the fridge and the table

The process of learning, under supervision, to become autonomous begins at an early age. It includes learning to manage what appear to be insignificant micro-spaces such as the sweet jar or a supply of sweets or drinks kept in the bedroom. This is tolerated behaviour and it inscribes a small fragment of dietary practice within a territory that has been officially delegated to the child. The sweet jar is at once a 'supply of goodies' and 'proof of self-regulation' (Diasio 2002: 254). The freedom to pick and choose from it must not, however, lead to any infringements of the rules that have been established by the child's parents. If the experiment is successful (or if the parents abandon the struggle!), the material supports for this autonomy may be extended when the child reaches adolescence: a tray taken up to the bedroom, teatimes spent watching a film on the computer with friends . . . And as they grow older, they are granted the ultimate symbol of autonomy: a fridge. 'It means I really have a place of my own', says Julien. 'A little flat in my bedroom', adds Sébastien (cited in Ramos 2002: 120). Those young people who do have a fridge in their room (and, as yet, there are not many of them) feel that, quite apart from the practical advantages it has to offer, such an appliance means that they are beginning to leave their childhood behind them. They have marked out a self-governing space that gives some of their dietary practices a material existence.

Although they are very important in symbolic terms, the little spaces of a bedroom are of secondary importance compared with the experiments in autonomy that are going on elsewhere in the house. At certain times, no one in particular uses the dining table and it can

117

be 'squatted', and then there are the meals on the tray and the snacks that are eaten on the run. This extension of individual zones and times must, of course, be negotiated and in many cases the negotiations take the form of a long war of attrition. As Elsa Ramos (2002) notes, and as I learned from my own research, it is much easier to tolerate personalized meals (which are eaten when and where the individual concerned pleases) if the whole family is not at the official dining table at a set time. This is because what looks like a convenient arrangement when everyone has their own timetable takes the form of a challenge to the myth when everyone eats separately but at the same time. Aurélie, for example, tries to get her parents to accept her new ritual of pizza in front of the telly on Sunday night. Unfortunately for her, 'I don't always get my own way' (cited in Ramos 2002: 202). Her parents still think that they should all eat together.

Although no one says so in so many words, families tend to introduce a twofold system and keep the two dietary dynamics apart so as to ensure that this individualism does not interfere with family meals. They accept that their children have the right to behave as they see fit, provided that they accept some collective discipline when the whole family does eat together. They must let their parents know in advance if they are going to be out, turn up for meals on time when they are at home (even though they are free to eat when they like when they are on their own), respect at least some minimal standards of behaviour (even though they enjoy subverting them outside the home) and eat the same things as everyone else (even though they eat very different things when they are on their own). In that way, they learn to manage a sort of controlled schizophrenia and are always moving between systems governed by codes that are in many respects antagonistic. They are in a peculiar position and that influences their view of the actors involved. The same cannot be said of their parents, who go on putting up a stubborn resistance in an attempt to prevent everything from being individualized. Somewhat surprisingly, young people find it easy to lead this schizophrenic existence. Of course they constantly launch new guerrilla attacks in an attempt to extend their autonomous territory. And of course the existential lightness of living on snacks gives them an intoxicating taste of freedom, but family life still has its irresistible charms, even if they are restrictive. 'To be honest, I like it. It's very comforting,' says Frédéric (cited in Ramos 2002: 205). 'But it's true that having to eat at set times can be a bit of a drag at times.' Although they are inflexible, family meals are both satisfying and comforting, and they make a change from the uncertainties of adolescence. And although the young people themselves are not really aware of it, there is more to it than that. They may think that they put up with this old-fashioned discipline because they are obedient and they love their families. Without realizing it, they are in fact learning lots of little things that they will later use in their own lives. In their own way, they too will reinvent the world of family meals. Although they have no real sense of that future, they feel an intuitive attachment to the dated charms of eating together as a family. And their attachment to that model proves that family ties are still very important, even though our modernity is based upon autonomy.

Alone at last

These 'dated charms' come at a high price. The real reason why they are such a source of psychological comfort is that, for a moment, we forget that we are 'tired of being ourselves' (Ehrenberg 1998) and regress towards an infantile status. The freedom to eat what we like when we like, in contrast, gives us an exciting taste of freedom, of the lightness of being young and of a future that we are inventing for ourselves. When we first begin to live independently in a home of our own, we can break all the rules and enjoy an unbridled anarchy. 'What do I like best? Being able to be self-reliant', says Séverine. 'There are no set times, you're answerable to no one and don't have to tell anyone you'll be back at 10 or 11. And you can eat when you like' (Gestin 1997, cited in Singly 2004b: 266). Sudden impulses and a willingness to make the most of the opportunities that come along are the only things that matter. And this encourages us to eat convenience foods. It is not just because it is a symbol of freedom that Anne-Lise eats 'anything'. Spending time on housework and preparing meals seems anachronistic to young people. 'I never make any effort to cook' (cited in Singly 2004b: 267). The fridge is therefore more important than ever. It is a cornucopia and, once it is full, everything is there for the taking as soon as the door is opened. 'I really like picking at what's in the fridge when I feel like eating. Sausages, leftover salad, cheese, tomatoes' (Valérie, 25, cited in Garabuau-Moussaoui 2002a: 204). The ability to act on the spur of the moment and the unpredictability of immediate future (which will quickly prove to have its own physical and intimate attractions) adds to the symbolic importance of what we mistakenly see as a banal and functional gesture. Someone who eats alone has broken completely free from the restrictive discipline of meals and the exacting chore of having to cook. One word comes up again and again in the interviews: people 'peck' at things as though they were free-range chickens. Going to the fridge or other stores of food (the fruit bowl, the cupboards where the snacks and biscuits are kept, the sweet jar), they gather whatever they like and turn their homes into modest stand-ins for the Garden of Eden. 'I sometimes eat chocolate instead of a meal. I tend to do that in the evening. I also eat a lot of fruit. Sometimes I skip a meal and just eat fruit. Two or three pieces of fruit. A banana or an apple' (Isabelle, 20, cited in Garabuau-Moussaoui 2002a: 204). As I discovered in the course of a different study (Kaufmann 2008 [2005]), a deliberate refusal to cook and eat on an organized basis can give rise to an ill-defined but very real sense of excitement, even for older single-tons. It makes up for the hundreds of years when women were chained to the stove. For the first time in history, women can now try to live as autonomous individuals and prove to themselves that they are autono-mous on a daily basis by eating as and when the fancy takes them. Some go one step further in order to heighten their existential pleasure. Danièle, for example, has invented a game: she enjoys not knowing what there is in the fridge and making do with what there is in the evenings. She eats whatever she can find: a yoghurt, a bar of chocolate, a tin of pâté without bread . . . . A personal relationship with food can liberate young women from the usual female schizophrenia we dis-cussed earlier (the earth mother with a sylph-like figure), propel them into the purely rational world of diets and slimming (Ciosi-Houcke et al. 2002) and help them get away from heavy meals and rich sauces. My study of the lives of single women (Kaufmann 2008 [2005]) shows that the lightness they feel (and which suggests that they are more or less sticking to a diet) has more to do with the way that they just pick at their food, and that the nutritional values of what they choose to eat is of dubious value. The chocolate and cakes often cancel out the calorific benefits of the salads and yoghurts.

This youthful rebellion is also directed against the dining table, which is the rigid, haughty symbol of the institutionalized family. They make an effort to find furniture that is closer to the floor, softer and easily moved. They want to do away with the idea of disci-pline and make themselves feel at home by lounging around. 'I very rarely eat at the table. I use it as a desk. I always eat sprawled on the sofa bed. Off a tray' (Juliette, 22, cited in Garabuau-Moussaoui 2002a: 226). Everything revolves around the tray, which is really a table, but one that can be taken into other rooms. 'I get a tray and take everything into the dining room: a main dish, the mayonnaise, ketchup, mustard, the gherkins and a piece of cheese' (Paul, 21, cited Garabuau-Moussaoui 2002a: 226). 'I take my tray and put everything on it. I eat it all at the same time' (Juliette). Christine (26, cited in

Garabuau-Moussaoui 2002b: 227), in contrast, eats her meal in two stages, with a half-hour break in between; she associates dessert with complete relaxation. 'I snuggle up on the sofa to eat my yoghurt.'

Those who graze all the time live mainly on cold food and ready meals. This is 'cooking degree-zero' (Garabuau-Massaoui 2002a: 203). Heating things up is slightly higher up the scale, and the microwave is used in combination with the fridge (which may have a freezer compartment). Simple cooked meals (pasta, steak) are the next step. The technique is still elementary and the food is prepared quickly. And yet it is not unusual for beginners to want to add a personal touch and to be creative. This usually means adding various ingredients (often in the form of spices). Some of them can be quite out of the ordinary and the results can be unpredictable. But even when the process of deconstructing meals is at its most intense, a second, and very different, logic begins to make its presence felt.

Seduction

Meals are never completely deconstructed and the 'individual' model never really materializes. Some meals are eaten within a collective structure, such as a university refectory, and weekends often provide an opportunity to enjoy 'some good home cooking', as Anne-Lise puts it (Gestin 1997, cited in Singly 2004b: 267), even though she is an enthusiastic believer in 'anything goes' when she is on her own. 'Eating anything at any time' sometimes has its limitations. Mealtimes may even be set, within certain limits. And then there are parties with friends which definitely have to be planned if they involve eating together. They are often an opportunity to rediscover that meals, and even cooking, can be fun, or even to use an old family recipe. The cook has unconsciously observed how it is made and now turns it into a personal speciality. But the dining table is shunned and has to compete with seats that are soft and low or with picnics on the floor (Lehuedé and Loisel 2004).

The real change in their eating and cooking habits comes from an unexpected quarter when young people fall in love and become involved in relationships. This is presumably not unrelated to the sensual pleasures of food: the desire to do things properly and to make an effort to feed one's beloved is part of the grammar of seduction (Etchegoyen 2002; Frain 2004). Inviting a partner home for even just a simple meal is all it takes to throw the host's normal points of reference into confusion. He or she feels an overwhelming need to stop

121

improvising and deconstructing meals and to make something resembling a proper meal. This means using better and more expensive ingredients (Ciosi-Houcke et al. 2002). It also means that the structure of the meal is closer to the canonical form. Even the dining table can recover something of its old prestige. A conjugal bond is beginning to be forged and that involves an alchemy based on food or, to be more specific, on meals that respect the conventions. It takes more than feelings, words and cuddles to sustain love. It also needs to be grounded in very banal shared activities. Whenever possible, those activities should be pleasant and not without their sensuality. In that sense, there is nothing to beat sharing a meal. Sharing meals helps to create a loving relationship, just as it will subsequently create a family.

'When we first got together, we didn't see each other very often, but when we did, we used to make meals for each other. That went on for a year and a half. And then we decided to move in together and we did the same with what little money we had: meals for two, and meals with friends. I like to cook, and so does my boyfriend. It means a lot to us.' (27-year-old woman, cited in Ciosi-Houcke et al. 2002: 324)

When a couple have decided to eat together, they can no longer eat just anything whenever they like. And they do not want to do so, even though they do still enjoy a lot of freedom. Mealtimes tend to become regular, though there is still some flexibility. When she was living alone, Clémentine remembers; 'I ate when I was hungry. But now, even though we don't have set times for meals – we're still quite flexible – we know that we have to eat between 7 and 9 in the evening. And lunch is between 12 and 2.' Her grazing days are over: the beginnings of a system are beginning to emerge, and it provides a framework for practices that are more regular and more meaningful. For Juliette, who has just started a new relationship, the change has been sudden and rapid: 'My boyfriend moved in with me a week ago, and I've never done so much cooking in my life.' Complete spontaneity has become a thing of the past: they are beginning to project themselves into the future, and to plan ahead. 'It also means that we do the shopping together, choose what we want to eat together and plan for the week ahead' (Juliette, 22, cited in Garabuau-Moussaoui 2002a: 190).

A drink before the meal

Everyday meals change as relationships develop: when couples eat together on a regular basis, their day-to-day meals take on qualities they did not have when the partners were on their own. The same applies to special meals. Whilst couples who move in together very quickly settle into a routine (Kaufmann 2002b), the desire to disrupt the routine, to invent a new way of living together and to make it more intense is an integral part of falling in love. They want to find ways to become closer and to intensify their relationship. Rudimentary culinary skills are used to create the alchemy of intimacy, rather as though they were a magic wand. Laura is still under the spell: 'I got a surprise when I got home on Monday night: he'd made prawns flambéed in cognac with basmati rice' (Laura, 25, cited in Garabuau-Moussaoui 2002a: 191). The setting is important too: the way the food is presented, the way the table is laid, the background music . . . The idea is to create a total environment that transports the pair of them into a world of their own. Tony puts his heart into it and uses his imagination. His meals are colour-coordinated, and he alters the position of the table and the way it is laid, chooses special music and lights little candles. 'It creates an atmosphere. I make a big effort.' Dinner is a real feast and it encourages them to talk about anything and everything. The odd thing is that they do this every night, and there is therefore a danger that what was a special occasion will become a matter of routine. They have yet to reach that point, and they openly enjoy these magical moments. In more general terms, it is not unusual for these intense experiences to give birth to a new institution. Just like meals, parties can make families.

The emergent social bond transcends the banalities of compulsory socialization because even little rituals add a note of sensuality and have an obvious meaning. In that sense, the habit of having a drink before the meal is very revealing. Not all young couples have a drink before they eat, which is just as well for the nation's health. But the survey shows that many of them do so on a more or less regular basis. As the relationship gradually becomes more structured, they have to find ways of demonstrating their commitment to each other. Such moments help couples to bond. In Tony's case, the ritual takes place every evening and it is a prelude to a candlelit dinner. In Clémentine's case, the ritual is cursory and not a regular habit. Later in the life cycle, the decision to have a drink (which marks a break with normal practice) or to have a glass of good wine in Amandine's case, often signals a desire to revitalize the relationship and to 'find ways of being a couple' (Brenot 2001).

When couples first live together, more or less spontaneous parties add a touch of magic to what are beginning to become habits. It takes them a long time to become stable routines. Although mealtimes, for example, are much more regular than they used to be when they grazed on their own and are decided by mutual agreement, they are still very flexible and couples often eat later and later, as Tony puts it. When they have their aperitif and their candlelit dinner depends on what he feels inspired to cook. 'We often eat at ridiculous times, from 10 onwards, something like that.' Clémentine has decided on a time slot: between 7 and 9 in the evening. But when things do not fit in with her timetable, she has no qualms about looking at the TV guide. 'If there is a good film on', they are quite happy to take their time and to eat at the coffee table in the salon. Meals like that are out of the ordinary, and they have a drink first.

Birth of the family

Without really noticing it, the young couple settle into their new homes day by day. The very fact that they have furniture is an indication that they are gradually being integrated into a routine existence life that will regulate their behaviour. It is, on the other hand, possible to resist the process of integration in an attempt to prolong the existential lightness of being young. Madeleine recalls: 'We were together for five years before we had the children. Cooking never meant much to me. When we did invite people around, they all brought something to eat or drink.' Different couples change in very different ways and the way they eat is one indication of how they change. Some are very quick to begin to organize meals, others less so. Whether or not they lay the table, they all gradually come to feel that they are a couple simply because they repeat the same gestures day after day. They feel that their life trajectory has been stabilized and that it now has a structure they can share. This is a very special moment in their conjugal life and it can require delicate handling. The flames of passion die down, and whilst the new reassurance that comes from having a stable identity does give their lives a meaning, it cannot really compensate for the loss of the dubious charms of not having to make decisions, or the lack of ardent passion. Their conversations, in particular, lose their sparkle and they may even feel that they have nothing new to say to each other, especially at mealtimes. Having to sit opposite one another at the dining table can become something of a problem.

> 'You find yourselves sitting there like two idiots who have nothing to
> say to each other. You say to yourself: "Come on, we're not a little old
> couple!" But, over a meal, you do see yourselves as an old couple. You
> rack you brains in an effort to find something – anything – to say. That

124

didn't happen to us. You begin to wonder if you shouldn't rave it up a bit. You drink water all week, and by the time Saturday comes around, you've had enough of drinking water, damn it! No problem there! A couple of drinks and you never shut up. There may well be silences but, if there are, you don't notice them on Saturday nights!' (Cannelle)

Having another drink to liven things up or making sure, like Tony, that every night of the week is Saturday night are no more than palliative measures that hide, for a while, the fact that something is missing and that they have nothing to say to each other. And it is by no means certain that the conversation will be any livelier than it was when they first met and fell in love (Kaufmann 2002a). In the early stages of a relationship, the excitement and the realization that they know so little about each other helps fill the gaps in the conversation. But as the ritual of the meal becomes institutionalized, the silence becomes more deafening and indicates that communications are breaking down. Small talk can hide that fact for only so long. The couple have to find real topics of conversation that stimulate and excite them. It is at this point that they begin to talk about getting married and having children (and the two things often go together).

From this point onwards, meals take on a new dynamic which indicates that the couple have turned a very important page in their story. Their old carefree existence is gone, and they can no longer live for the moment and do things on impulse. Their lives are now part of a future family project which, more so than at any other point in their lives, transcends and does away with the desire to be independent. The old awkwardness at mealtimes is gone, and there is a lot to talk about now that they are partners in the future family firm. As a result of their everyday conversations, a couple of lovers have become a parental couple. As they think about what they will have to buy and what changes they will have to make, they imagine how their lives will change. At this point, they are often under a lot of illusions. When, a few years earlier, they met and fell in love, they imagined that having a partner would not change their lives and that they would still be themselves. They now believe that they can have a baby and still go on enjoying all the attributes of youth. Tony says that they will still go on his trips around Europe on his old motor bike. What about the baby? No problem: he'll find some way to take the baby with him on the bike. Tony has yet to learn what a baby really is and does not realize that, as soon as it is born, it will profoundly change the identity of its young parents, that it will completely disrupt that system of values and that, whether they like it or not, a whirlwind of new activities will inevitably plunge them into a round of domestic tasks that have to be done day after day. The couple have not just turned a page in their story; a whole new biographical chapter has begun.

The main change in their identity is that the couple's life now centres on their child: nothing could be dearer to them, not even their own lives. This leads to the first change in their dietary behaviour. This period in their lives is especially conducive to reflexivity (they read, analyse and discuss anything that has to do with babies) and they suddenly develop a new interest in what they eat. Many girls once had an interest in what they ate in the sense that they had an obsession with dieting. Their interest now centres on nutrition and health (eating properly for the baby's sake). It is, for example, very unusual for young people living on their own or with a partner to eat fresh vegetables (because of the work and the complex household management involved), but they now become one of the couple's favourite foods (Ciosi-Houcke et al. 2002). As soon as the child can eat soup and puréed vegetables, its parents often learn to eat them too. The high point is reached when the baby can eat at the table with the rest of the family; this is the moment that marks the real birth of the family (Ciosi-Houcke 2002). Despite the amount of work involved – and the exhaustion that follows – the family symbolism of the dining table and table manners is irresistible. 'For the moment, my daughter still eats separately, but when she does start to eat with us, there will be a lot of changes. We will have to buy a dining table to start with. It will all be very traditional: knives on the left, forks on the right.'[1] 'It's only recently that I've begun to enjoy laying the table properly. It used to be "knife and fork" and that was it. But now that he can eat at the table, I make much more of an effort' (32-year-old woman, cited in Ciosi-Houcke et al. 2002: 327). What they eat changes too. Young people adopt a real strategy of avoiding main courses such as roasts and stews (Garabuau-Moussaoui 2002a). Couples who have just moved in together know nothing about slow-cooking techniques, but they quickly learn when their children are old enough to eat at the table. The pressure cooker that was only used occasionally suddenly becomes very important (Kaufmann, unpublished study). It is the perfect symbol of the radiant warmth of the family that eats together. And is automatically associated with the image of the earth mother.[2]

[1] 29-year-old man (cited in Ciosi-Houcke et al. 2002: 327). He obviously has yet to assimilate the tradition he wants to pass on, as he puts the cutlery in the wrong place.
[2] The use of the French term *cocotte-minute* is significant. This piece of kitchen equipment was transposed from the world of industry (pressurized steam) in the 1950s. The (male) engineers who developed it tried for years and years to impose the term self-cooker

A breathing space

This is the beginning of the long period during which meals, which have become a weighty institution, begin to structure the family. But practices and representations quickly diverge. Whatever the 'communion' ideal may mean to their parents, children begin to express their desire to be independent at a very early age, either by refusing to join in the collective ritual or by demanding something else to eat. The recurrent war between the family and individual autonomy has begun. As the children reach adolescence and then become young adults, they extend their spheres of independence and eventually move out of the family home. For their parents, this once more revolutionizes family meals. It is not just that there are fewer people around the table. What is commonly described as the 'empty nest' syndrome is characterized by a more relaxed rhythm as the motivation generated by the dynamics of the social bond loses its impetus. Mealtimes become more peaceful and less intense. The cook (who is usually the mother) realizes how much effort went into making meals for all those years and especially when the children were young. She sometimes begins to wonder how she managed to do it all. This is especially true of families in which individualization has finally put an end to family activities. Maïté is, of course, an extreme example: 'When the children were younger, I used to put more on the table because we were all there. But we rarely eat together now, so . . .' it is ham sandwiches all round and whatever is in the fridge.

When she thinks of the days when everything revolved around the family, the cook is amazed. Where did she find the energy? And why didn't the weight of having so many things to do feel like an even heavier burden? As she begins to shed it (or begins to want to), it seems to become even heavier. Even though she is now doing less (or would like to do less), everything seems, paradoxically, to be getting more difficult. And it is at this precise point that she has to begin caring for her elderly parents. The in-between generation, and especially the mother, finds itself at the hub of a whole network of multiple services, and that can be more than she can take (Attias-Donfut and Segalen 1998). Fifty-eight-year old Yvette is on the edge of a nervous breakdown: 'I've got granddad to look after, and he wants his meals at set times, and then she leaves her daughter with

(*autocuiseur*) because it was more technical. To no avail: *cocotte* [the onomatopoeic 'cluck cluck'; *ma cocotte*: 'sweetie'] does much more to capture the family tenderness that is slowly simmered in the kitchen, usually by the mother.

127

me. I can't say no because I would look as though I wasn't a proper grandmother. But when I have to cook for the whole lot of them I sometimes feel like taking to my bed and staying there' (cited Attias-Donfu and Segalen 1998: 70). Even though she is only 52, Marjolaine too has almost reached that point: 'Having a lot of people around really is a chore, it has to be said. And as you get older, it becomes even more of a chore. You've given your all. For years and years.' But because she loves cooking and wants mealtimes to be convivial, she devoted herself body and soul for years and made an effort even when she could not face peeling all those vegetables. It is because she made so much effort in the past that she is so tired at such an early age. And because her children really enjoy family meals. 'But they expect everything to be done for them. It's a habit they've got into.' Marjolaine is, and always has been, the only cook in the family: neither her husband nor her children have ever given her any help. She is torn between two contradictory impulses: she wants to go on using meals to make her family, and she wants a break from it all. At the moment, the latter impulse is obviously the stronger of the two, given that it has taken her children so long to become independent. It is as though there was a time lag between that point in life when she feels she has to slow down – and she has now reached that point – and a structure of family practices that has lasted a little too long. For Madeleine, in contrast, the two moments have coincided, and she is definitely enjoying the feeling that her day-to-day life is becoming more relaxed. 'Oh yes, when the children were still at home, I used to rack my brains about what to cook. Everything's cool now. The number of times I say to myself: "What shall we have to eat?" And then take something out of the freezer.' The quiet joy, which she scarcely dares admit to, she feels as she experiences this new lightness inevitably reminds one of Danièle, the single woman who enjoyed not knowing what she had in the fridge. Madeleine too feels that she is now a liberated woman.

So much for the bright side. But there is also a dark side and it can be hard to come to terms with it. Life has certainly become easier and more peaceful but there is a price to be paid: meals are no longer what they used to be. A lot of effort went into creating a bond and a vital dynamic. They may not always have been easy but the conversations were always lively. Even the cook's task has become less onerous. 'We were talking the other evening, and we realized that there was a whole series of meals that I used to make when the girls were still at home. I don't make them any more. I'd forgotten about them' (Charlotte). A quick lexical analysis of the interviews allows us to identify the terms that are used most frequently: meals used to be 'important' and 'interesting', and now they are 'simple'. 'There used to more of us here for meals, so mealtimes were more interesting' (Maïté); 'I used to take more time over it, for one thing . . . but now, when I decide to make a meal, simplicity is the decisive factor, Now that there's just the two of us, it doesn't matter so much' (Hortense). Life has become simpler, and quieter.

The children come home

Except when the children come back at weekends, or for some family occasion. Then there are a lot of mouths to feed. Things are even livelier when they bring their partners and when the house is filled with the chatter of the grandchildren. There is now a striking contrast between ordinary meals, which are very simple and quiet, and the occasional noisy gathering. Meals are now organized around two different family configurations, particularly as it is unusual for the whole family to get together. And because big family gatherings do not happen very often, they become potent symbols. 'It matters a lot when the children are here. We'll be having them for Christmas and New Year' (Babette). Although she is no great stickler for form, the table is properly laid. There is more food than usual, and it is chosen more carefully. And the cook does not care how long it takes to make lunch because she is once more carried away with the idea that she is doing it for the family. 'I really like cooking something special' (Babette). Babette does not prepare big feasts; it is just simple home cooking. It only takes a minute. Eugènie has turned her *pot au feu* into a ritual, and it has become the emblem of togetherness. 'Oh, a *pot au feu* is delicious! It's something I haven't made for a long time . . . when there's just the two us . . . it isn't worth it . . . .' So she rings her children, but not to say: 'Would you like to come over on Saturday? I'll make a *pot au feu*.' She inverts the terms of the equation, and the *pot au feu* becomes the excuse for the invitation: 'We're having *pot au feu* on Saturday. Are you coming over?' And they always come because they love her *pot au feu*. They also love the alternative, which is *potée* [hotpot with pork and cabbage]. 'Or else it's *potée*. They love that! Love it!' The immense pleasure they get from her meals makes her very happy (even though she does not say so to them) and revitalizes her: the family blood runs quicker in her veins.

An irresistible force compels parents to make a big effort, and they forget about the new simplicity of their quiet little meals. Partly out of sense of duty and partly because they want to be seen to do the right thing. So they make an effort to ensure that everything is perfect. As the family invitations become less frequent, the stakes become higher and everything has to be perfect. The food has to be first class and the table has to be nicely laid. This is another paradox, which I also observed in my study of how love affairs begin (Kaufmann 2002a): the desire to make a big impression and to make everything look authentic can lead to a certain amount of play-acting and pretence. We become less 'natural' because we want to make a good impression. Charlotte's anecdote is very revealing in that respect. When her girls were young, the house was full of noise and bustle and she did not always have the time to make the perfect meals she dreamed of making. She used to laugh about this with her husband and it became the subject of the kind of standing joke that all families have. They are like magic words that always make everyone laugh, even though they have become stale. The children began to take the lead and make sure the joke is repeated. 'Oh, my youngest used to say: "What's she going to make for tea? Will it be out of a tin, a foil container or a plastic bag?"' The parents no longer find the joke funny. They probably wish they'd never made such a big thing of what was just a joke. They now find it embarrassing and over the last few years they have done all they could to banish it from the family memory. And they are very careful not to lay themselves open to criticism. 'I buy ready meals when there's just my husband and me.' But there are no tins when the children come for a meal. Never. 'I always do something special.'

The sense of duty and the fear of making a bad impression are, however, of secondary importance. The injunction is born of a deep and indefinable desire that encourages her to cook, without pausing to ask why. She is cooking for love. That impulse is, however, the complete antithesis of the desire to have a breathing space. So it all depends on the domestic and relational context (whether or not the cook has to do everything herself, the children's willingness to spread their wings, the grandparents' situation). There is a subtle dialectic between the genesis of the social bond and all the hard work; if the burden is too heavy, the cook feels that she has had enough. Suzette thought she could not go on. She really panicked when her son announced that he would be coming home for lunch every day. 'That gave me a fright.' It was not that she already had enough to do in the kitchen but that, having given her all when her children were young, she now wanted a long rest. Her husband did not come home for lunch and she had rediscovered the delights of just having a tasty light snack. Her snacks required little or no preparation and she ate more or less when she felt like it. She had come to a new arrangement with herself and rediscovered aspirations she thought she had forgotten. Her son's announcement was a frontal assault on an existential world that she found very attractive. At first she felt disappointed (how was she going to manage?) and guilty about feeling disappointed. But the family reflex drove away her gloomy thoughts; she wanted to make something really tasty for his first meal with her. And now her passion for cooking is growing by the day. Because she wants to make something nice for her son, the old reflexes kick in. It is almost as easy as it used to be. 'My son comes home for lunch now. At first I said to myself, "Oh no, It means a lot of work for me." When I'm on my own, I make do with a slice of ham. In the end, I surprised myself because I make things that take quite a lot of time: *blanquette de veau, osso buco.* Things like that. Strangely enough, I don't mind all the fuss. It's better for him because he gets a good meal. And it's better for me. So it suits both of us.'

Family love-feasts

In many cases, the fact that the children are now independent means that the family will, to some extent, grow apart before it wants to get together again for a meal. The usual schema is that of a biographical trajectory in three stages. It begins with intense family activity and day-to-day guerrilla warfare to prevent the family from breaking up. Then comes the need for a break as the children's reluctance to leave home becomes both tiresome and irritating. And then, in a final reversal, ordinary meals become simpler but there is also a new desire to get the whole family together for a meal.

The change is just as spectacular from the children's point of view. As teenagers and young adults living at home, they wanted more and more independence, and finally moved out. They were quite happy to be left to graze. We have, however, also seen that, whilst they wanted their independence, the prospect of family meals was not always viewed with horror. Even at this stage, family meals had their attractions, and their attractions grew once the children had organized their own domestic structures. They stop trying to get away and are happy to go home. There are many reasons for this. At the most material level, there are of course strictly dietary considerations. The joys of grazing soon prove to have their limitations. Given that the system (or anti-system) they have set up can scarcely allow them to eat better even though they would like it to, using structures that act as service-providers – restaurants or, better still, mum and dad – provides the

131

solution. Their parents have similar preoccupations. They are vaguely worried by the disorganized way their children are eating and try to make up for it in some way by giving them garden produce or doggy bags, and by inviting them home for meals. 'The children don't have time, so they live on convenience food, even sandwiches sometimes. So when they do come home I make a deliberate effort to make the traditional meals my mother taught me to make' (Madeleine). They are fed, even stuffed, and they could not ask for anything better. 'I stuff myself. You wouldn't believe how much I eat. Mum thinks it's funny. I don't normally eat like that' (Cannelle). They eat more than they need to because a full stomach reassures them, takes away life's worries, both because they feel that they are sated and because they enjoy rediscovering the things they used to like. As Tzvetan Todorov notes (2001 [1995]: 66) they need to be held, cradled and enveloped because they want 'comforting contact' with something familiar. That 'primary behaviour' does not completely disappear as they grow up. Even when their desire to be independent is at its most destructive, being held, just for a moment, is still good for them. They need to rediscover familiar landmarks, to revert to old habits and, most important of all, to bathe in a family 'atmosphere'.

> 'When I go back home, it does me good to feel . . . the family atmosphere. It's a bit like sailing into a port. It feels stable, and I'm obviously very close to my mother. It's the same with my little brothers: when I haven't seen them for a while, I miss them. When I go back home, it's a bit like being inside a cocoon. I feel I'm safe, as though I was inside a shelter.' (Anne-Marie, cited in Ramos 2002: 209)

The family atmosphere is at its most intense and enveloping at mealtimes. Now that the family is together again, everything feels warm and harmonious, and even the food tastes better than ever. 'They always find it really good to come home!' (Babette). There is more to tasty food than rediscovering the taste of childhood: because they are all sharing the same pleasure, the family comes back to life. *Agapê* is a Greek word meaning love (*Eros* is another word for it). Convivial agapes around a table have the same etymological root as expressions of a feeling of loving friendship, and that is no coincidence.[3] On such occasions, families do commune and do experience something that is very intense. Even more so as the family grows up and as the children, who are now young parents, bring their babies with them

[3] In historical terms, agapes were banquets in which the tables groaned with food, and at which human beings communed with the gods. When the Eucharist took on a symbolic value, they were banned.

for a meal. Their identity has undergone a mutation and they are becoming caught up in their own domestic revolution as they rediscover the benefits of eating at the dining table, disciplines and table manners. That intuitive realization now adds a new dimension. The new parents look back at their own childhood and now have a very different perception of how their parents behaved towards them. The idea of transmission and of a line of descent becomes almost palpable. All at once, they see themselves as a link in a chain.

The meals themselves are not always all peace and harmony of course. Just as the weight of the domestic burden can discourage parents from using meals as a way to make a family, the strict discipline and the cultural generation gap can put children off. If there are too many differences in the way they and their parents do things, or if the invitations come too often, they eventually stop wanting to go home. And it is in fact not so much the desire to be together that matters as what actually happens when the family is together. There is an obvious discrepancy between the way family gatherings are represented (they are idealized because their symbolic weight means a lot to everyone) and what actually happens (they are not always as pleasant as we say they are, or as we tell ourselves). It is as though everyone was trying to convince themselves that they are perfectly happy when they sometimes want to run away, just as they did when they were teenagers. Christmas and New Year are the classic symptoms of the discrepancy between what we imagine is going to happen and what actually happens. In the current climate, in which our urban environment encourages flights of fancy, we look forward to family get-togethers because we expect them to be happy events that will be warm and communicative. Reality, on the other hand, is stubborn and the dream never quite comes true.

> 'I can almost taste the turkey in advance. My mother does me potatoes to go with the chestnut stuffing. They're the best potatoes in the world! But it has to be said that Christmas can also be a real drag. It never lives up to expectations. You turn up thinking it will be like a Christmas card, with all the music and the stars, like a fairy tale. And then you come down to earth and you say to yourself: "Damn it, this is boring!" The worst of it is that you feel guilty because it isn't the way it is on the Christmas cards. And then next year, you still fall for it, and it's the same every year.' (Cannelle)

And the parents who organize everything may not always be bursting with enthusiasm in the way we would like them to be. Claudine Attias-Donfut and Martine Segalen (1998) found that all the people

133

they interviewed said that Christmas dinner was a very important family occasion. But they also said that it involved a lot of work when the family took on the dimensions of a tribe and when their parents got older. Then there is another problem: who is going to take over from the in-between generation? The growing tensions and irritation can destroy the harmony we expect to experience when we eat together. One woman told the interviewer that she had reached the end of her tether because she had to do everything herself. She had come up with a drastic solution: 'It's always the same ones who do all the work, and the rest of them don't raise a finger. I think we should do away with Christmas and then there would be no problem' (cited in Attias-Donfut and Segalen 1998: 12).

The beginning of the end or a new start?

Now that the children have left home and are living independently, a new chapter opens for their parents. They now have to provide meals for three generations. When the generations get together, there are a lot of mouths to feed and, whilst they look forward to that, it involves a lot of work. 'When Christmas is coming up and you've invited the family, you rack your brains to come up with something that makes a change from quick and easy meals' (Madeleine). And after having been parents for so long, they are back to being a couple again and eat facing each other across a dining table. In a sense, they revert to the lightness of their younger days but they are older now and have become less inventive and less confident. They have settled into a new routine. 'Now that the family circle is smaller, we are beginning to become a bit more set in our ways. There's no denying that' (Madeleine). Why try something new when a lifetime's experience of cooking means that you can easily make simple meals? 'These days, there's less variety and we tend to eat what we've always eaten. And at our age . . . I don't experiment as much as I used to, that's true. How can I put it . . . I'm . . . I'm like everyone else . . . I get by on what I already know' (Madeleine).

If, however, we listen carefully, we quickly realize that experience and familiar routines that have developed over the years are not the only factors involved. Hortense begins by pointing out that she finds it hard to break old habits as she gets older. 'We're not going to change the way we live at our age.' But listen to what she says next: 'Try something new? Not now that there's just the two of us.' Now that the children have left home, married life isn't what it was when

134

they were young. When they were young they were willing to experiment and were committed to working on their new relationship. Now that they are always on their own together, Hortense feels that she no longer has either the energy or the motivation. In a sense, she just cannot be bothered. This helps to explain why routines have become so important: their socialization now has a greater structural effect on individuals because they have lost the ability to make the subjective projections that make the effects of their socialization so disappointing (Kaufmann 2004) 'When there's just the two of you and you know your husband won't create a fuss, you don't go to so much trouble' (Anneth). So Anneth does not go to so much trouble and life becomes easier. There is, however, a high price to be paid: as the routines become simpler, they lose their intensity and she is beginning to feel that she is watching her own life from the outside. When the children leave home, something else happens too (and in many cases there is only a short interval between the two things). Retirement also encourages their parents to stop trying, and acquired habits become a form of self-protection. The ensuing process of 'letting go' has been analysed in detail by Vincent Caradec (2004). Meals are both a very accurate indicator of how far the 'letting go' process has gone and a major factor that determines whether it will slow down or accelerate. Just as meals helped to make the family when it was effervescent, they loosen the bond once they degenerate into something that is just routine. The tone used by the interviewees when they talked about different periods in their lives is very revealing. They were cheerful, even enthusiastic, when they talked about having a lot of people for a meal (even when they were describing how tiring, and sometimes even exasperating, it could be) but suddenly began to speak more softly and in a monotone. They sounded almost sad when they described what meals were like once the children had left home. Eugénie's answers were brief and unenthusiastic. Her tone was flat and lifeless. That was because she was talking about a period in her life that was less lively. And then she suddenly began to speak more quickly, with a new rhythm to what she was saying, and with more energy and emotion. 'It was mainly when my husband was working, when he was away from home and came home on Friday evenings. Oh, you know, it was really . . . really . . . I'd make something like grilled salmon . . . something out of the ordinary.' Nowadays there is no 'something' and everything is ordinary. Madeleine's tone changes too. As we have already seen, she rarely cooks anything new. But when she was being interviewed, she suddenly sat bolt upright when the recent past was mentioned, and became quite animated as she relived it: 'I often used to swap recipes with the women I worked with. "Look what I've found" someone would say! "You can't imagine how good this is".' And we would talk about it, and copy out this or that one. When we went back to the office on Monday morning, we'd discuss them. "Oh, that was good . . . that wasn't nice." And so on and so forth.'

A whole range of factors converge and help to accelerate the letting-go process: the need for a break, the awkwardness of being just a couple again, the television that drowns out the conversation more and more . . . Then there are dietary concerns and medical advice as to what to eat. It is just when the family becomes less demanding that the minor worries about health associated with old age begin to make themselves felt. The advice is usually the same: don't be greedy and reduce the size of the portions. 'Less' is the key word during this period in their lives: less inventiveness, less muscle tone, less on the plate, less time in the kitchen (half as much; Guilbert and Perrin-Escalon 2004), fewer people for meals, conversations that are less lively, less enjoyment of food. Everything becomes more bland and smaller. Except when it comes to dietary issues which are now very much on their minds (Guilbert and Perrin-Escalon 2004). Whilst they may be mentioned only in passing, dietary concerns can combine with the other factors that encourage couples to let go simply because they mean that they eat less. Eugénie put it very well when she said at one point in her interview: 'When my husband was still working . . . it was heavy work. Now, he's like me and doesn't do anything, so we don't eat much. And you have to be careful at our age.' Whilst the logic of reflexivity can get out of control, it can also have the opposite effect of encouraging people to experiment. Whereas (as we saw in Part I) reflexivity can lead to a loss of reference points for someone who eats alone and may encourage bad habits, it can also have the opposite effect of reactivating a social bond that is becoming sclerotic. Eugénie may well sound sad when she talks about having to eat smaller portions but she livens up a little when she describes how she and her husband are trying to improve their diet. 'Now that we're retired, we have a much more balanced diet. I try to keep it light, salads and things like that. I don't mean I make anything complicated but it makes a bit of a change.' Babette has already gone a lot further down the same road. On her doctor's advice, she had decided to go on a diet together with her husband. Quite apart from the fact that they now talk more about dietary issues, this has given her the opportunity to change the culinary habits of a lifetime and she has begun to cook lighter meals. Health issues help to encourage a new commitment to married life: eating well so as to protect the quality of life for both partners. This does not mean that Babette has lost interest in cooking. Her new recipes often take longer to make (about two hours on Sunday mornings) than the old ones.

There is nothing inevitable about 'letting go'. Some couples find the biographical transition that begins when their children leave home difficult to handle but others use it to give their relationship a new dynamism. Now that their children are not the factor that brings them together, a new interaction between husband and wife begins, and it is part of the broader process of 'taking on a new identity' (Caradec 2004). This is therefore an especially decisive moment, as the couple may either begin to let go or energize their relationship. Various kinds of activity can be used to do so: sport, cultural interests, travel, or even sex. But, because they are alone together day after day, ordinary meals, and the quality of the conversations they have over them, are probably the most important. Breaks from routine can also be important because special treats show that the partners are still committed to one another and that the relationship is still alive. The survey revealed that, at this stage, they begin to have a drink together before the meal, just as they did when they first fell in love. This is not entirely risk-free (it can degenerate into a chronic alcoholism that means they will never break the habit) but it is an easy way to create intimacy at little cost to either partner. 'You need to celebrate the end of the week,' says Babette. So, diet notwithstanding, it is 'port on Saturday evening and at Sunday lunchtime'. In Hortense's case, it is port on Friday, Saturday and Sunday. This is a new ritual and a clear indication that a new phase in their lives has begun. She and her husband are once more a couple and it is not always easy to find other ways of saying that they are. 'We never used to have an aperitif like this, not every week. Now we have one on Friday evening, Saturday evening, and Sunday lunchtime. It's something we can share. Something of a treat. We always have a drink in the lounge, and then eat in the dining room.'

Doing something out of the ordinary and using meals as a way of revitalizing a marriage is not, however, easy, as couples typically spend less times on meals at this point in their lives (this explains why having a drink before the meal is so popular: it does not take long). Avoiding this schizophrenia involves some delicate manoeuvres. Charlotte is a case in point. During the week, she cooks something quick. 'It has to be said that I'm even more alone than ever, now that I'm with my husband all the time. We just have some soup, some bread and cheese, a yoghurt, and that's it.' But while they are having their soup or yoghurt, they never stop talking about food and planning

137

the meals they are going to have with their children. She makes lists two days in advance. So they lead two parallel lives: a frugal married life and an extravagant family life, and they contrive to combine the two without any difficulty. The problems start when the children are not there for Sunday lunch. There are just the two of them there for what is usually something of a feast. What shall it be: frugality or extravagance? Simplicity or intensity? They have found a solution: something out of a tin but not just any tin. It has to be something they brought back from their last holidays (they always bring a lot back). It does not take long to cook but it does remind them of a high point in their married life and it breaks the routine. Eating whatever is in the tin gives them a lot to talk about, as it means they can relive the holiday they enjoyed together in a new setting. Madeleine, in contrast, secretly dreams of staging a coup in the kitchen and of how she would be its first casualty. Now that she no longer has to cook for the family, she has lost all interest in cooking and her marriage. She no longer makes any effort and, as she put it, gets by on what she already knows. But at the same time she has developed a passion for new kinds of cuisine that are both light and modern. She loves eating in restaurants. So why not try to make the same things at home? 'It's a paradox, because it would be ideal at our age.' Unfortunately, 'It's complicated!' It is complicated because this is not a technical decision that can be made outside the context of her marriage. Madeleine finds herself in a social situation in which the repetitious nature of married life is a source of psychological reassurance. It is therefore difficult for her to spark the revolution she secretly dreams of sparking. The improvised rituals that can revitalize a marriage are impossible if the couple are really caught up in the letting go process.

Meals and families

As it accumulated, the data from the survey allowed me to confirm that there is a very close relationship between families and meals. What I originally saw as just one hypothesis amongst others therefore gradually proved to be my main line of research. At every stage in the life of a relationship, meals both help to create bonds and serve as an index of the quality of family life. We have seen how the family cycle in particular – from the days when everything revolved around the children to the danger that the parents will 'let go' when they leave home – imprints its rhythms on meals. Biscotte's story is in itself a summary of the problematic. Her early married life was bland in both culinary and marital terms. Rebelling against her mother, who urged her to do more, she refused to devote too much of herself to cooking: a woman's destiny was not to be found in the kitchen. As a couple, neither partner could find a way to break the routine and there were few rituals to bring them together. This was not unrelated to the fact that neither of them was deeply committed to the relationship. When they had children, Biscotte did, however, manage to cook proper meals: for the children. She was the only one to make an effort. The relationship turned sour and ended in a divorce. At this point, she became a fanatical cook in an attempt to keep the family together. 'I cooked from morning to night.' She made lots of cakes, even though she was not very fond of them. She lost interest when her children left home. She once tried to make herself a proper meal. 'But when I sat down at the table all by myself, I couldn't eat it.' She prefers to live on snacks: a piece of cheese, a yoghurt, a piece of fruit. She has discovered that she is usually not very hungry. She has lost interest in cooking and sitting down by herself at her big dining table gives her a mental block. The contrast with the scenes she remembers is striking. 'I used to cook for a family who liked nice things and I knew that they would enjoy what I made.' She enjoyed the fact that they enjoyed her cooking. That was when she had a family and when they ate together.

Biographical trajectories aside, many other contexts make it clear that there is a close connection between families and meals. It is well known that meals are the focal point of big family get-togethers which can be very intense. Olivia does not feel at all tired, despite all the work Christmas involves. 'There are 25 or 30 of us, but I'll go on doing it for as long as I can. Being able to get together, to see each other, is a real joy.' It takes only a glance at her photo albums to see that many of the events in the illustrated history of her family myth have been immortalized for posterity in photos of meals (Kaufmann 2002b). 'We've always celebrated the big events in our lives by having a meal. When we finished paying for the house, getting exam results . . . things like that. We've always had a meal to celebrate. The children can still remember' (Madeleine). The same close relationship can also be observed in less grandiose contexts, as when the family group tries to resist the forces that might disperse or individualize it. Joël Meissonier (2002) takes the interesting example of men who live in the suburbs, spend a lot of time commuting to and from work, eat lunch away from home and get home late in the evening. The most functional solution would be for their wives and children to eat early and on their own, and for the commuters to grab something to eat on the way home, or even to eat on the train. But functionality is not the issue: the symbolism of the family is at stake. 'There are some things you can't give up, and one of them is the family meal', says Mr Ranime (cited in Meissonier 2002: 231). If they did not eat together, there would be nothing to keep the family together. The group holds out as long as it can, even though 'the children say "I'm starving"' (Mrs Lescure, cited in Meissonier 2002: 230). Suzette's husband gets home late too. She does not have to deal with children who complain that they are starving; there are 'just the two of us' in the evening now. But there are many reasons why she should not have to wait for her husband to get home. First, she has become used to eating on her own and having only a light meal (or had got used to it, until her son began coming home for lunch). Her husband likes his independence (but does not share her liking for light meals), watches a lot of television and would be quite happy with a meal on a tray in front of the telly. Neither of them says much at mealtimes, and their meals are not really moments of intensity. And it is precisely because they do not have much to say to each other – which suggests that their marriage is not all it might be – that they insist on having a meal in the evening. It is as though it was the one thing that kept their relationship alive. 'When he gets home late at night, I think it's too late for me. But I make the effort to wait because . . . It's better when we're together, even if we don't have much to say to each other most of the time, we always have something to say at mealtimes.'

Both relational extremes – intensity and fragility – are a great encouragement to use meals as a way of revitalizing the bond. The intensity of the attractions of love and of caring for children encourage it but so does the strain of letting things go, growing individualization or the break up of the relationship. It takes even more effort to use meals as a means of strengthening a relationship or a family when one partner is not there. Claudine Marenco cites a woman who is separated from her husband:

> 'Well, there's no family atmosphere because her dad's not there . . . despite that, I try to create . . . a family atmosphere for my little girl, so in the evening I sit down at the table with her, even if I'm not hungry and we have a proper meal, with a little hors d'oeuvre, a main dish, and then cheese. It's a proper meal . . . I make myself sit down with her and eat with her, so that we're a proper family despite everything.' (Marenco 1992: 248)

But using meals in this way when the relationship is weak is not always easy, especially when the partners begin to quarrel. Close intimacy over a meal table can make things worse, just as it can encourage intimacy. Jacqueline Burgoyne and David Clarke (1983) found that the people they interviewed spontaneously told stories, which were often both long and detailed, about food when they mentioned being divorced or remarrying. Describing the events that led up to their divorce, they mentioned their loss of appetite at the table, weight loss and plates being thrown; when they began a new relationship, they recovered their appetite and began to enjoy sharing meals again. Unfortunately, that was not what happened to poor Mrs Graham. After her divorce, she tried hard to cook for her three girls. Eating together was their way of being a family. They invented a new kind of meal and an extended teatime replaced dinner. She thought she had rediscovered love with Martin. The mealtime ordeals showed that it was just a dream. She could not be bothered to make him a separate meal and he could not fit into their system. What seemed to be a prosaic detail proved to be a sign that they had a serious problem.

Non-families and non-meals

That there is a close connection between family ties and meals can also be demonstrated in negative terms: non-family situations clearly encourage unstructured meals. The people who were interviewed said so quite spontaneously, and often compared the different experiences they had been through. 'Now that it's just the two of us, we eat more simply', said Melba. Couples whose children have left home eat less than they did when they were at home. But people who live alone (or eat alone) eat less – much less – than couples. 'Oh, when you're on your own you don't make so much of an effort. When there are two of you, you force yourself to eat' (Maryse). 'Cooking is something you do for your family. Because when you are on your own, you tend to cook less' (Anneth). 'Oh, when I'm on my own, I'm not going to spend two hours cooking! I do something quick' (Bélangère). Various biographical situations can lead to a growing disenchantment with both cooking and eating. When we are young, the jubilatory intoxication of existential lightness encourages us to live on snacks and everything gets smaller when we begin to stop making an effort. Leaving those situations aside, people who are on their own definitely lose interest in cooking and food, especially if they are middle-aged. To be more accurate, they lose interest in cooking and in ordinary meals. Single people often lead very active social lives and make up for the drabness of the single life by inviting each other home for meals and especially by eating in restaurants with groups of friends (Kaufmann 2008 [2005]). At home, every meal is simple and quick: they spend little time on cooking, eat smaller portions and lay the table quickly. When, that is, there is a table: many single people do not have dining tables because they do not like the family symbolism. Single people, like young people, tend to make a point of eating sitting on soft, low seats that can easily be moved around. The single life encourages them to go on trying to prolong their youth because it means that they have no commitments and that their future is still ahead of them. And that influences the way they cook and eat their meals.

It is common for some members of the family to eat on their own. As a rule, that is not a problem for those who live on snacks and have a fridge. But what happens when it is the cook, who is used to slaving over a hot stove even when she does not feel like it, who eats alone? As a rule, she slows down, loses interest in cooking and realizes that all she wants is something light. Melba spends her Friday evenings alone because her husband plays sport. 'It's the end of the week, and I get a bit fed up with cooking.' She is happy to graze. Suzette began to cook again when her son started coming home for lunch, and quite enjoyed it. But she could remember something she enjoyed even more. 'I didn't eat a lot: fruit, cheese. I didn't eat a proper meal, and I didn't cook. I'd got used to the quiet life and to eating alone in front of my favourite TV programme.' Biscotte has been on her own for longer and completely refuses to have anything to do with food or cooking: 'I've lost interest.' She eats very little: 'I don't eat anything, nothing at all. Not interested. A bit of cheese, a yoghurt, some fruit but nothing cooked.' She dislikes the dining table and its family symbolism. 'If I sit there by myself with a plate in front of me, I completely lose my appetite. I'd rather have a piece of cheese and eat in front of the telly. I can manage that.'

What we have just described is, of course, a model that gives a schematic picture of how most people behave. Not all single people (or people who are living alone for the moment) live on snacks. Some of them like their food and some even enjoy cooking. They are such keen cooks that the absence of any family input does nothing to curb their enthusiasm. It is interesting to look at what forms it takes. Single men tend to eat big meals because they are either greedy or hungry. Jean-Pierre Corbeau (2002) cites the example of Boris, a forty-year-old bachelor with a very hearty appetite (he weighs over 120 kilos). Even he rarely eats at the table when he is at home and would rather live on snacks or go to a restaurant with friends. Single women tend to cook because they have a passion for cooking and cannot stop themselves. Candy sometimes makes proper meals for herself when her children are away: 'I find it relaxing.' Prune has always cooked because doing so is part and parcel of the ethics that governs every aspect of her life: 'Even when I was single, I used to make veal olives, with peas from the pod and carrots.' Some people never lose their appetites, or their enjoyment of cooking. But all, or almost all single people, dislike having a dining table in the middle of the room because it is the most potent symbol of the close link between families and meals.

The first meal

It is especially interesting to study the first meal that marks the existence (which in some cases is by no means certain) of a new family tie. Such meals are problematic in two senses. Like any meal, they have to bring a group together and the need to do so is all the more urgent in that the closeness of the relationship presumably represents the beginning of a lifelong commitment. But, given that modern societies are both individualist and reflexive, it is quite normal for both partners to stop and think before they commit themselves, to try to observe each other and to determine the quality of the ties that are being established. Meals should therefore both speed up the familiarization process and be used as critical instruments that allow them to test the water. The two things are of course contradictory, as I found in an earlier book that looked at the first time couples have breakfast together (Kaufmann 2002a). Most of the interviewees described a delicate combination of two things: an eroticized desire to embark upon a new relationship and the shock of encountering strange eating habits or disconcerting table manners. Agathe, for instance, was very taken with John but began to wonder what she was getting herself into when she found herself trying to eat a huge sausage sandwich in an unmade bed with John; she was more used to bone china and dainty cakes. Then there was Vincent, who was disconcerted by the cultural gap between his urban habits and the rural world Aglaé lived in. 'I didn't like the milk at all. It was straight from the cow, and I wasn't used to the strong taste.' Aglaé, for her part, sat in silence at the other end of the big table, scowling at the glass of water and the aspirin in front of her. Was this really the beginning of a passionate affair?

Reflexive individualism has destroyed the institutional nature of the ritual banquets of old, such as the wedding breakfast feasts that once signalled that two families had become one (Segalen 2003). Nowadays, little rituals (such as a drink before the meal) are cobbled together after the event to give the relationship a little sparkle and excitement. There are, however, still some situations in which a meal sanctions a new bond and they are of particular interest. The decision to introduce a new partner to our parents is one such occasion. The choice of partner has already been made and the parents make an effort not to interfere, much as they may want to (Cosson 1990). The introductions are therefore not – officially – an examination and are supposedly no more than a rite of passage as a new member is welcomed into the family. In a return to the tradition of the 'clanship of porridge', it is once more a meal that brings about the extension of the group. Mathilde Perrot (2000a) has made a study of these special meals. The first conclusion to be drawn from her work is that the survival of this foundational ritual probably results from a mistaken perception on the part of the actors. They assume that, because meals usually give rise to wide-ranging and uninhibited conversations, they can, ideally, give rise to little rituals that are both well suited to the times in which we live, simple and authentic, and flexible and relaxed. 'It's easier to talk over a meal than over a drink. Eating gives you something to talk about. It breaks the ice and gets the conversation off to a good start. It's more convivial' (Mrs Simonet, cited in Perrot 2000a: 36). Every effort is made to try to defuse and normalize the situation, to behave as though nothing important was at stake and to pretend that this is just an opportunity to get to know one another over a nice meal. 'It wasn't a formal introduction, or as though it was for life. It wasn't as though he was Mr Right; he was just someone I was with at the time' (Delphine, cited in Perrot 2000a: 29). 'Making it official is putting it a bit strong. It was a way of showing them I was living with someone I loved, that I was going to spend the rest of my life with him, even if no one said so in so many words. It was . . . perhaps I should say it was a way of making it official. That's overstating it, but there aren't many other ways of putting it' (Marie, cited in Perrot 2000a: 27). The meal very quickly reveals the terrible intensity of the social mechanisms it has set in motion. Normal conversations over a meal are as relaxed as they are because everyone already knows everyone else. And now everyone has to get to know everyone else very quickly. We are surprised to discover that, whilst it may be relaxed, sharing a meal is not as straightforward as we imagined it to be and that the meal is in fact a lengthy procedure that has rules. 'Meals are little plays. They last quite a while, and that allows everyone to observe everyone else at their leisure' (Javeau 1984: 93).

Being forced to be on very close terms as we sit opposite each other has the opposite effect to what we expected: the relaxation is an illusion but the anxieties and tensions are very real. A lot of play-acting goes on and these meals have none of the simplicity and authenticity we had hoped for.

The pressure actually begins to build up long before the moment of truth arrives. Pauline recalls how her mother gradually began to feel the stress.

> 'It was supposed to be just a simple meal. Just a simple meal together, but that wasn't all there was to it by any means. She had tried to make an effort. And she thought the usual tomato salad with onions wasn't good enough. So she made a proper meal. Boiled beef with carrots. And it was 30 Celsius in the shade! She meant well, but it just so happens that Benjamin isn't very keen on boiled beef and carrots at the best of times, never mind when it's thirty degrees in the shade. Mum felt really awkward.' (Cited in Perrot 2000a: 35–6)

Emilie was very impressed when she went for her first meal at her boyfriend's parents' place. 'It was the dining table they use at Christmas and it was sumptuously laid.' Paradoxically, the parents also feel that they are on trial and do not want to let anyone down, so they tend to try too hard. The young couple feel that they are about to sit an examination and they try to get ready for it. The son or daughter provides a detailed description of the family's way of doing things and of all its members so as to allow his or her partner to make a good impression and not to put their foot in it. Juliette's main worry was her father. 'Mum was nothing to worry about, but I warned Vincent that dad might ask some awkward questions, and that he was probably in for a short interrogation, a sort of test to find out how he felt about me, to find out if he was intelligent, sensitive, that kind of thing' (cited in Perrot 2000a: 38). Sylvain thought that Gwénola could have done more to help him and would have liked to have been briefed more thoroughly:

> '"You have to tell me what I have to talk to him about, what subjects we can talk about . . . because I have no idea." So I said to him: "Oh, I don't know. Just talk to him about holidays. He likes travelling, or about the stock exchange . . . You don't want to talk about that? You're right, you don't know anything about it. That's true! Right. Well, don't mention football, because he doesn't like it. Oh, I don't know! We'll see!"' (Cited in Perrot 2000a: 38)

Conversation and table manners are usually central to the way families construct meals and can prove to be very delicate issues.

Finding something to talk about is the first obstacle. The need to establish an instant familiarity with people we do not know means avoiding the many topics about which we might disagree. 'Avoid so-called difficult topics, like politics, the unions, religion. And avoid getting into discussions, at least that day. Don't criticize the Pope's line on condoms. Avoid things like "What do you do for a living?"; "I'm unemployed"; "Can I get you a drink?"; "No, I've been going to AA for years now". Just don't put your foot in it' (Mathieu). There is another taboo subject: the parents have to avoid asking too many searching questions as that might give the impression that they are weighing up the girlfriend or boyfriend, and especially their career prospects. They find it very difficult not to be curious. 'He wanted it to be friendly. But they still asked him "What are you going to do afterwards? What about your studies, in the medium to long term?"' (Sophie). The best thing to do is to stick to small talk but that rings false over a meal that we intuitively feel to be a rite of passage and the stress makes it feel all the more important. How can we talk about anything and everything at such an important time? I have described elsewhere (Kaufmann 2002a) how people make small talk when they first have breakfast with a new partner precisely because it is such an important occasion. And that can create problems. Mathieu, who had failed to grasp how delicate the situation was (and who suspected that they took a dim view of what he did for a living – he was a professional photographer), was on the point of exploding: 'I was beginning to lose it because they were showing no interest in what I do. As soon as I started to talk about what I do, they changed the subject and said: "OK, that's fine, how are things? Why don't you give him some chicken?"' (cited in Perrot 2000a: 48). When the conversation becomes difficult, we can always talk about the food we are sharing.

Good manners can also be a problem. The guest is not familiar with the family's way of going about things. The parents have made more effort than usual because they do not want to make a bad impression. The young hopeful who wants to be accepted by the family tries to be on his or her best behaviour. Nothing is as easygoing and relaxed as it is supposed to be. 'I made an effort to sit up straight, pulled my chair up to the table and concentrated on using the right knives and forks. I forced myself to drink some wine, but not too much because you're acting a part and you don't want to look like the local wino!' (Gwénola). 'Try not to put your foot in it, have a drink, but don't overdo it. Don't swear every time you open your mouth . . . Unless they do! Watch for the signs that tell you that you can relax. And have a second helping, and say it's good! And don't use your fork as though it was a shovel!' (Delphine, cited in Perrot 2000a: 40). Mathilde Perrot cites an interesting counter-example. The boyfriend kept putting his foot in it (he had knocked over a chair by hanging his heavy biker's jacket on the back of it). Once they had got over the shock, the family decided to make a joke of it. He was very young and no harm had been done. The poor lad's gaffes (and his girl-friend's embarrassment) had made it perfectly clear that this was not the start of something serious. Everyone breathed a sigh of relief and turned it into a joke. But when it is a real, and somewhat stuffy, rite of passage, it structures the group into a unit with surprising speed. And yet nothing important is said. That is not the important point. The important point is that a collective discipline with a long history (which explains why it is so rigid) has been imposed without anyone realizing it. The issue of where everyone sits at the table is one index of the extent of the mutation that has occurred. 'You don't catch on at first but by the time it comes to the second meal, you've got it!' (Benjamin, cited in Perrot 2000a: 67). 'The fact that you sit in the same place for the next meal is a fairly obvious indication that the family group has adopted you' (Perrot 2000a: 4).

Taking sides

'The shock . . . the culture shock' (Perrot 2000a: 67). Pauline still shudders when she recalls the first time she met Benjamin's parents. It takes only a few seconds for a meal to reveal how different our partner's family is. Mathieu was impressed by how much money Sophie's parents had. He had concluded that his own manners had to be beyond reproach. He was mistaken: he had misjudged the situation and did not understand her family's way of life.

> 'I'd had enough of talking about food. There was no conversation. Sophie's parents have money and they're more middle class, but in terms of their attitudes, they might as well be working class. They shout at each other at the table. At home, we don't watch telly; we eat and we talk to each other. At their place, everyone just sits down. My family are more old-fashioned. When I first met Sophie's parents, I wanted to make a good impression and show I'd been brought up properly, so I stood waiting for her mother to sit down first. He father told me to sit, and he laughed when said I was waiting for the mistress of the house. To begin with, I waited for her, but I quickly came to understand their codes of behaviour and felt embarrassed.' (Cited in Perrot 2000a: 66)

The anecdote captures the awkward situation in which he found himself: paradoxically, he felt that he was in the wrong because he was trying to behave properly. In such circumstances, our usual response is to re-establish our self-esteem by falling back on our own values and taking a critical view of our surroundings. And that is what Mathieu did. 'In the end, I decided I wanted to keep my distance. I'd been well brought up and I didn't want to "slum it". I stuck to my own values because I wanted to be respected for what I was' (cited in Perrot 2000a: 66). The familiarization ritual of the 'clanship of porridge' had failed to work. Mathieu could not empathize with Sophie's parents' family culture and the meal was proof that he could not. Sophie had to choose between her new relationship and her family. Received ideas notwithstanding, it is not unusual for someone in her position to side with her in-laws rather than her parents (Lemarchant 1999). It all depends upon the fragile equilibrium that the new couple are trying to establish. When one partner takes a dislike to his or her in-laws or even quarrels with them, the other partner has to choose between the relationship and their parents. In this case, Sophie took Mathieu's side and not that of her parents. 'When we're with his parents, we talk a lot, but not so much with mine. When we're with his parents, the telly is turned off, but with mine we go on watching the news. It's all a bit shallow' (cited in Perrot 2000a: 66).

Meeting Pauline's parents was a culture shock for Benjamin too. But unlike Sophie, Pauline immediately sided with her parents. Benjamin found himself in a minority of one, faced with a group that was both united and hostile. Pauline admits that she overreacted but says that she could not control herself. 'I find some things really offensive, like eating with your knife, for example. I can't stand that. Benjamin does it because that's the way he was brought up. It was very intolerant of me, very prim and proper, but I can't help myself' (cited in Perrot 2000a: 42). Suspecting that something like this might happen, she had, however, made careful plans for that eventuality, and had carefully briefed both parties. Her advice to her parents was very general and ethical: 'I told my parents Benjamin was from a fairly modest background so that they wouldn't be too offended by some of the ways he behaves.' Her advice to Benjamin was more practical and designed to improve his table manners:

'I spoke to him about this and we had a row, so I spoke to him again and we had another row. I told him early on that it wasn't really done, or at least not at my parents' and certainly not at my grandmother's because she's a stickler for things like that. It was for his own good, a way of making sure that he didn't get pigeon-holed, that his attempt to integrate did not get off to a bad start. He took it as a direct, personal attack on him, the way he's been brought up and his parents.' (Perrot 2000a: 42)

Pauline is convinced that she is in possession of a universal truth (good manners) and that she is motivated by love: she wants to give Benjamin a foretaste of what she imagines their future life together will have to be. Benjamin feels that he is being judged, put down and humiliated because of what he and his family are. He is, for a moment, reluctant to criticize his family in an attempt to save his own skin. 'It's true, everything is very informal at home' (cited in Perrot 2000a: 42). But he came under renewed attack and all hell was let loose halfway through a meal. It was the way the used his knife that triggered it. As usual, he cut himself a piece of cheese and used his knife to put it in his mouth. Pauline had been watching his every move throughout the meal and immediately noticed his mistake. Her parents had seen what he did but said nothing. It was Pauline who rebuked him in front of everyone, thereby demonstrating that her parents' opinion meant more to her than anything else, including Benjamin. The meal had shown where the balance of power between the two groups lay and it was not in his favour. 'I said to her: "Is that what you call education, telling people off in front of everyone?"' (cited in Perrot 2000a: 42). But the way he said it showed that, to all intents and purposes, he and his family had been defeated. One aspect of the couple's future together had been decided over a meal, in micro-struggles around the table and with sidelong glances at how they all used their cutlery. A banal knife had helped to decide someone's fate.

Talking about the weather

Meals, mealtime conversations and table manners establish family ties in a very concrete sense and shape the configuration of the groups involved because they are rituals that are repeated day after day. The liveliness and intensity of festive occasions have the foundational effect of defining the meaning of the relationships between people who do not otherwise get together very often. Conversations over meals and table manners also construct other kinds of social ties with colleagues or friends and the meals in question may be eaten in restaurants, or at home if the family network is open to friends.

Friendship is a living bond and it changes as it develops. Friendships die or at least fade away when the logical development of everyone's centres of interest can no longer sustain the synergy (Bidart 1997). Once again, meals allow us to see how things stand, all the more so in that dinner parties are becoming less and less institutionalized. Attendance is no longer compulsory and they increasingly reflect nothing more than a desire to spend some time together (Lehuedé and Loisel 2004). Table manners are becoming less strictly codified and less reliant upon protocol, both because informal meals (pasta, an omelette) can be improvised on the spur of the moment and because dinner parties are planned a long time in advance. In the latter case, the goal is to make the meal a special event and to create an atmosphere. Creativity is the order of the day in terms both of the food and the setting, and that matters much more than the way the table is laid.

Ideally, the guests share a pleasant moment of intimacy and sensual communion. They enjoy eating together but they also enjoy the atmosphere. As at home, difficult and boring topics of conversation (politics, work) therefore have to be avoided. The minor polemics that do arise are more contained than they are at home: the important thing is to get the group to gel in a positive, friendly way. There are two topics of conversation that cannot be avoided: children and holidays. The various families that gather together compare their dreams of what it means to be happy and try to share them. This group logic is especially obvious from the self-control that applies sanctions to anyone who talks too much about themselves (Lehuedé and Loisel 2004). Conversely, the dominant note has to be one of self-effacement and generosity if the group is really to come to life. When that happens, the happy experience of sharing a meal helps to create lasting ties of friendship.

These friendly gatherings are not very frequent. The stakes are therefore far from negligible. What becomes of the friendship depends on the conclusions that are drawn by each of the families (and each family immediately comes to its own). It is therefore logical to heighten the intensity and the feeling of togetherness. A variety of devices are used: special table settings, sophisticated food, large amounts of alcohol. And above all, an effort is made to be as open as possible and to make the exchanges more intimate. Ordinary conversation is not enough, nor is kindness or cheerfulness. Whilst they are part of the group, the guests have to open up to each other and do so in all sincerity. Some topics of conversation are always banned and, if they do come up, it is obvious that the party has been a terrible disaster. The most obvious is the weather, which is something to be discussed with strangers or during polite exchanges with the neighbours. If more than a few seconds are spent discussing the weather, it is a sign that everything is very superficial and that the meal is not going to be a success. And that the ties of friendship are unlikely to last.

A short history of tables (Part II)

The dining table is still central to the construction of bonds both between friends and within the family. I began to tell its story in Part I. It can be summed up very quickly. The dining table is descended from the sacrificial altars that were used to make offerings to the gods. In the Christian West, dining tables were in use for a long time before they became permanent fixtures, despite the foundational reference to the Last Supper. The meaning of meals was too indeterminate. It was unclear whether they were convivial rejoicings or symbolic religious gatherings (Verdon 2002). When the civilizing process began to centre on table manners, the dining table became the focus of a public performance. The fact that these short-lived spectacles took place in public did not mean, however, that the table was a permanent fixture. Planks were simply put on trestles for the duration of the party. What we now call a dining table is a recent invention dating back to roughly the eighteenth century. It then became a permanent fixture with a specific function, and chairs were placed around it. 'Chairs were not really everyday objects during the Middle Ages. A chair was an attribute of the sacred, and reserved for kings and holy images. Commoners sat anywhere they could: on the floor, on mantelpieces, on cushions, chests or benches. Where they sat depended on their rank, but they all sat remarkably close to each other' (Roche 1997: 190). Three-legged chairs first appeared in the fourteenth century. But it was some time before they were arranged around tables, and it was only in the seventeenth century that the canonical arrangement (chairs placed opposite each other around a table), which we now take for granted, emerged. Duflot's print *The Benediction* (after Lebrun) dates from the beginning of that century.

> It depicts a family gathering, with the father and children seated, and the mother standing. The spiritualized atmosphere probably contains an allusion to the Last Supper. The banality of an everyday meal cannot be divorced from the vision that renders all things unto God. The table, which is a modern invention (people managed without tables for a long time), is now found in many different social situations. (Roche 1997: 191)

151

The Christian world used this new object to introduce a symbolism in which sacred references coexisted with a social form that was still tentative but beginning to solidify. As we saw in Part I, it was slightly later, or in the nineteenth century, that a whole society's cult of the family came to crystallize around the strict discipline that had all members of the family group sitting facing one another. We now know that the material object which made that arrangement possible existed before those ideas became established. In historical terms, the dining table has played a central role; it helped to produce the modern family.

Ever since the beginnings of modernity, the table has played an increasingly important role in the world of work as well as in the domestic realm (though this is probably just a strange coincidence). It is a basic tool for the administrations and other bureaucracies that are an intrinsic part of reflexive societies (Weber 1992 [1922]). It is also a prime tool for all the intellectual professions and service industries that are expanding so rapidly. Fewer and fewer jobs involve physical contact with earth, iron or coal; the number of desk jobs is steadily rising. Organizational and working methods are also changing. Hierarchical command structures are giving way to discussions and negotiations and they, like training sessions, take place around a table. People sit facing each other in the canonical way whose genesis has just been traced.

This synergy undeniably gives a certain power to the table and yet it is difficult to grasp the full extent of that power because the table itself seems to be so banal. And yet its structuring materiality does produce social forms on a daily basis, both at home and in the office, and all over the world, without the actors realizing it. Although its essential role is discreet, it exudes a symbolism that is not without its effects. The culture of colonialism, for example, used tables to impose its models for bureaucracies, education and meals. In societies in which custom required people to eat sitting on the floor, and with their hands, rigid table manners introduced socially distinct places in European restaurants. The colonists went home but the tables remained. Tables are one of many indicators of how the Western model has influenced the rest of the world. The conclusion is inescapable: it is now normal to sit upright at a table, even in Arab and Asian societies that were used to different physical postures. If, however, we look more closely, we find that the dining table's hegemony is neither clear nor systematic. In Japan, for example, it is common for several types of table to exist side by side within the same house. Although Western-style tables are making rapid inroads in China, they are confined to the dining room, and low tables continue to be used in the lounge (Desjeux et al. 2002).

It is amusing to note that, at a time when dining tables are becoming more common in the non-Western world, the West is discovering the new delights of low tables, which make for much more relaxed styles of eating. It is as though, now that the age of hegemonic influence is over, a world consensus is emerging around the idea of having a variety of different tables in the house. They do not, however, all have the same meaning: the reasons why we use high or low tables vary enormously (Desjeux et al. 2002). We all use them in different ways, just as we use meals to structure our families in different ways.

Just a table?

As we saw in Part I, dietary practices are becoming highly individualized and the traditional role of women is being undermined (which helps to promote their legitimate emancipation). Convenience food is becoming more popular as a result and less time is spent in the kitchen. But as we saw in Part II, the dining table has, despite all its historical tribulations and all the different uses to which it has been put, an effect on how family groups are structured. Before we pursue our discussion of culinary issues any further, and before we look at what goes on in the kitchen, it seems appropriate to ask whether a dining table (in combination with a fridge or freezer) might not be enough to make a family. Dietary and nutritional issues aside, can meals still create family ties? Do we still need meals to make a family and, if so, why should that be the case?

A few of the people interviewed for the survey answered that question in the negative and said that a table was all that was required and that there was no longer any need to cook. Karim Gacem's example of the Pécheur family is an emblematic case. Without going into great detail, it is worth pointing out that Pascale, who is the mother, has had a major influence on the way her family eats. As a feminist, she refuses to be confined to the kitchen and, having experienced anorexic episodes in the past, is not prepared to spend her days slaving over a hot stove. 'Even when it's just a matter of heating up ready meals, it makes me want to throw up' (cited in Gacem 1997: 76). It is not just that the table plays a structural role even though no one cooks. The dining table has little to do with the pleasures of gastronomy. 'Food does not matter very much to us. It's just food.' The dining table itself is an indication of how little interest they show in what is on their plates. It is a garden table covered in oil cloth, which is flatteringly described as the 'tablecloth'. The glasses are jars that once contained mustard, and it shows. The knives and forks are laid almost at random. It is, as Simon puts it, 'a complete shambles' (cited in Gacem 1997: 79). The absence of style masks the fact that the conversational function of their meals is highly institutionalized and that the table's characteristics are conducive to this. The table is round and small and the way the group sits around it encourages discussions. 'There we all are around the table, all facing each other' (Pascale, cited in Gacem 1997: 67). The group dines on the words that are exchanged rather than on what they are actually eating and the whole family is used to lively discussions and a high level of noise. So much so that the slightest silence immediately gives the impression that they are living in a void. 'I really hate it when you can hear the flies buzzing. I really don't like it when we sit down at the table and no one says a word. I feel like running away' (Pascale, cited in Gacem 1997: 70). For the Pêcheurs, the dining table does seem to be all they need to be a family. This is a lively family with a genuine communal spirit. The group is more institutionalized than appearances might suggest. Although their individual independence means a great deal to the Pêcheurs, mealtimes are governed by a group ethics that does imply a certain discipline, and especially a punctuality that allows the whole family to eat together. Pascale is reluctant to admit it. 'We're not going to start to dictate how many mouthfuls everyone eats per minute. We're not going to waste any energy on introducing rules' (cited in Gacem 1997: 83). She does, on the other hand, have to admit that the group gets very annoyed when one of its members is late for a meal. The dining table structures the time the family spends together all the more in that its individual members have greater freedom elsewhere.

This model of a life organized around two distinct blocks of time (with conversations over a meal as a counter-balance to independence) is not, however, very common. In some cases, there is no real group likely to compensate for the growing individualization of practices. In extreme cases like that of Maïté's family, everyone makes their own sandwiches and eats separately during the week. Whilst many households do not take things that far, convenience foods and takeaways leave the dining table to work its magic all by itself; it now tends to serve the defensive purpose of preserving what is left of the group. 'Even if it is only for half an hour, it does mean that we do all get together', says Melba, whose ambitions do not extend far beyond that. Even the Pêcheurs find it difficult to live up to the high standards of their model. The obligation to sit opposite one another for intense conversations inevitably triggers a desire to run away, especially for children. The dining table is then abandoned in favour of meals on trays in the lounge, which is the lair of a monster that is strictly banished from the dining room: the television. The parents try to coordinate movement so as to ensure a minimal degree of family life. 'Eating together does mean that there is a certain closeness', says the father (cited in Gacem 1997: 67).

It takes more than a dining table to create a family. Conversation does create bonds but it is difficult to manage. If it is just one ingredient among others, it can take the form of pleasant chatter that creates no problems. If, however, we expect too much from it, there is a danger that it will become both tiresome and a source of tension. As we have seen, the communal ideal tends, rather, to be based upon a reasonable syncretism. Conversation does have its part to play but it must not go beyond certain limits. Satisfying the need for food, and the enjoyment of food, are also primordial elements in this syncretism. This is especially true when meals mark a departure from the usual routine. Even a minor break from routine can give the family the feeling that this is a real event. The meal itself is an important factor and so is the manner in which it was made. That is because it is part of a history (old memories and very recent practices) that means something to the family. Home-cooking adds a further dimension that can enhance the syncretism.

We can see this if we take one last look at the Pêcheur family. Laurent, the father, has a secret longing for a very different kind of family meal and for the smells that once permeated the house and announced that a gastronomic ritual was about to begin. He has no regrets about the choice they have made and loves the fact that they have so much to say to each other over the dinner table, especially as he cannot see himself slaving over a hot stove: 'I find that making a meal really is something of a chore' (cited in Gacem 1997: 101). But almost without realizing it he has quietly begun to cook and has invented a new ritual. 'We have breakfast together. It's a family tradition we've gone back to. It was the same with my parents' (ibid.: 102). Everyone made their own breakfast for years but Laurent has discovered a new kind of quality time. 'I want it to be a real family moment' (ibid.). He did not make a fuss about it. It happened gradually because he was willing to prepare things in advance and because he felt an irrepressible need to do so. There is a lot of food (toast, orange juice, various hot drinks) and the table is properly laid. The lighting is soft and there is background music on. The contrast between this and the family's tasteless evening meal is striking.

155

Everyone in the family has, curiously enough, been slowly won over by this world of elementary sensations. And the most surprising thing is that they are so taken with this atmosphere that they almost forget to talk to each other. The Pécheurs have become unrecognizable. 'Even when we're running late, we have a quiet breakfast. We can hurry later. It's very calm. We don't say much, but we start the day together' (Pascale, cited in Gacem 1997: 103). Cooking has allowed them to find a new way of being a family. Clémentine confirms this. Immediate sense-perceptions are very important. 'Being together over a meal you don't want to eat is not really being together.' The family feels more together when the meal tastes good. And the work that went into making it creates a dynamic that involves and affects the group even before the meal has begun. 'Now that I've started to cook, I'm trying to get the family to follow my example' (Clémentine).

What magic allows the solitary work that goes into cooking to bring people together as a family? It is time to open the kitchen door and see what's cooking.

Part III

In the Kitchen

THERE IS COOKING AND THERE IS COOKING

The chef

Making meals is obviously an activity that does a great deal to help to create family ties. There is, however, more to it than that. The individual who does the cooking also has more personal dreams and interests and they are both rich and complex. We will now look at them in more detail. But first we must decide just what to call the person who does the cooking. Until now, I have, for the sake of convenience, allowed myself to use the term *la cuisinière*, given that it is usually a woman who does the cooking. Statistics, however, do not really alter the fact that the assumption that it is a woman who does the cooking might be very politically incorrect from the point of view of equality between the sexes. It might, in a sense, encourage women to remain trapped in their traditional role. Although it is unusual for men to do the cooking, French uses the masculine noun *chef* to describe anyone who cooks.

As we shall soon see, an impressive range of alternatives is available to the cook. She (or he) must constantly choose between various types of food, between quick and slow styles of cooking and between different types of meal, and these choices have nutritional implications as well as an impact on the form of family that is being constructed. Without even realizing it in most cases, cooks are always making decisions and their implications are more far-reaching than they might imagine. A cook is much more than someone who works in the kitchen. A cook is someone who is in charge, a leader [*chef*]. He may not give many orders but the person who is in charge of the kitchen in fact holds the destiny of the small domestic group in his hands. Now the term 'chef' is very familiar in the catering industry.

159

For other reasons, it is used in the professional sense to refer to the person in charge of what is indeed a very male environment (the almost military hierarchy of kitchen brigades). As we shall see, it is not inappropriate to use the same term to refer to whoever is in charge of the home kitchen because it is definitely the chef who takes the decisions (he or she may consult other members of the family but is usually in sole command and may find it a lonely responsibility). The only problem is that *chef* is a masculine noun even though 'he' is usually a woman. We have to bear that in mind, and in what follows it will have to be taken for granted that *le chef* is a woman if we wish to get a better picture of the real nature of the division of domestic labour.

Two worlds

Most of the people interviewed reacted to my first questions in the same way, and it is very revealing. They either wanted to know what kind of cooking the survey was about (or, to be more specific, which of two kinds of cooking it was about: the everyday meals they tried to make as quickly as possible or the meals they cooked for pleasure or because they had a passion for cooking, and on which they spent a lot of time) or talked exclusively about their passion for cooking. It was immediately obvious that 'cooking' was something that went on in two very different worlds and further investigation showed that one was systematically contrasted with the other. Clémentine's immediate response was to say: 'It depends what we're talking about.' She went on to make a distinction between 'day-to-day cooking', which she compared to housework, and 'Cooking', which was part of a very different world. Candy even refused to use the word to describe what she saw as a somewhat off-putting day-to-day activity. She tried to find another word to describe it but could not do so. Throughout the interview, she made it clear which of the two categories she was referring to. Many other people made the same distinction: one form of cooking took place in the repetitive everyday world of the race against the clock and 'domestic chores' (with all that term's unflattering connotations) and the other took place in a world of creativity and impulsiveness that was quite out of the ordinary. 'Cooking is more creative than other forms of housework. On the other hand, I don't like having to cook every day' (Biscotte). 'Cooking day in, day out, two meals a day, at lunchtime and in the evening, is not much fun; it's just another form of housework. But cooking myself is something else.[1] Just making something different, and having the time . . . .' Melba's final words are not as insignificant as they might seem. 'Something different' is not just a variation on a theme; it is a break from routine that attempts (successfully) to enliven family life. The inversion of the relationship with time is an even greater mystery. There is never enough time and, because there is never enough time, having to cook every day is a pain. The relationship with time can, however, be inverted; when there is more than enough time available, the other form of cooking becomes a pleasurable activity.

In the minds of the people who were interviewed, the distinction is perfectly clear: their lives are divided between two completely different worlds. And it is true that two contradictory action regimes and thought regimes are at work. As we shall see, however, the distinction between the two is neither stable nor watertight. They constantly overlap because the physical actions involved are the same in every detail. This puts even more pressure on the cook who constantly has to choose between two contradictory positions. The clarity and forcefulness of their answers indicate that cooks always have two models in their minds, and that those models have a different influence on what they think and do. This schematic picture tends to exaggerate the most obvious differences between the two worlds in which they live. The inversion of the relationship with time is, for example, very often related to the opposition between 'weekday' and 'weekend'. The distinction is not, however, as clear-cut as their more general comments might suggest. Savarin admits, for instance, that he does make 'quick and easy' meals at weekends and that his passion for cooking can be revived during the week 'when the opportunity arises'. Paule-Dauphine often goes back to the theme of a 'break from routine'. What she actually does in the kitchen, on the other hand, could not be more routine. It is part of a well-established action-system with which she is very familiar. 'I'm very much a traditional cook.' She exemplifies the social complexity that lies behind the simplified models because, given the state of her marriage, the routine she is describing is determined by the structure of the meals she cooks. In an attempt to stop getting into a rut, she persuades her husband to take her out to restaurants to eat something different and try something new. She never tries to reproduce these experiments at home and falls back on a tried and tested routine. Because she is thinking in terms

---

[1] The verbal slip is delicious. She obviously meant to say 'cooking itself'. We can only conclude that 'cooking myself' reveals that her commitment to cooking involves some underlying issues to do with her sense of identity.

of abstract models, she imagines that the contrast between the two forms of cooking is greater than it actually is: the realities of everyday life are much more complex than her models. Anneth becomes somewhat confused and her answer to the question is quite contradictory. 'Cooking is just like another form of housework. It's nicer than the rest of the housework because it allows you to do what you want to do and to do something special for your friends or family.'

The *ancien régime*

These forceful descriptions of the contrast between the two culinary models are all the more noteworthy in that this bipolarization is, in historical terms, a recent phenomenon and has yet to affect the majority of the population. A far from negligible proportion of cooks still, like Paule-Dauphine, operate within a very regular framework that does not change. There is no real difference between what they think they are doing and what they actually do. The framework within which they operate is characterized by a sense of duty and the need to get on with things, and is based upon the traditional role of the woman who devotes herself body and soul.

It is, of course, this bipolarization that turns the cook into a *chef* or leader whose every decision affects the family's future. The chef has to strike a balance between the quick and easy meals that have to be made because the traditional role of women has changed, and because his or her personal commitment inverts the relationship with time. Both models centre, however, on the individual subject. Autonomous, emancipated individuals tend to make quick and easy meals; being creative in the kitchen gives a meaning to the lives of those with a passion for cooking. This is quite in keeping with the complementary images of the individual that dominate our second modernity (Kaufmann 2004). It is not surprising to find that the distinction between these two ways of cooking is a recent development that took place at some point in the 1960s or that it does not affect the whole of society to the same extent. The few interviewees who always cook in the same way according to the survey are therefore of great interest in that they exemplify a way of life that is on the verge of extinction. Its most remarkable distinguishing feature is the weight of the binding structures that make their bodies an element within a system that is already in place. There is little or no difference between their thought regimes and action regimes, and life goes on as expected, both in the kitchen and at the table (hence the highly institutionalized and ritualized Sunday lunch). This does not mean that the individual at the centre of the system (who is, as it happens, a woman because this action logic takes up so much time that it is impossible unless the woman is confined to the home) is no more than a support for the structure, or that the cook neither thinks nor feels as an individual. On the contrary, and as has always been the case, some people like cooking and are good at it, whilst others do not like it so much and are not so good at it. Individuals' interest in cooking, and their culinary skills, varies considerably (and has always done so). Such variations are now a key factor that explains individual levels of commitment. Under the *ancien régime*, cooking was simply something that had to be done. Cooks (and in this context we are talking about women) did what they had to do, whatever the circumstances. With, of course, varying degrees of enthusiasm and success. In the far-off days when the rural population lived on soup, there was little difference between one household and the next. As standards of living rose, as more products came on to the market and as more free time became available, the differences became more pronounced. Some women did their duty and nothing more whilst others became real artists. Although the subjective shifts of perspective that mean that cooks suddenly move from one culinary world into another had yet to develop, their general position was characterized by their degree of commitment which varied from one family to another. Leaving aside their specific features, the following examples have been chosen because they illustrate the different ways different women fulfil a role that still has much in common with the *ancien régime*. Eugénie illustrates one extreme and Prune the other.

Eugénie feels that her way of life means that cooking is an inescapable duty. She defines it in ways that are at once very specific ('for my husband') and extremely vague ('all sorts of other reasons'). 'At times, it really is because I have a duty to my family. You say to yourself, "Right, I really do have to make a meal. For my husband, and for all sorts of other reasons." But if you're on your own, you don't cook. Ultimately, you have no choice.' She feels she has to cook. Although she does not want to, she settles down to her task as best she can. 'When I cook, I cook; I try to do my best, but it's not my cup of tea. I don't really enjoy it. It's not a chore but it's something that has to be done and that's all there is to it. I've never had a passion for it.' She just does what she has to do and goes on doing what she has always done; everything about her life is predictable. 'Keep it simple' . . . 'Don't make life difficult for yourself' . . . the expressions come up again and again and hammer home the ethical principles that determine what she does. 'I don't make life difficult for myself. I tell myself that simple things are the best. I do things I know I can do. I don't bother with cookery books and all that, and I don't do anything fancy. It's just one more thing that has to be done, and it's soon over and done.' It doesn't take long. It is just one more thing that has to be done, and she knows she can do it. Although she is not very keen on cooking, the idea that she could live her life differently never enters her mind. 'If you don't cook, if you don't do the housework, what do you do?' She may not be very enthusiastic about them but her domestic duties take up most of her time.

Prune also gets on with her life without even thinking about it. But she does not find cooking difficult and is both a competent cook and a passionate one. She makes no distinction between what she has to do and what she wants to do and that makes her forget that she has no choice. 'I never get bored, not even with peeling vegetables.' She is so involved in what she is doing that she would rather be on her own in her little kitchen without anyone to disturb her and devote herself to the things she loves (cooking, mealtimes, her family). There is something magical about cooking and it is her hands that work the magic. That is why she likes to make slow-cooking meals that require a lot of preparation. 'With a stew, it's you that adds the taste . . . the ingredients . . . how long you spend on it . . . you decide everything.' Because she loves spending time on it and does not mind how long it takes, Prune feels that she is making something more than a meal. Her mind is full of images: images of the past (the big family meals she enjoyed as a girl), images of the immediate future (the next meal) and images of her family. Her dedication to cooking is her way of creating a family. And she is a very traditional cook who makes the same things day after day and meal after meal. This explains her hostility to change and exotic foods. 'What is fried rice, when all's said and done? It's just an omelette with peas. With a stew, it's you that adds the taste . . .' Prune is 33. Although she is young (and very attached to the modernity of an affectionate and relational family), she is perpetuating an extreme (and rich) form of the culinary model of the *ancien régime*. Cooking is a vocation.

Lightening the burden

In their different ways, Eugénie and Prune both exemplify what is now an unusual stance. The obligation to cook is now seen as intolerable. Feeding the family is acceptable but devoting oneself body and soul to it is not. Time constraints, combined with work commitments, are in themselves enough to make it impossible. Then there is the desire for personal emancipation, especially for women. Cooking is either something we do because we want to cook at times of our own choosing or a burden that has to be made as light as possible. The new products and services that free us from the burden of cooking to at least some extent are therefore widely used. An acceptable meal can be prepared in just a few minutes. Those who have opted for 'quick and easy' meals have clearly rejected the cook's traditional role. It may seem paradoxical, given that this way of cooking is so undemanding, but the common complaint that it can be 'a pain' is highly significant. Although she does not particularly enjoy it, Eugénie refuses to describe making meals as a 'chore'. That is because she still accepts the idea of duty and does not project herself into alternative identities: cooking is her whole life. In the modernity of the first culinary world, in which the ideal model of speed becomes too demanding, the slightest little thing that takes time (a lettuce that has to be washed, a jar that is difficult to open) can suddenly make us feel physically tired or irritable. When things get difficult, it is always a sign that we have more than one identity. The individual who is surprised to find that the task in hand takes a few more minutes than expected mentally stands back from it and sees what he or she is doing from the outside, rather as though a different part of his or her identity was an outside observer. His or her other self says that this is a waste of time that could be put to better use (either at work or for leisure activities).

Functionalist representations of new products and services notwithstanding, quick and easy meals mean that we have to develop some very subtle tactics. Except when the use of individual ready meals is taken to extremes (as at Maïté's, where everyone makes their own sandwiches), the 'speed' model must not always be there in the cook's mind; the dream of being able to do everything quickly has to be adapted to real life. In order to avoid that danger, the cook has to retain at least some notion of her duty to the family (which means that the cook's old role has not been completely forgotten). She may not have a duty to make cordon bleu dishes but she does have a duty to give the family a decent meal and to put food on the table. The issue of routines has not been completely resolved either. In the pre-modern system, actions were structured by routines, and the body itself acquired habits that were themselves an integral part of the old traditions. This is what Guy Thuillier (1977) calls the 'ancien régime'. In theory, modernity emancipates individuals

165

and allows them to be both free and creative. In practice, the free individual makes only sporadic appearances and tries at other times to reconstruct the old habits in a bid to reduce the mental pressure and make his or her actions more fluid. Torn between contradictory injunctions (save time/provide a proper meal), the cook's degree of commitment constantly changes. As we shall soon see, there can be brief outbursts of passion while she is making the most banal of everyday meals. She does not usually succeed in working in one mode for any length of time. Depending on the context or the moment, she may either adapt to the 'speed' model or fall back on the idea that it is her duty to make a meal for the family (in which case she tries to rely on routines that make the task easier). Alternatively, she may decide to be more creative and to add a personal 'touch' (which disrupts her routine). The survey shows that the idea of duty tends to predominate. The cook is convinced that she is justified in spending more time on the task in hand, does not stop to think how long it will take and begins by reactivating some basic routines. 'If I press the "mash" button inside my head, the machine starts. It does it all for me' (Cannelle). Once the more demanding but routine sequence has been set in motion (mashed potatoes in Cannelle's case), the cook can invert her relationship with time. She wants to work fast and suddenly time flies because she is totally 'caught up in what she is doing' (Giard 1994: 216), just as she was under the old regime. When circumstances (lack of time, a sudden feeling of exhaustion) demand it, she may suddenly decide to make something that takes no time at all. 'Sometimes I say to myself: "I can't be bothered tonight, so it's just a slice of ham and a green salad", and that's it. There are times when you just can't be bothered' (Hortense). The individualization of practices and the new role played by the fridge accelerate the process still further. 'In any case, there's always the fridge. If they don't like what's on offer, they can fend for themselves' (Amandine). The cook has a whole range of supplies in store and can therefore adapt meals to the needs of the moment. The freezer, for example, means that a meal can be made very quickly when circumstances dictate that no more time is available. The freezer means that the cook does not actually have to be in the kitchen and can just eat like the rest of the family.

These variations in action regimes and degrees of personal commitment explain the underlying feeling that 'quick and easy' meals are somehow difficult. I analysed how these mechanisms operate with respect to housework in an earlier book (Kaufmann 1997). We acquire the ability to develop very routine gestures because our action schemata are stored in an infra-conscious structure of the brain. It is not magic or some abstract habit that causes Cannelle's mashed potatoes to 'make themselves'. The very specific schemata she has internalized mean that she knows precisely what she has to do next; it has become automatic. The variety of action regimes implies the existence of a range of other possibilities (opening a tin rather than making mashed potatoes) relating to different action schemata (both conscious and infra-conscious). As a result, competing schemata emerge and lead to a cognitive dissonance which always make us feel that things are difficult. This is not the case with Cannelle who concentrates so hard on her mashed potatoes that the process is automatic once she has begun to make them. In most cases, however, the fact that there is, at least in theory, a quicker alternative means that the slightest delay (such as having to peel the potatoes before we cook them) introduces a feeling of annoyance.

The underlying idea that 'quick and easy' meals are difficult (which, whilst it may not last, is a source of annoyance) is exacerbated by their negative ethical connotations which make things worse. Even the idea of doing one's 'duty' by one's family fails to live up to the dreams of a lot of cooks. And the mismatch becomes even greater when the cook decides, for some reason or other, to save even more time. Although she tries to convince herself that she is quite justified in doing so, she cannot help feeling a certain guilt and that can be very annoying. Surprisingly, Amandine is the perfect example. How can she feel guilty when she cooks three different meals a day (one of them featuring her husband's famous Cretan diet) and when her sons are always so critical of her (they complain about a lack of variety but always insist on eating the same things)? And yet it takes only one comment for her to tell herself that she could have made something else and showed greater commitment. 'It's true that I do feel guilty sometimes and I tell myself I'm overdoing it. I buy ready meals.' 'And sometimes I forget: "Oh damn, I made that the night before last!" And they notice: "We've already had that once this week!"'. One of the problems with quick and easy meals is the belief that we have to give people what they want to eat; the spirit of self-sacrifice and love implies that we know in advance what they want. A failure to anticipate their desires or, more paradoxically still, too great a desire to do so, can make the cook feel both guilty and uncomfortable. Charlotte still works but her husband is retired. Although he likes his food, he rarely cooks. She hates the fact that he has recently got into the habit of coming into the kitchen 'to see what's cooking'. Because she is always in a hurry, she knows she cannot make the things he likes.

Charlotte senses that her other self could, if the context allowed it, be a more 'loving' cook. That is why she finds everything so difficult.

A sudden fancy

The *ancien régime*, which was both monolithic and institutionalized, has given way to two very different action-models. Cooks do not know which way to turn and are worn out because they cannot come to a decision. The first model – 'quick and easy' – appears to be simple but is underpinned by two contradictory logics. The second, in contrast, forces the individual to concentrate both mind and body on the task in hand. This state of mind is governed by specific mechanisms. The same is true of the feeling that things are difficult which results from a cognitive dissonance. In the second model, the emotional impulse is the most important factor; cooking is a passion. It is like the great passions of old but it is also what Christian Bromberger (1998) calls an 'ordinary passion'. Ordinary passions are an important feature of the societies of our second modernity, in which there is always a danger that the reflexive individual's self-doubts and questions will induce a sort of existential schizophrenia. The cook therefore has to find some way to put the shattered meanings of his or her life back together again and cobble together some sense of self-identity, even if it is no more than temporary (Kaufmann 2004). There are several ways of doing so but none is more effective than passion. Even a minor passion for something very simple can be all it takes. Passion sweeps us away: everything makes sense and seems obvious, and we no longer feel the deadly chill of reflexive modernity. Nothing could be more modern than a minor passion.

The people who were interviewed captured the emotional nature of the new culinary regime perfectly. The recurrent use of one central term was particularly significant: 'I want to.' Its content is ill-defined and can change quickly but it refers simultaneously to a desire to be creative, the expectation of personal pleasure and a wish to give one's love to one's family. Wanting something is usually a sudden impulse and it overcomes us when we least expect it to, just like the great passions of the past. 'Even during the week, I sometimes come up with an idea, or suddenly want to make something. I often feel sudden impulses just like that' (Marjolaine). Wanting to do something allows us to forget the pressures of everyday life. Suzette says that she does things 'on impulse' or, rather, 'used to' because 'that's all over now. I can't do it any more. I've become very calculating.' She feels all the more nostalgic for her old impulsiveness in that she now finds it much more difficult to cook and in that her marriage is no longer what it was. Passions make life easier but we cannot feel them to order.

Cooking for love makes family ties more intense because, thanks to another paradox, we feel, as individuals, that we just want to do something. Desires, which simply made the cook's job easier under the *ancien régime* (and which were repressed by the bourgeois model for table manners) now do a great deal to promote an enhanced socialization. The changing position of delicacies within the general architecture of meals is in that sense very revealing. They were once the inevitable centrepiece of the meals that cooks produced at regular intervals. They now tend to indicate that something special is happening and that something has changed: they indicate that the cook has abandoned the 'quick and easy' model and has discovered a new passion for cooking. She obviously expects something in return, because it is not exactly easy to love without being loved in return. Amandine is well aware of it. She would really love to be able to give more of herself and to give her family a treat, thanks to the magic of her cooking. Unfortunately, the only reward she gets is indifference and rejection, though her daughter is the exception to the rule. Cooks can do nothing on their own. But once the people they are cooking for have made it clear what they want, the impetus to make it has to come from the cook.

Unlike love itself, cooking for love does not always imply any long-term commitment and is not very time-consuming. Sudden fancies and momentary impulses can easily trigger sequences of events that do not last long. It takes only a moment to decorate a dish, and only a gesture to add an extra ingredient. This second action regime sometimes comes into play when we least expect it. It can even happen to Mäité. During the week, it is ham sandwiches all round. But on Sundays: 'You can't live on sandwiches all the time. I have a little more time to spare, so I try to do something a bit special.' When she is asked to go into greater detail, the list of Sunday treats is not, unfortunately, very long: steak, escalope, chips, pasta . . . She suddenly becomes more animated: 'Sometimes we even have . . . .' What comes next is something of a let-down. Sensing that her answers are making a poor impression, Mäité makes an effort to describe what other treats she can come up with: 'The pasta isn't always the same. I try to ring the changes, so we have spaghetti, tagliatelle, things like that.' The interview was drawing to a close when she happened to mention desserts. Desserts? Yes, she makes home-made desserts every weekend. But desserts are different. She does not begrudge the time she spends on them because she loves making desserts. 'For some reason, I love making them.' She likes making them so much that she thinks about nothing else as she does so, which is why she forgot to mention them. When she is making desserts at the weekend, she is in a different culinary world and her whole family joins her there. 'It's just as well because we all like our food in this family.'

There are strict time limits to Maïté's moments of passion, and they are highly ritualized, which somewhat reduces their impact. Like any passion, the passion for cooking feeds on the unexpected. This explains why this mode of action is very often part of a bid to be creative: the cook becomes excited because she is being creative and the treat comes as a surprise to the family she is feeding. 'I quite enjoy trying out new recipes. And it makes a change' (Marjolaine). The second action regime disrupts all routines, from kitchen to table. The cook makes a mental effort to come up with something new and the novelty turns the meal into an event. The logic of married life and family life mean that we inevitably get into habits. Whether they mean to or not (and in many cases they are not opposed to this, though they may not say it), family members protect themselves by getting into habits that make life less tiring in mental terms. They also make life more boring. A sudden passion for cooking therefore looks like a convenient way of disrupting the routine for a while. It does so to only a slight extent but that is commensurate with the ease with which it can be done. Whilst it may not alter the nature of a relationship, creative cooking can spice it up. Olivia was interviewed three weeks before Christmas and could think of nothing else. She wanted 'a change from the traditional turkey'. A change from turkey meant a slight change of lifestyle. As she thumbed through some magazines, she came up with an idea: chicken in coconut milk. Chicken in coconut milk is not just chicken. It transcends chicken. Last year, Olivia and her husband had a holiday in the West Indies, and coconut milk obviously brings back memories of the sun and the scent of the islands. It also meant she was setting herself a challenge. Cooking chicken in coconut was something no one in the family had ever done before. It would be quite an event. 'Like a party, so I wanted to make something special.' But she soon began to have doubts: what would the coconut milk do to the meat and wasn't there a danger that it might be too sweet? So she decided to devote two weekends to testing her recipe. Both she and her husband began to experiment with chicken in coconut milk. A sudden fancy inspired by reading a magazine had triggered a joint undertaking that took several weeks.

Candy is not especially fond of chicken in coconut milk or of anything else that is exotic. She will eat exotic food but that tends to happen during the week when she buys ready meals or frozen food. She prefers 'traditional cooking', and she has time for it at weekends. And yet she had as much to say about creativity as about pleasure and passion. 'Cooking at the weekend is one of my leisure activities. Even when I'm on my own, I cook myself a little something. When I say "cook", I mean I create something.' She has her own way of being creative: she works intuitively, without bothering too much about measuring things carefully and without following a recipe. But as she improvises, she does follow certain rules and does respect a tradition. 'I always make shepherd's pie the way my mother used to make it.' Because her improvisations are intuitive, Candy does not realize that what she is saying is somewhat contradictory. But the real reason why she does not notice that she is contradicting herself is that she is convinced that she is creating something, though she would find it hard to say just what it is. She is creating a family life that is intense, spirited and anything but routine. The paradox is that she is at her most creative when she is being most respectful of a tradition that restores the link with the generations that came before her. By making shepherd's pie the way her mother used to make it, Candy really is inventing something. Cooking for love works in mysterious ways.

Hidden difficulties

The two culinary action regimes constantly overlap. In most cases, cooking for love is for weekends, and quick and easy meals are for weekdays. I have already explained why it is difficult to integrate quick and easy meals into a fully coherent model: because we are always eating different things, we have no fixed points of reference and that makes everything feel difficult. The feeling that things are difficult is neither acute nor overwhelming, like cleaning windows, for example, which is often seen as a job no one wants to do. The feeling comes and goes, nags at us and makes us irritable. And besides, not everyone hates window cleaning (though many people do). In the same way, not everyone sees cooking as a chore and there are a lot of individual variations. Babette has to think hard before she can remember when she last found it difficult ('Well, I really must have been out of sorts that day'). Melba and Suzette, in contrast, always feel that it is an unpleasant task. 'It's a drag, it's often a drag, but you force yourself to make a meal' (Melba); 'Having to cook every day is a real bore, a real drag' (Suzette). As a rule, it was, however, unusual for the interviewees to complain about having to cook, except in the specific contexts that we will look at in a moment. When they did complain, they did not say much and spoke softly, even ruefully. The responses were strikingly different from those I obtained from a previous survey about housework (Kaufmann 1997) when the respondents talked a lot about how hard they found it. The peculiar nature of the difficulties inherent in making quick and easy meals explains some of the differences. There are specific reasons why 'quick and easy' meals can be difficult, and those reasons are both irritating and hard to define. That may explain why we do not always perceive them as difficult but we also ask ourselves whether day-to-day cooking is as straightforward as the answers might suggest. This is basically a methodological problem: does asking questions encourage the interviewees to hold something back? Interviews can be a very effective tool and they do help us to understand social processes because the individuals involved can express themselves with an astonishing sincerity (Kaufmann 1996). Very few people lie deliberately but they do sometimes lie to themselves. The researcher must therefore learn to tell when they are hiding something. In this case, it is obvious that they are not telling the whole truth. Fortunately, one of the questions used in the interviews makes it possible to tell when that is the case. That it does so is pure coincidence in that the question was designed for other purposes. At the end of the interview, the subjects were asked to ignore the contingencies of the present and to describe their dream of perfection. Prune, for example, described a fairy-tale garden, with chickens, rabbits and goats, and told the interviewer how she would make cheese the traditional way. Prune, however, is an exception. The vast majority gave a different answer and it was always the same: not having to cook. They would stop cooking at once: 'So as to have time to do other things' (Belangère); 'Sit down and be waited on' (Candy). Tony adores cooking for love. He is an artist who creates masterpieces every night of the week. Throughout the interview, he talked about how much he enjoyed cooking. When he was asked the last question, his tone of voice suddenly changed and revealed what he really felt about having to cook. 'I would employ people, all sorts of cooks. Then I wouldn't have to bother.' He paused for a moment, presumably thought about his passion for cooking, and then made the same point again. 'I'd park myself, and eat. I'd do other things. I'd take up photography again.' He used to be a keen photographer but had more or less given up that hobby when he began to devote all his energies to cooking.

We hide the fact that we find cooking difficult for many different reasons. The first is that it is difficult to give a fully balanced picture of everything that cooking entails. For anyone who is passionate about it, cooking is emotionally charged and therefore an attractive prospect. It is mentally stimulating, and that makes us forget that many aspects of what we are doing are completely banal. Cooking for love provides individuals with an image with which they can identify; they can see themselves as creating family ties by sacrificing themselves for the sake of love. Then there is the alternative way of cooking which is much more fragmented and difficult to understand, even though we tend to idealize it. A passion for cooking does not mean that making meals is easy. Carried away by their enthusiasm, cooks often find themselves out of their depth. They also forget what it entails (having to face the washing up when their enthusiasm fades). When they look back, they forget about all these collateral problems. Their passion has to remain pure and unalloyed. Take the example of Savarin. Like Tony, he becomes very passionate when he talks about cooking; it is a creative and enjoyable leisure activity and he never finds it a bore. 'It's not a chore at all; I really enjoy it.' So why is he sometimes happy to eat frozen pizza? 'When I get home late, it's too late and I don't feel like cooking. We want to spend the evening together, and I don't feel like spending my evening in the kitchen.' Sadly, real life is not simple and cannot just be divided into two parts. There are lots of evenings when Savarin neither gets home in time to cook nor gets home too late. He cannot decide what to do. He often gets caught up in something and then realizes that he is trying to do too much, or says to himself that he should have just heated up a frozen pizza. Cooking is not an activity like any other. Because it always involves an element of self-sacrifice, it forges a family bond. And we find it hard to admit to ourselves we do not actually enjoy making the meals that make a family and that bring a lively group together around the dining table. If we did so, we would feel terribly guilty and so we say nothing because to do otherwise would be unacceptable. It is easier to forget about the minor torments of having to cook every day.

Coming up with an idea

We repress our minor problems but not the major ones. They are too important to be denied. In certain specific circumstances, we can no longer conceal the fact that we are finding everything very difficult. This can happen when we are short of time, when we feel that we are the only ones who are making an effort or that we really cannot be bothered. The routines we have internalized break down and having to shell two kilos of peas begins to look like a never-ending task. But we usually find things difficult for more specific reasons, and almost all the people interviewed agreed that it has nothing to do with the physical problems involved. The problem is usually inside our heads. Paradoxically, we both feel tired because of the build up of ideas that get us nowhere and have the unpleasant feeling that our minds have gone blank. When that happens, the cook 'cannot think of anything'. 'Oh yes, there are times when I say to myself, "What am I going to make for lunch? What am I going to do?" It's hard, very hard, when you can't come up with an idea"' (Paule-Dauphine).

Although it is usually assumed that 'coming up with an idea' is a simple, technical process, it in fact plunges us into all the complexity of culinary alchemy. At this particular moment, it suddenly becomes obvious that we have a vast range of choices to make. The cook has to know what there is in the store cupboard, what everyone likes (and it is unusual for all members of the family to like the same things). She has to choose a set of criteria (nutritional value, taste, family dynamics) and think about both the meals she could make and the dynamics of family interaction at mealtimes. She has to think in the long term and vary the menu (which means remembering what she has made recently). She has to take advantage of what is on offer in the supermarket. As we saw in Part I, the way we think about food is becoming more reflexive and that adds to the mental pressure. There is a question mark over everything we eat and a constant outpouring of nutritional advice in the media. The important thing to remember is that, whatever we choose, it will never satisfy everyone. All the criteria we use are deeply contradictory. Different people like different things; things that taste nice are rarely good for us; if we save money, we sacrifice quality, and so on. Whatever we choose, it will probably be unsatisfactory for one reason or another. Whatever we 'come up with' by way of an idea for a meal is likely to meet with criticism (when we eat together as a family – friends always say they like what we give them) because everyone has their own idea about what a meal should be. Even if a whole team of researchers in the human sciences collaborated with one family to help it make the perfect choice, they would fail because the criteria are so complex. And we have yet to mention the greatest difficulty of all. The real reason why she cannot make up her mind is that the cook is uncertain as to how far she wants to commit herself (is she making something quick and easy, or cooking for love?) and as to what kind of social bond is being forged (is it individualized or collective? Routine or creative?). 'If you don't want to get into a rut, you really have to rack your brains every day' (Suzette). But when we are not swept away by passion, love is the most tiring thing of all.

Cooks therefore develop ingenious tactics in a bid to make their lives easier. They avoid things that take up too much time (when they are not in the throes of their passion for cooking). The need to work fast and to improvise reduces the range of choice. Even Prune uses that tactic: 'I check what's left in the fridge.' Tony has a whole range of tactics and they are highly sophisticated. He always has an alternative in mind. He plans ahead but does not concentrate too hard on that mental task, knowing that he will improvise if he has the opportunity to do so. His plans can be updated if need be, or abandoned. 'I try to plan ahead, but often . . . it depends . . . on what's in the fridge, or what I feel like . . . I had planned to make a *pot au feu*, but I found myself making lasagne.' His second tactic is based upon the material indicator of what fresh produce he has available. He buys large quantities of vegetables to last the week but without worrying too much about what he will actually make. He then takes the vegetables as a starting point and chooses those that are still fresh. Several other people said they did the same. Basically, they concentrate on strictly technical and dietary considerations and marginalize the relational implications of the decisions they make because they are more difficult to manage. There are two ways of doing this. Either they improvise on the spur of the moment in terms of their culinary technique, or their passion for cooking means that 'coming up with an idea' is all part of the fun. It is the in-between areas that cause the real problems. Prune looks in the fridge to see if 'the leftovers' will give her an idea. But she too has other principles and they are very demanding: she will never make the same thing twice in the same month. 'Sometimes, you get really pissed off with yourself when you can't come up with an idea, especially when you can't be bothered. What am I going to make?' The only real way for the cook to avoid feeling this mental pressure is to decide on the basis of one criterion which is usually chosen for arbitrary reasons. All at once, things begin to look simpler and easier. 'It might be the time it takes to prepare, or just the fact that I feel like eating one thing rather than another' (Clémentine). We will encounter this way of going about things on more than one occasion. Because making a meal means taking lots of incredibly difficult decisions, it is, in intellectual terms, primarily the art of making things less complex. We have to convince ourselves that our culinary choices are not really very complicated. That is why we find it so hard when it takes so long to come up with an idea. Our inability to make a decision reveals something we cannot afford to admit to. It is because cooks refuse to face up to that fact that the mental effort involved becomes even more unpleasant. 'I don't feel like cooking, so I really have to rack my brains' (Candy). Madeleine's answer to the final question about her dream was unusual. Unlike almost everyone else who was interviewed, she did not want to do away with the manual aspects of cooking. The only thing she would like to be rid of is the need to come up with an idea:

'Right then, I'm going to be futuristic. I'd get a computer. I'm not too fond of computers, but I'd like one for this. To be able to say, today's Monday . . . these are the vegetables I have . . . and this is the meat . . . I click on: "What menus do you suggest?" And it prints out the perfect menu, or two menus, and I choose which one to make. And it would print out a recipe telling me how to make it. Tonight, for example, there's some leftovers. I ask the computer, and it tells me: you could make this . . . this or that.'

All cooks have their own ways of resolving this difficulty. Suzette tends to leave things to the last moment. This method has its drawbacks: a sudden lack of inspiration can give rise to an unpleasant feeling of existential emptiness. 'You've got into the habit, and have been cooking for I don't know how many years, and suddenly your mind goes blank and you don't know what to make. Why that day rather than another?' Hortense prefers to plan ahead on a regular basis. 'It's unusual for me to do things at the last moment. Over breakfast, I say to myself: "What are we going to have for lunch?" And I don't leave it until 11 to do the shopping.' Sometimes she even plans things two days in advance, 'always over breakfast'. Bélangère sometimes plans her meals a week in advance. She doesn't make lists but 'It's all inside my head'. But she also has to plan for the immediate future. She makes very specific plans: 'I'll make this, this and this. I make a mental list.' It is the mental effort involved that makes 'having to come up with an idea' so difficult. 'It's really hard when I have no idea what to do. And when I still have to come up with something. I really begin to worry when it gets to 5 or 6 and I still don't know what we're going to eat!' (Marjolaine). To make matters worse, there is also something else to worry about. Once the cook has 'come up with an idea', she then has to draw up a plan and work out a timetable. 'The other worry is always having to think ahead.'

Passion changes everything: what was a chore becomes a pleasure. Even when the cook has a passion for cooking, a more relaxed relationship with time (holidays, retirement . . .) is in itself enough to lighten the task of having to think of something. Hortense, for example, spends her weekdays quietly leafing through her recipe books looking for something to make next weekend, and reading the 'How to Make Better Meals' pages. Madeleine's enthusiasm grows when it comes to desserts. She forgets her dream of having a computer to tell her what to make. When she is thinking about desserts, she lets her imagination wander through a realm of pure delight and loses her inhibitions. 'I really enjoy thinking about desserts.' But there is thinking and thinking.

'What would you like to eat tomorrow?'

Cooks feel very alone when they cannot come up with an idea and that makes their job even more difficult. At such times, they let slip something that sounds like a cry for help, though they may not put it in so many words. 'Oh, they're never any help! Sometimes I can't think of anything. So I ask them: "What shall I make?" And they say "No idea"'. Bélangère's distress call is not addressed to anyone in particular. The main virtue of her cry for help is that it helps her to recover her psychological balance. She also hopes that it will make her family understand how intense and complex her job is. Unfortunately, her cry for help is so abstract that the other members of the family do not feel concerned. They all have their secret likes and dislikes. But they also have a vague feeling that answering the question would involve a lot of work, especially in that it implies making a collective effort (even expressing a personal preference would mean taking a stance and putting their own needs first; they do not want to appear selfish). As usual, they would rather leave the decision to the cook, even if it means that their hopes will be disappointed. Bélangère's response to their silence and lack of interest is to ask more specific questions. Unfortunately, her husband has already settled down comfortably and retreats still further: 'Oh, don't ask me.' She now feels even more alone and the mental pressure increases. The cry for help has had precisely the opposite effect to what she expected.

Some cooks have realized that, although it is therapeutic, the cry for help has to be used in moderation and that they have to avoid formulating it in terms that are both abstract and demanding. They should either ask for help without expecting to get an answer or address specific questions to specific members of the family. That is the tactic Babette has adopted. Coming up with an idea is 'really the only thing that bothers me'. She speaks directly to her husband, calmly, but firmly:

'sometimes I ask him: "What you do you want to eat?" "Whatever you like" . . . "You really are beginning to get on my nerves"'.

She has, however, been very clever. She did not ask him to come up with an 'idea', which implies making a mental effort. She asked him what he wanted: 'How can I give you what you want?' It is difficult to tell the difference between real love ('I'll make whatever you like') and subtle diplomacy ('Tell me what you like and I will come up with something'). It does not matter: the problem is so tricky that even this ingenious solution proves to be unproductive. 'Whatever you like', replies her husband. Her partner's lack of interest makes her even more annoyed. And repeating the question does nothing to improve matters. Her husband is convinced he is acting in good faith: he does not want to force her to make what he likes or to give orders: he will be quite satisfied to find a meal in front of him. Faced with such a lack of interest, which makes her feel even more alone and misunderstood, Paule-Dauphine has come up with what she thinks is a brilliant solution. Rather than speaking in general terms or asking what people want, she makes a suggestion just to provoke a reaction.

'Sometimes I make a suggestion: "Should I make . . . ?" He is not exactly enthusiastic and says "If you like . . .". So I say: "Well, you come up with an idea, then!" And he says: "Oh, do whatever you like." I've already spent enough time trying to come up with an idea and there comes a point when I've had enough.'

The difficulty of these one-way exchanges touches a very sensitive nerve. The cook has asked for help because she felt alone and at a loss as to what to do. This is not just a matter of mental fatigue and nor is it a strictly personal problem. Cooks make meals, and meals make families, but when she sacrifices herself for the sake of love, she is simply giving them what they want. And before she can do that, they have to tell her what they want. Unless they say what they want, her self-sacrifice becomes sterile, thankless and painful. When she asks questions, the cook is often asking her family what they want as a way of stimulating both the family dynamic and her desire to cook. 'I'd like it if, every now and then, they would tell me "I'd like this or that"' (Babette). She wants them to tell her what they want because that would add an emotional dimension to their exchanges. But she does not ask them too often and her questions are neither specific nor insistent, as that would turn the cook into a servant who can be exploited at will. 'It feels good when my husband or the children say: "You haven't made that for a long time." And I say "You're right, but that doesn't mean I'm going to, you know." But it's true; sometimes you do run out of ideas' (Hortense). Cooking is an unstable form of alchemy and there is always a danger that what was an emotional exchange will become just a chore. It is not just in fairy tales that carriages turn into pumpkins. In order to ward off that danger, Clémentine has come up with a clever tactic that combines a cry for help and emotional exchange with an element of self-defence: 'Sometimes I ask him: "Should I do this or that?" But they are both things that I want to make.'

Inside the cook's head

Having to come up with an idea when you cannot think of anything makes everything feel difficult because this unpleasant experience is the complete antithesis of the ideal that dominates culinary practices: everything should go smoothly. The *ancien régime* imposed a framework that could regulate actions, and what remains of it (usually a set of routines) should trigger automatic physical reactions. Quick and easy meals should reduce the range of choice and make it easier to give the family what they want (and offering them a choice between pizza margherita and pizza quattro formaggi makes the cook's life easier). Passion removes all doubts because we get carried away. An inability to come up with an idea means that neither of these mechanisms is working and, because the cook is trying to do everything, she ends up doing nothing. Everything has to be done in a hurry, so it should be easy to decide what to make. Coming up with an idea also means that the cook's actions must be part of a controlled action regime.

Once the machine has been set in motion, various mental images may come into the cook's mind, but they are not unpleasant and so do not increase the mental pressure she is under. They are not, however, just any images. This is because every form of involvement in the activity of cooking implies a specific cognitive activity. When we are cooking for love, we see sets of images (of the family, of meals, of the culinary masterpiece that is being made) that we use to construct a virtual identity for ourselves. We become actors in a delightful play that we act out in our heads (Kaufmann 2004). Routines based upon well-established infra-conscious schemata allow our minds to roam free (daydreams, random associations). Some cooks have music on in the background; others pay more attention to what is on the radio.[2]

---

[2] They listen to the radio but do not watch television, as it is too distracting and prevents the cook working properly. Television is reserved for mealtimes, when they tend not to have the radio on.

Paule-Dauphine has got into the habit of listening to the radio during the week and regularly listens to her favourite programmes;[3] her hands are busy but her mind is elsewhere. When they no longer have to think about what they are doing, Charlotte and Maryse prefer to sing. 'When I started to cook, I had to concentrate. But now I can think about all sorts of different things, and sometimes I sing' (Charlotte). 'If I don't know the recipe, I concentrate. If I do, I don't think about anything and I sing' (Maryse).

Charlotte and Maryse do not always sing while they are cooking. Before they can sing, their automatic reflexes have to empty their minds. When they are cooking something new or difficult, or when something goes wrong in the kitchen, they have to 'concentrate' or consciously think about what they are doing.

> 'I think about what I am doing, and nothing else. I think about the sauce, about how to make it thicker . . . cook on low heat for so many minutes . . . I really . . . that's all I can think about. Even when I've made it before, it's always new . . . "That's going to burn . . . what do I do to stop it?"' (Prune)

The cook is completely caught up in what she is doing and thinks about nothing else. 'When I'm cooking, I'm completely caught up in what I'm doing' (Biscotte). So much so that the mental pressure can feel enormous. This is not, on the other hand, the mental pressure that results from the inability to come up with an idea and it is usually not unpleasant. The cook is not thinking about anything but does not feel the usual strain. 'I think it's because I really like cooking. I concentrate on what I'm doing, and my recipe is all I can think about' (Candy). Concentration focuses the individual's mind on a few simple ideas and those ideas are reassuring because they have a very concrete outcome.

There is, however, one thing about having to concentrate that can become mentally exhausting or even stressful: we need to have a plan and get the timings right. That is simply because concentration breaks up the unity of the present. Cooks have to manage many different kinds of time and to project themselves into the future in order to remain in control but they still have to concentrate on what they are doing. Assuming that everything is more or less under control, they may be able to improve their concentration and become even more involved in what they are doing. But once things begin to go wrong, their levels of anxiety and mental distress rise and planning ahead

---

[3] She spend one to two hours a day cooking.

becomes difficult. The danger of this happening is so great that cooks develop various tactics to minimize the intellectual task of planning ahead. They rely even more on the automatic reflexes that tell them what to do next. This explains why they are reluctant to use appliances with complicated programmes, such as ovens, coffee-makers and food processors (Desjeux, Alami and Taponier 1998). Timers, on the other hand, lighten the load by helping them to remain in control of particular time-sequences. 'I really could not manage without it because I often have to think about so many things . . . too many things' (Marjolaine).

We very rarely take this into account when we think of what is involved in cooking a meal. Being a cook means having a real 'intellectual ability to plan ahead' (Giard 1994: 222). This becomes immediately obvious (in a negative sense) when a beginner suddenly find himself in charge of the kitchen. This happened to Mr Chapman who suddenly had to feed his children after his divorce. He had no idea that cooking could be so intellectually complex. When he started, he found it hard, very hard, to make something as simple as a Sunday lunch. He was all over the place. One thing was ready and everything else was not: the meat wasn't done and the potatoes and the beans were ready. Or the meat was done and the vegetables had already gone cold. It took a lot of effort, and a lot of trial and error, to get it right and to make sure that everything was ready at the same time (Burgoyne and Clarke 1983: 36). Practice does make it possible to internalize these time-sequences as certain gestures become automatic. Even Mr Chapman was able to learn that lesson. The same method cannot really be applied to everyday meals which are as repetitive as they were under the *ancien régime*. Once we begin to improvise, we suddenly realize how difficult it is to project ourselves into the future and to work to a timetable. Hence the need to come up with more subtle techniques. Bernard Conein and Eric Jacopin (1993) have, for example, demonstrated that cooks constantly rely on objects that act as signs telling them what they have to do next. They might, for instance, cut a lump of butter in two, and leave a knife on one lump to remind them to cut it up later. The knife acts as a reminder of what they have to do next, and a simple piece of visual information acquires an intellectual meaning. The cook obviously has to get into the habit of doing so at some point in the planning stage but the purely manual and intuitive act of putting the knife on the butter reduces the mental pressure. 'The effort that goes into using spatial and perceptual data as the basis for a plan is minimalized' (Conein and Jacopin 1993: 68).

'Making mud pies'

Tony also finds having to coordinate everything mentally exhausting. 'Time-management is the hardest thing of all . . . making sure everything is properly cooked and hot . . . making sure it's all ready at the same time.' Apart from that, the great thing about every other aspect of cooking is that he finds it relaxing. 'I'm not thinking about anything. I'm thinking about what's cooking, about how it will taste. I'm not really thinking about anything else, and that's why I find it relaxing. It means I have to concentrate.' For Tony, thinking about nothing and concentrating are synonymous (even though the two activities could not be more different in cognitive terms). Both mean that he does not have to think about existential matters that might become distressing or stressful. 'Cooking is my tranquillizer, the only thing I know that reduces the stress. It gives me a breathing space when I get back from work.' In the same way that some people go for 'long runs' until they experience the extreme exhaustion that produces 'a solar well-being which dissolves the tension' (Porel 2003: 62), Tony immerses himself in the more playful activity of cooking. It can have a therapeutic effect. Candy does the same: 'Cooking helps me relax; it means I have fewer things to think about.'

In order to achieve that result, a few principles must, however, be respected. The idea that things are difficult must be avoided at all cost and there must be no mental pressure. The cook must therefore either be passionately involved in what she is doing or fall back on well-established routines. She has to be completely focused. The therapeutic effect is greatest when she can concentrate exclusively on simple physical tasks. Forget about cooking, forget about everything. Your hands are the only things that exist . . . your hands and the elementary sense of touch . . . the physical feel of the ingredients 'throughout all the peeling, chopping, kneading, cooking and mixing that goes into turning ingredients into a meal' (Frain 2004: 97). Such gestures help us to rediscover all the touchy-feely pleasures we experienced when we were children and the sensual delights of 'a very small child playing with mud pies' (Châtelet 1977: 30). 'Cooking also means making mud pies and kneading them' (Desbiolles 1998: 24). Regression that takes us back to our childhood is the best form of therapy.

A child is a magician who creates wonderful worlds by fiddling about with things. Cooks do precisely the same, the only difference being that their daydreams can become real. As they cook a meal, they make a family. The experience is not always pleasant; indeed, it can be both unpleasant and tiring. And there are always doubts because a cook has to choose between hypotheses that are completely contradictory. The ability to make things less complex and to concentrate on the task in hand is the pinnacle of the art of being a cook. Or, better still, to make it as concrete as possible, to make things respond to the slightest touch. The cook's hands crystallize the new syncretism on which the family is based as they make the meal it is about to share. Cooks sometimes have the vague feeling that they are shaping the future of their family as they knead their dough. The future is in their hands. They are their family, and their family is in their hands.

Time inverted

The other great thing about doing things with our hands is that we exist in the present tense and have a very special relationship with time. It alters the way we experience time. It makes time stand still and does away with its terrible tyranny. It is not because we have time that we are no longer short of time; it is because we are no longer working against the clock that, suddenly and almost miraculously, we do have time. This inversion of our relationship with time does not come about by chance and we cannot just will it to happen. There are specific reasons why the relationship with time becomes inverted and cooking allows us to understand them.

Let us begin with the *ancien régime*. Culinary practices were part of a constant process of constant socialization. Cooks knew precisely what their role was and it was described by books on household management. Cooks certainly dreamed but their dreams did not take the form of projected identities that could affect the way they did their job (Kaufmann 2004). The time that was available to them was therefore a raw material that was both soft and neutral and it was perfectly adapted to their system of practices. The rhythm was regular, and usually quite slow. 'If you are going to cook traditional meals properly, you have to have the time. It takes a lot of time' (Madeleine). For someone in her position, the main problem is not the lack of time. The problem is that there is too much time. Having to 'kill' time when you have too much time on your hands is like standing on the edge of a threatening existential void. Maryse still talks about having to kill time, which explains why she does not want a dishwasher. Both cooking and washing up by hand 'keep me busy'. It makes a virtue of necessity. 'I enjoy it. I like taking my time. I should have lived in the 1950s. People took their time in those days.'

Our second modernity has completely changed our relationship with time. Time used to be the same for everyone but we now have a range of options. Individuals' involvement with time can take various different forms. The constraints of life may, however, reduce the number of available options. Women of working age who have to cope with the demands of work but who still have family responsibilities often have to do everything in a rush and are always short of time (Fagnani 2000). Even in the most extreme situations, they still have to juggle with their time and that demands a lot of nervous energy. Contemporary societies encourage us to project ourselves into different identities and to imagine 'possible selves' (Markus and Nurius 1986) that may inspire projects for the future. The problem is that, whereas we can have a lot of possible selves, very few of them can ever become real. Individuals who once had to say goodbye to their imaginary identities because they were so improbable now have to say goodbye to identities that are eminently possible. When they find themselves in an unpleasant situation, they wish their lives were different, and they can be different. Time is therefore no longer a raw material that is soft and neutral; it has become a commodity that is in short supply and there is never enough of it because there are so many possible scenarios. As time speeds up, we seem, paradoxically, to have less and less of it. As it accelerates, it encourages us to project ourselves into the future and it becomes more difficult to time things. This explains the peculiar nature of 'quick and easy' cooking; it becomes a chore because we do not have time to cook, even though we work faster and faster and are always in a hurry. This is not because we are short of time in the objective sense that time can be measured in absolute terms. It is because of the discrepancy between what we do and how we represent what we do. Although they work quickly, cooks dream of being able to work even more quickly because they want to be elsewhere and doing something else (eating, relaxing, working . . .). And it is precisely because their minds are elsewhere, because one of their other selves has taken over, that time flies. They have to be either completely oblivious to what they are doing or fully involved in it before time can slow down and stand still.

When we concentrate fully on some manual task, time stands still. A simple but well-established routine can have the same effect. The cook's actions are perfectly timed because she is not thinking about what she has to do, so she can daydream or listen to the radio. Although it is difficult, complex time-management allows her to concentrate on what she is doing: the cook is fully involved in what she is doing. Although she does not really have all the time in the world, time does stand still. The way our relationship with time is inverted therefore varies greatly, depending on which method we use. From that point of view, the passion for cooking is quite remarkable. It obviously does not expand time as effectively as a routine that has been completely internalized. When we are in the throes of passion, time can flash by (which does not mean that things are not difficult). We do, however, have a different sense of time. We have a strange feeling that the time is passing very slowly and gently. Because she does not notice the 'passage of time' (Prune), the cook feels that she is sacrificing herself for love because she becomes sensitized to what the family wants. Family life becomes more intense. '"Hmm, that's delicious. How do you manage it? Where do you find the time?" So I say to them "You just have to let it simmer, that's all". "Yes, but come on. Only a grandmother makes meals like that"' (Prune). The important thing is that, because she is doing something she really enjoys, the cook wants to savour the experience. Because she is working with her hands and has a routine, she has more time but she is not deliberately manipulating time. Once she starts cooking, her perception of time changes. 'When you want to cook – and I mean really cook – you have to have to take your time, really take your time' (Olivia).

There is cooking, and there is cooking. Almost everyone who was interviewed began by making a distinction between two very different action regimes. The real difference between them is that they involve very different relationships with time. The interviewees were quite explicit about this. On the one hand, they made quick and easy meals, wished they could make them more quickly and complained about not having enough time. 'I very often buy things that need little or no preparation, like salads, ham, soup, steak' (Charlotte). When, on the other hand, they are cooking for pleasure, they take all the time they need. 'I spend more time on it on Saturdays and Sundays, a lot more time.' Charlotte contrasts weekdays (quick and easy meals . . . and sometimes they are very quick indeed) with weekends, when she indulges her passion for cooking. She does have some time during the week but she spends it planning for the weekend: she looks up recipes, discusses her plans with her husband and begins to make shopping lists two days in advance. Biscotte projects herself still further into the future. 'I spend a lot of time thinking about what I'm going to make. It takes me all week.' When the weekend comes, the plans are, sadly, usually abandoned. Biscotte's passions are purely platonic. But when she takes refuge in her culinary dreams, she does to some extent experience a different kind of time. She is cooking for love, has more than enough time, when the cares of everyday life cease to exist. This feeling may not last long, but even cooking an ordinary meal can have its unexpected moments of passion. 'When I'm enjoying myself, I don't care if it takes another quarter of an hour' (Clémentine). Time goes into reverse. Melba described at length the difference between the two ways in which cooks experience the passage of time: 'There are times when you get behind with things, and there's no time for dreaming.' And there are times when she feels that she has all the time in the world and that dreaming is not just permissible, but advisable. She also explains how this inversion of her relationship with time changes her body rhythm. When she is 'behind', her movements are quick, brusque and devoid of emotion. At the weekend, she works more slowly and at a leisurely pace as she listens to music. Things take longer but everything feels easier.

Madeleine recalls her past. She recalls having to hurry to keep up because there was no time to make everyday meals. 'When we were still working, we didn't have any time during the week.' Doing everything in a rush allowed her to have some time to herself. 'But at weekends, we had all the time we needed. And it gave us a chance to talk.[4] Weekends were more convivial.' Now that they are retired and that their children have left home, those constraints no longer apply. But there is still a great difference between weekdays and weekends: 'We eat very simply during the week.' Madeleine has no qualms about leaving things to the last moment and relies on whatever is in the freezer. Meals are quickly over and done with. 'But at weekends, a lot of thought goes into it. By Friday, I'm saying to myself, "What am I going to cook on Sunday?" And I make something different. We need a change.' The idea that there are two different kinds of time goes some way towards explaining the tradition of having something special on Sunday but it does not explain everything. Madeleine has taken a deliberate decision to cook different things during the week and at weekends. She needs a change of rhythm and has to live a double life.

The personal touch

The people who were interviewed emphasize the weekday/weekend distinction. And basically, they are right to do so because these contradictory models do divide their time in two. The distinction is not, however, as clear-cut as they suggest. Madeleine, for instance, talks

---

[4] She is thinking about mealtimes; they spend more time over meals at the weekend.

about 'the weekend' but she is both exaggerating and oversimplifying things, and this helps to conceal the fact that the evening meals she makes at the weekend are light (and often quick and easy) and that a big lunch on Saturday is not a regular event. Sunday lunch is the only real 'weekend treat'. Passions are, by definition, intermittent and they certainly cannot be institutionalized. They are beyond our control and are therefore subject to variations. The cooks dream of weekends when time passes slowly and gently, and when making a meal is a relaxing and sensual activity; real weekends are much more unpredictable. Time does not fly during the week and not everything is a routine chore. On the contrary, the week can be livened up by brief outbursts of passion (and, although no one will admit it, they can be more intense than they are at weekends).

The idea of simplicity and speed is dominant. The cook does not set herself overambitious goals. Because she somehow combines sequence of routine actions with ready meals, she no longer experiences the difficulties she has when she is working against the clock. And suddenly the fancy takes her.

'You can't help yourself. It's an art form, and I'm not joking when I say that. A sudden fancy takes you; you feel like doing something, and you have to do it. I'm not saying it's a great work of art. It might mean no more than slicing gherkins finely to make the ham look special. Well, you don't have to, and you didn't plan to use gherkins: you feel inspired, and then you have no choice in the matter. Even when you don't have a lot of time, you have to add a personal touch.'

Because she is joking, Cannelle is exaggerating somewhat. But she explains the impulse to add a 'personal touch' very well and she is being perfectly sincere. Gherkins are not really her speciality, which is making generous use of spices, and that may be distorting her analysis of the personal touch. It is widely believed that adding a personal touch just means adding something in the way that one adds salt or pepper. And in many cases that is true. But the more highly developed ways of adding a personal touch are much more interesting. Adding a personal touch is basically a way of changing one's position, of inverting (for a brief moment) one's relationship with time: everyday fare with a hint of passion.

It need scarcely be pointed out that we cannot control our passions. Adding a 'personal touch' sometimes involves doing things that take much longer than we expected. It is often that way with Cannelle and her spices. She thinks she just adds something but she in fact tastes the food, corrects the flavouring, thinks of something else she can add, and so on. The gratuitous and unexpected 'personal touch' instantly makes her feel an existential intensity that she does not always feel when she is making a meal that has been planned a long time in advance and that requires a long-term emotional commitment. Most of the time, however, the personal touch is channelled into the register of 'modest inventiveness' (Giard 1994: 300). At a more pragmatic level still, it is often used in homeopathic doses to lessen the deadly effects of the routine or to make it less of a chore. The cook makes a gesture towards emotional commitment because it is physically stimulating but is very careful not to go too far in that direction. It really is not a great work of art. 'I'm not going to get it over with as quickly as I can but I'm not going to spend hours on it either' (Hortense). The 'artistic' sequence is integrated into an overall economy and there are limits to the cook's commitment. 'I improve things by adding a personal touch. I have to think of something that is different, easy to prepare and not too expensive' (Clémentine). Making meals day after day means that we are constantly trying to reconcile thought and action regimes that are quite contradictory. The personal touch is a seed of passion planted on stony ground and the cook never gives it time to come into full bloom.

'A lot of organizing'

The emotional involvement may not last for long, and its intensity may vary. Adding a personal touch, which can mean anything from the casual addition of something extra to ardent artistic inspiration, takes only a moment. Sudden fancies can involve a longer commitment. Think of the way Tony creates a ritual atmosphere for evening meals during the week. One-off events are even more intense and involve both a lot of work and a lot of advance preparation. Such occasions include Christmas and New Year, inviting friends home for a meal, as well as the special meals that are more frequent in certain families and which mobilize the whole family.

It all starts with the decision to make a meal. In some cases, the decision is impulsive and easily reached but some people take a long time to reach any decision because they are choosing between two different lives. They can either go on with their normal lives, which are quiet if somewhat boring, or they can have a sudden burst of enthusiasm. 'For me, taking the decision is the hardest thing of all. Once the decision has been taken, I can't see how you wouldn't go through with what you've started. Once the decision has been taken,

I don't care how long it takes' (Suzette). The second stage, the length of which varies from one person to another, is devoted to daydreaming. The imaginary projections, which mark an existential break from normality, are pleasant. Our minds can roam free because the real mental work has yet to begin.

> 'You tell me I could obviously spend my day doing something other than think about what I'm going to cook on Friday evening. But I find it relaxing. It stops me having to think about job applications and things like that. Or about staffing problems, given the nature of my job. I find it relaxing. But that doesn't mean that I don't have to think about Friday's meal. You have to be rational about these things.' (Candy)

Cooks do not daydream for long. They have to adopt a different cognitive attitude, stop playing with pleasant images, begin to think more calmly and focus on what they are about to do. The plan begins to take shape and the cook becomes a strategist whose every thought is focused on the battle that lies ahead. 'When I have guests coming, that's all I can think about' (Hortense). The final plan is drawn up just before battle commences. This is not a quick and easy meal with a personal touch, or a sudden fancy; this time, everything is planned in advance. As Candy said more than once, it involves 'a lot of organizing'. This is hard work. 'Having guests means a lot of work because everything has to be planned' (Melba). This is very serious work, though the outcome (cheerful conviviality over the meal) will not be serious. 'I get up early because this is a serious business' (Charlotte). The first stage in organizing a meal is an intellectual process, and making lists is an important part of it. 'I have to get organized. I write things down. I make a list of everything I need. I check to see what's in the house to make sure I don't buy what we've already got. There's a lot of organizing to do, a lot to think about. I think that's the hardest thing about planning a meal' (Candy). As the time comes closer, some things fall into place. 'I organize everything ahead of time. I need to know what I'm going to cook, and need to know that I have everything I need' (Candy). Amandine begins think about her Saturday night guests on Friday. 'There are a lot of little things to get ready. I peel lots of vegetables, and put them in bowls overnight.' There is a place for every job in the cook's mental timetable for the meal she is making and she tries to fit it in with all the other things she has to do in an attempt to coordinate everything perfectly. There are functional reasons why everything has to be planned in advance (it leaves the cook free to make last-minute changes) but the preparations are also visual signs that lighten the mental burden slightly.

Everything builds up to a crescendo. Even though the fact that the food preparation has been done takes away some of the pressure, the cook gradually finds herself caught up in a crescendo of activity. Her intense concentration (which focuses mainly on coordinating things) makes the coming event more intense and exciting. Everything is part of the build-up: the sauce, the family (or friends), the table decorations, the smells. She thinks of all these things but in no particular order and without making any distinction between the various levels of reality to which her idea refers. The one thing that has to take priority is getting everything ready, in the most concrete and most urgent sense of the word. Her hands are the centre of the world and their every movement is focused on a single culinary creation. 'I really like it! Especially when everything is nicely presented, smells good and all the rest of it' (Amandine). 'I do everything: I've started, so I'll finish' (Suzette). The grand finale comes when everything is at last ready, preferably just as the guests, who have already arrived, are sitting down at the table. What happens next is very interesting. The cook should be able to relax now and should enjoy both the compliments and the meal she has just made. Unfortunately, she is no longer very hungry. 'I could quite happily serve them what I've cooked, but without eating a thing myself. That would not bother me at all' (Charlotte). The interviewees came up with a lot of technical explanations as to why this should be the case. The cook has tasted everything, sampled everything, had a lick of everything and often more than was strictly necessary: there are no surprises left. 'I could still smell it so much that I didn't want to eat any of it' (Clémentine). All that is true but it is of secondary importance and the real explanation lies elsewhere. We have only to watch the cook at the table: she is a little distracted as though she was recovering now that the excitement is over and was immune to any other passion. 'Afterwards, when we're at the table, it's not unpleasant, but in fact it's all over and done with and it's no longer the same. It's what comes before the meal, preparing the meal, that is the real source of pleasure' (Amandine). The more complex the organization, the greater the intensity and the stronger the emotions, the greater the distance between the cook and what she has cooked. She has identified with her meal so much that she cannot bring herself to eat it. This explains why some cooks develop tactics (simple meals, advance preparations) that allow them to feel more relaxed in both physical and mental terms. But, to go back to our distracted cook at the table, what Amandine says is not actually true: everything is not over and done with. Despite the emotional release, she feels that she is still on duty. 'There's still something on my mind: is it cooked properly, is it . . . ?' (Clémentine). It is only when the guests are on the point of leaving that the pressure really drops. 'When it's time for coffee, when it's over and people are about to go home, then you feel happy. You can relax then' (Clémentine). For the cook, the meal itself is a sort of in-between time that is difficult to describe. She no longer has to make an effort or concentrate but she cannot really relax either. Her mind is no longer on 'organizing' the meal but she still cannot stop thinking about it. The tension has eased off but she cannot really relax. She is not really there and her mind is elsewhere.

Stress

Some cooks prefer not to prepare things in advance so that they can relax over the meal, whilst others would not give up the lonely pleasures they enjoy before the meal for anything in the world. There are also great variations in the types of emotion that accompany the crescendo. The greatest variations relate to the intensity and quality of the stress the cook is under. All, or almost all, cooks experience at least some stress when they have to organize a complex meal but that is no more than the effect of extreme concentration. That kind of stress is the result of the mental pressure they are under but some cooks also becomes stressed because they worry about how well their skills will be judged, and about their own attitudes towards the meal. Their anxiety can take different forms. Some cooks do have only limited skills and know it (some openly admit it and joke about it but other finds dinner parties torture). Others are much more gifted but lacking in self-confidence. Amandine is like that, probably because she always has to put up with unkind comments from the family. 'I'm really frightened I'll mess something up. I always feel I'm something of an amateur.' Some cooks are very confident about their skills and are very relaxed. 'I'm not afraid of taking risks. When we have guests, I like to make something I've never made before. It's a way of discovering new things' (Savarin). Biscotte is an extreme example. She uses new recipes, never tries them out in advance and is not shy about talking about what she sees as her failures in front of her guests.

And then there are those who, whatever their level of competence, suddenly feel that they are on trial. They did not think about this (or did not think about it seriously) when they took the decision to make a meal because their minds were full of images of conviviality and the meal everyone was about to enjoy. Because there are so many things to organize, their anxiety levels inevitably begin to rise as time goes by. And they cannot really understand why they are becoming so anxious. What are they worried about? They are going to enjoy a nice evening with friends. So why worry? Yet some cooks get very anxious indeed. 'The stress! The stress! I can't sleep the night before because my mind is in turmoil' (Paule-Dauphine). Even so, she is calmer than she used to be. 'When I was young, I really did get into a panic.' For most people, however, it is the other way around. Take Suzette: 'On big occasions, I panic more than I used to . . . because . . . even going shopping stresses me out, and so do a lot of other things. I don't enjoy it so much.'

A cook in the grip of anxiety does not really understand what is happening to her. Some even try (usually in vain) to make themselves see reason. The problem is that there are reasons why they get into this emotional state. As we have seen, cooks dream of communing with a group of friends and of dinner parties that are all sweetness and light. But, as we have also seen, the guests will talk about how the evening went. Friendship is a living bond and its quality is determined by high points such as meals. Friends speak with forked tongues. They are very sincere at the dinner table when they speak as though the communion was perfect. But when they all go home, they speak in analytic terms. The stakes are therefore high. It is not only the cook's performance as an individual that is on trial. The social bond and the future of a friendship are at stake and that is much more important. The cook has much more than just a meal to worry about. The lucky few who do not feel any anxiety are happy because they know nothing about this dark side of meals. Such naivety is, alas, no longer tenable when experience reveals what the cook refuses to see is at stake. Witness Maryse's story about the aunt who, years ago, organized the family's great ritual meal. She got the idea that they needed a change: quail with grapes. 'None of has had ever eaten quail! Serving us quail! The very idea!' She raises her voice, sounds shrill, still not understanding how her aunt made such a terrible mistake. The story of the quail has become a sort of negative myth in the family. Quail with grapes, which a lot of people like, has become emblematic of the loosening of a bond but it is more likely that it was simply a sign that it was breaking down.

Aftermath

Unfortunately, the cook cannot relax once the guests have gone home. There is the washing up to be done. 'I love making meals, but I hate washing up and putting everything away afterwards. Scrubbing the bottom of the pans and things like it. I hate all that. And to make matters worse, I like to put them away clean, so I have a problem' (Amandine). All cooks say the same. Even those who do not usually find washing up a problem complain that it suddenly feels like one chore too many. Their bodies begin to feel heavy. The shapeless leftovers smell bad and defeat the normal routine's ability to structure things. The unusual nature of the objects that have piled up – and there are a lot of them – and the unusual pattern of the day all conspire to disrupt the routines that make normal life so easy. The cook is naked, has no points of reference and finds herself in a world that is not exactly inviting. The cook may find what happens next unpleasant but it is of great interest to a sociologist. Let us recall the previous episodes. A decision was reached. Pleasant day-dreams gave way to the mental pressure of having to 'organize it all'. Timing everything was difficult and she had to concentrate. Being so busy was stressful. All those stages represent a change in her action regimes and thought regimes. The ordinary framework of socialization and the peaceful life that revolved around old habits were left behind as the cook projected an imaginary identity into a future that she had to create. Because she always kept that goal in mind, she had all the energy she needed. That is the great difference between well-established routines and projections: the projections have to generate the constant supply of energy that keeps the cook going. Stress, anxiety, idealized images, auto-suggestion, technical rationality . . . it all helps to convince her that she is making progress. But when the guests have gone home, this mental structure suddenly collapses because it has served its purpose. The cook is drained of energy but that does not make it any easier to slip back into the old routines. So what does she do next? Olivia explains: 'After the party is over, it's absolute chaos, that's true. What a chore! All those plates and things . . . but you have no choice in the matter. It's all part and parcel of giving a dinner party. And then you forget, and only remember the good bits.' She uses two different tactics. She convinces herself that she has no other option and tries to think about it as little as possible, as though it was a well-practised routine. But at the same time the memory of an enjoyable evening does give some meaning to the last jobs she has to do. 'Nobody likes it, and I'm no exception to the rule. But once you get down to it, it's all part of giving a dinner party' (Eugénie). She makes one final effort, even though her heart is no longer in it.

The mechanisms behind making a meal are extraordinarily complex.

The people interviewed succeeded in explaining how some of the cogs work, and they did so with talent and lucidity. But they inevitably simplified them. Their distinction between weekdays and the weekend was too clear-cut. And it was only the aftermath – after the guests had gone home – that was described as a bore. But the build up to the meal was not unadulterated pleasure either. There was the mental pressure of organizing and coordinating everything, and the various levels of stress. Negative feelings had to be recycled to generate energy. There were also moments when everything felt physically difficult: there were so many daunting objects and raw materials (vegetables to be peeled, things to put away, things to be washed up . . . .) that they could not be included in the imaginary projections that gave her the strength to go on. 'It's always chaos. So, I tidy up. It has to be done, so I just get on with it' (Candy). Because she cannot rely on her familiar routines, the cook has to be a skilful alchemist who can use positives to cancel out negatives and who can convert negative feelings into energy (Kaufmann 1997). This is the emotional price that has to be paid by anyone who becomes caught up in an action regime inspired by passion, even if it is only an 'ordinary' passion. 'Passion is an ordeal we cannot escape, a drama based on an inextricable mixture of joys and pains' (Bromberger 1998: 28). The higher the Sisyphean mountain of 'all that organizing', the more unpleasant the emotional aftermath and the more the cook has to work at finding the imaginary reserves of energy she needs to reach the summit. Her energy may flag for a moment, and what she is doing may seem meaningless, but she keeps going (because she has to). But once the initial impetus has gone, everything feels like an effort. 'I find it hard when we have a lot of people round and I have all those potatoes to peel. Things like that are hard. Having a lot of people really does make for a lot of work' (Marjolaine). Having a lot of people round is not always a chore. The cook simply has to identify with an existential projection that marks a break from routine. She has to want to enjoy herself and be prepared to get caught up in the swing of things.

Recipes

The cook who embarks on organizing a meal that is out of the ordinary steps outside the framework that usually structures her actions (established roles and internalized routines) and, thanks to a combination of imagination and energy, enters a world in which she invents the culinary and relational future. Unlike the 'personal touch', which is a momentary impulse, this alternative register of action requires 'organization'. We rely upon conscious points of reference rather than our usual habits. Other supports are welcome because they can shore up this complex structure of lists, sign-objects, and so on, but it may put yet more mental pressure on the cook. This is where recipes come in. They are precious because they tell us exactly what to do. They are sometimes used to make something different, even though the meal itself is nothing out of the ordinary; in such cases, it is the recipe, and only the recipe, that makes the difference. Conversely, the cook may choose to make a meal she has made many times before for a dinner party, in which case it is the meal that makes the occasion, and she wants to be sure that nothing goes wrong. The survey shows, however, that cooks very often combine the two tactics: they are not afraid to try out something new even though the relational stakes mean that they are under a lot of pressure. The explanation for this paradox has to do with the overall logic of the process: her involvement in a different existential process encourages her to abandon her routines. But it has more to do with the coherence of the cognitive modes the process involves. Having abandoned her usual habits, the cook (whose head is full of images, emotions and thoughts) tends to rely more on the reference points she has memorized and to be very disciplined. This explains another paradox that emerged from the survey: the cook sticks closely to the recipe when she is making something she has never made before and does exactly what it tells her to do, rather as though she was back at school. Some cooks are more intuitive than others and always interpret the recipe in their own way and in the light of the knowledge they have already accumulated. They tend to do this when they are making meals which do not matter very much (like Olivia, whose great speciality is using up leftovers) but follow the recipe on big occasions. Suzette, who is not an intuitive cook, provides a perfect description of the strange nature of the relationship between the cook and her recipe: 'I really like making new things but I do not have much imagination. When I'm making something I haven't done before I'm always looking at the recipe.' Paradoxically, it is because they do exactly what the recipe tells them to do that cooks like Suzette can be innovatory. 'Stick to the rules. When you don't know what you're doing, you stick to the rules' (Bélangère). Because the cook obediently follows the recipe, she finds it easier to enter a new culinary world that allows her to get away from her old routines. Such observations do not just apply to cooking: individuals do not become more creative and freer simply because they work alone. Cooking is always a social activity. Other

195

people's experience (as recorded in recipe books, in this case) helps us to reinvent ourselves.

Recipes also have their other uses: they are guidebooks for beginners. Novice cooks have to establish routines rather than get away from them. Clémentine's grandmother gave her a cookery book when she was first married. Clémentine laughed at what she saw as a gift from a different age. Her grandmother was living in a different world: modern women do not begin their adult lives by learning to be good cooks. Clémentine put the book on the shelf and forgot about it. One day, she opened it. It has become her 'bible' and she now uses it almost every day. She shops only twice a month and buys in a lot of groceries but has little idea of what she is actually going to cook. When it is time to make a meal, she decides to cook, say, chicken, and consults her bible. 'Right. How do you cook chicken? What goes with chicken?' She 'concentrates hard', follows the recipe to the letter and quickly becomes disoriented when everything does not happen just as the book says it should. Her book is already stained (because she uses it a lot and not because it is old). More experienced cooks often hang on to their first 'bible'; it may have become a little battered but they are still very attached to it and think that it cannot be bettered. 'New cookery books are all very well, but they're not the same. The old ones really do teach you the basics' (Madeleine). Experienced cooks still refer to their old recipe books from time to time when their reflexes or memories fail them. Some constantly update them. Paule-Dauphine, for instance, has a notebook and keeps it up to date by copying out her favourite recipes.

Recipes are now usually used for different purposes: they are instruments which mark the beginning of a different existential process. This explains why there is a considerable discrepancy between the current interest in recipe books and the use that is actually made of them. Whilst we dream of leading a different life, it is not always easy to make the dream come true. Our cupboards are full of recipe books, to say nothing of the newspaper cuttings we will use 'one day'. We never do. 'If I see a recipe I like, I cut it out. You should see how many I've collected!' (Olivia). Maryse also cuts out and collects lots of recipes but she never looks at them again. Yet as she cuts them out, she really does believe she will use them which is why she goes on collecting them, even though her cupboards are already overflowing. And she regularly watches a food programme on television. 'Oh, there are some simple recipes. And they work. You can make them another time.' Has she used them often enough to know that they work? No, she almost never uses them. But it's obvious that they're good, you can tell. It's almost as though she really had tried them out. In practice, Maryse prefers to stick to what she knows and very rarely uses new recipes. Is she being illogical? To say so would mean overlooking the fact that life is not purely rational. Making something out of the ordinary requires a great deal of imaginative effort. The imagination knows no bounds and we have to daydream for a while before we can come up with alternative scenarios. We think beyond the actual meal we are planning to make. Some cooks, like Maryse, would rather not go beyond that stage. Candy goes through with her plans a little more often than Maryse and that allows her to believe in her fantasies, even though they are obviously far removed from the meals she actually makes. It has to be said that she spends a lot of her time dreaming about how cookery could change her life. She also watches food programmes and reads lots of magazines. 'Sometimes, I spend an evening browsing through cookery books in the lounge. And I say to myself: perhaps I should make that this weekend.' These imaginary identifications are not restricted to a clearly defined preliminary phase, though that is when they are at their most intense. They provide an alternative that is always there in the cook's mind. The sudden, unexpected decision to add a 'personal touch' indicates that the cook is referring to an alternative model. That is why the collection of recipes in the cupboard is not entirely pointless. The recipes may well have turned yellow with age but they represent a storehouse of dreams: another life is within reach.

What triggers the cook to spring into action can vary greatly. In Candy's case, it is something about the recipe itself. She becomes fascinated by its technical side and cannot wait to try it out and make it part of her personal repertoire. Anneth is more drawn to the logic of pleasure. She wants to experience new pleasures and she wants to share them with the people she loves because she loves them. A new recipe? 'Well. You want to taste it, and to give other people a taste. I want to introduce people to the things I like.' The cook is not always sure which is more important: creating something personal or the loving self-sacrifice. This is because the two things are closely intertwined. A cook produces both something personal and a social bond. In some cases, the meal is no more than a means to an end: she either wants to 'make a family' or to share a meal with friends. But, sometimes, the social bond is a convenient excuse for something more selfish. It can be a form of self-fulfilment. As a rule, cooks alternate between the two positions and make little distinction between them because of the syncretism of what they are doing.

Variety and variations

Breaks in our action regimes are intrinsic to the most recent developments within modernity. Together with the growing number of products that are on offer, this makes it more difficult to 'come up with an idea'. In the far-off days of the culinary *ancien régime* (in traditional rural societies), all meals followed the same pattern and that, combined with the poor choice of available foodstuffs, meant that people ate the same things on a regular basis. The daily meal took the form of 'repetitive necessity' (Roche 1997: 257). During the nineteenth century, a greater variety of produce became available in urban areas but the bourgeois model (using table manners to instil family values), which was structured around the idea of a strict order, inevitably meant that meals did not vary a great deal. 'Regularity leads to habits, which in turn guarantee regularity, and therefore order' (Marenco 1992: 127). It was not until the early twentieth century, and above all the First World War, that a combination of factors (including improved canning techniques) finally overthrew that restrictive order (Vanhoutte 1982). At the same time, the new science of nutrition began to place more emphasis on the need for a more varied diet, first 'to ensure that the stomach does not grow weary, and then on the grounds that a more varied diet excites gastric secretions and thus stimulates the appetite' (Marenco 1992: 159). The physiological importance of having a varied diet had in fact already been emphasized by many earlier treatises on dietetics, and it exacerbates what Claude Fischler (1993a) calls the 'paradox of abundance', or the contradiction between the need for variety and fear of the unknown. The cook's life became more complicated as she (and most cooks were women) tried to resolve the contradiction. How could she reconcile the routines that made her day-to-day work easier (as she internalized infra-conscious schemata) and the reflexivity that disrupted her routines because such a variety of things was available? We are now familiar with cooks' favourite techniques: they use subtle combinations and are not above using weasel words. Semantic shifts introduced the principle of variation as a substitute for variety. 'I'm not much of a one for health food, but I do try to give them a balanced diet. I'm not going to make them pasta every day for a fortnight. As a general rule, I don't make the same meal twice running' (Savarin). Her final rule suggests a practical norm (not the same meal twice running) but it is far removed from her claim to be providing her family with a varied diet. Taken to its logical conclusion, Savarin's principle means that she could provide a varied diet based on two types of food.

The people who were interviewed did not have a lot to say about the need for a varied diet which, if it were taken to its logical conclusion, would make the cook's life a hell of mental fatigue. Because they did not notice the semantic shift, they talked about their real guiding principle: the variation technique (or, at an even more basic level, the technique of not serving the same thing two days running). They were all, in their own way, quite clear about this. Suzette and Prune represent the two extremes. Suzette (I would rather not think about Maïté and her ham sandwiches) regularly makes the same things: 'It's a practical solution because there is less to worry about. On Saturdays, for example, I know it will be roast beef. If it's Saturday, it's roast beef. The children like it. It's easy' (Suzette). Prune goes to the opposite extreme and never makes the same dish twice in the same month. Such major variations, which logically mean a varied diet, are unusual. Suzette is more typical (when she gets away from her set meals) and avoids serving the same kind of meat twice in the same week ('Not the same thing twice in one week'). On the other hand, she often makes stews and admits that she always makes enough for the next day; there are exceptions to the rule. 'As the old saying goes, it's better when it's reheated.' Maryse makes a point of 'not having meat every day. One day, it's meat, and the next it's fish . . . it depends. You can't make the same thing every day. But coming up with something different is a problem. That's true.' Paule-Dauphine follows more sophisticated rules: 'I always try to cook fish three times a week. If we have meat, and we've already had beef once, I'll cook pork or veal.' But it is Babette who gives the most revealing answer:

'Never! We never have the same thing twice running!'
'Why not?' asks the interviewer.
. . .
'Why would you feel bad about making the same thing twice running?'
'That's what I ask myself.'

Babette thought she had definite principles and said so quite explicitly. She suddenly realizes (and says it in all sincerity) that what her rule means is not exactly clear. Its main virtue is that it is eminently practical and it does often become a matter of routine: she automatically serves the same meals in a different order (without repeating them) and that lightens the mental burden.

The variation principle results from a contradiction (between the nutritional benefits of a varied diet and the need for an internalized order as a guide to what to do) and cooks resolve it by cobbling together a rough and ready solution. They are not too fussy about the meaning of what they say. Recent developments in the way they cook and the meals they serve do, on the other hand, give a new content to what was until now a fairly abstract principle. The variation principle has a relational purpose. Cooks now make meals that represent a group communion. The dream is, sadly, far removed from reality and the conversation, for instance, does not always live up to expectations. Even when it does not, satisfying the group's most basic desires can sustain the emotional exchange. As the sad story of Amandine shows, the cook can certainly abandon the attempt to be creative and give in to highly individualized and very regressive desires (pizza with mayonnaise in front of the telly). But she can also go on trying to educate her family about food thanks to the surprise effect of well-calculated variations. 'He said to me that the salmon we had the other day was good. Really good. And it made a change' (Maryse). Variations thus acquire a new meaning: they make a change from a repetitive diet that has become over-familiar. We should not, however, take too idealistic a view of this and have to understand that cooks ring the changes because they want to avoid negative comments (the family have completely internalized the variation principle). 'Sometimes, it's the children who say: we've already had that once this week!' (Maryse). 'I always try to vary the menu,' says Paule-Dauphine, who admits that she does so mainly because she is afraid of hearing her husband saying the words she dreads: 'Not again!' Even Suzette is always on edge about her Saturday roasts and is well aware that even a casual remark could change everything. 'No one says anything, no one objects and there's no problem. I know I shouldn't always make the same thing, but it's convenient.' The cook is torn between making her job easier and sacrificing herself for the rest of the family. It is a constant dilemma.

— 6 —

COOKING, COUPLES AND FAMILIES

Transmission and autonomy

In Part II, I made it clear that we have to be very suspicious of the deceptively linear history of soup when we analyse meals. There have always been quarrels over definitions, from the divine exaltations of the distant past to today's profane communion. Much the same applies to the history of meals. The researcher is, quite logically, tempted to fall back on a very technological and descriptive evolutionism that takes us from wood-burning stoves to induction hobs, or from hand-plucked chickens to pre-packed chicken fillets, rather as though the way we cooked evolved only as a response to contextual changes or to the appearance of new products. The fact of the matter is that the real changes occur outside the action regime. The difference between cooking and meals is that the major changes in the way we eat are recent and are essentially bound up with our second modernity. We have already looked at one such change, namely the transition from a single action regime, that defined practices in institutional terms, to the emergence of autonomous cooks who are in control of their own culinary destinies but torn between two very different action regimes, namely the rapidity that makes everything easier and a passionate commitment to cooking. The breakdown of any direct transmission from one generation to the next is another decisive change; that tradition has been destroyed by the growing individualization of culinary practices, especially amongst the young to whom the tradition was once passed on. The two principles are contradictory: we cannot have both individual autonomy and transmission.

The growing autonomy of the future cook cannot be divorced

from the growing autonomy of the individual consumer. The same individual who gains his or her independence by conquering tiny territorial spaces from the sweet jar to the fridge also comes up with strategies that offer an alternative to family meals. The dominant characteristic of all these strategies is that they are subversive. Young people may not be actively hostile to their parents' world but they do want to be different, to spread their wings and to establish their own identity. When they eat on their own, their choices are governed by their own likes and dislikes which they share with their age cohort. When they first begin to experiment, apprentice cooks tend to be subversive, not to say anarchic. They are inventing a new world. 'One time, I added chocolate to my ravioli. I was 14 or 15, and I just wanted to see what it would taste like. I did it once. Never again' (cited in Garabuau-Moussaoui 2002a: 106). Isabelle Garabuau-Moussaoui's informants also talked about 'crisps with Nutella' and 'cornflakes with bolognese sauce'. 'I was more inventive. I mixed anything and everything together. We experimented a lot', added Pascal (Garabuau-Moussaoui 2002a : 106). It is easier for them to experiment and to concoct strange mixtures if they use things that are easy to handle (small cold starters, desserts or pâtés in the case of those with more experience). Isabelle Garabuau-Moussaoui notes that this fascination with starters and desserts is quite in keeping with parents' refusal to allow their children to make main courses, and especially to use the oven. This concern for children's safety is often a very convenient excuse for the cook who, whatever he or she may say, is in no hurry to lose his or her throne and who wants to retain absolute control over the main meal. Young people find it all the easier to accept this arrangement in that they are not really inter-ested in the kind of meals that are the family's culinary heart because they are heavy, complicated to make and ritualized. Basically, they are still individuals who graze rather than eat. Their experiments are purely for their own benefit and that of groups of friends and, when they do cook, they rarely get beyond almost instant snacks. When they reach the next stage of their apprenticeship, they begin to cook more but their 'experiments' often take the form of adding personal ingredients (spices, grated cheese, cream, ketchup). They begin their apprenticeship intuitively by adding things that mean something to them because they are part of their identity but then adopt an encirclement strategy. Once they have adapted the begin-ning and the end of the meal to their liking, they move inwards, begin to make main courses and gradually reconstruct whole meals.

202

Mothers and daughters

Apprentice cooks do not encounter any resistance as they strive for greater autonomy because their parents do not try to pass things on in the way that their ancestors did. Cooks, in particular, let them get on with it and concentrate on their own tasks. The passing on of ancestral traditions has in fact been more of a mythologized model rather than a real practice for several generations now, especially when it comes to cooking. Cooks once clung onto their role all the more in that it was already losing its lustre and had already forgotten to teach their daughters to cook. Indeed, they often kept a few secrets to themselves. A cook whose place was taken by her daughter was quickly relegated to the status of an old woman (Verdier 1979). Women therefore tried to teach their daughters to cook without giving up their position and refused, for example, to allow them to use the oven themselves (this is obviously the origin of the modern parental ban). It was therefore not difficult for cooks to continue what was already an established trend. The survey showed that, even in earlier generations, many young women did not know how to cook when they first moved into a place of their own. Maïté cannot remember why that was the case. 'My mother cooked a lot, but I didn't learn anything from her.' Candy did not even know how to cook a steak. Melba improvised because she had to: 'I taught myself how to get by.' It was unusual for mothers actually to teach their daughters to cook but it was also striking to find that different generations had such different levels of skills. A lot of mothers who were cordon bleu cooks had daughters whose culinary skills were either rudimentary or non-existent, and vice versa. Olivia has a real passion for cooking and sees it as an art form. But she does not take after her mother. 'She didn't cook at all.' Olivia is self-taught and learned by trial and error. 'I remember I once burned a roast!' Mothers who are cordon bleu cooks and who do want to pass on their knowledge to their daughters often find that their efforts are not appreciated and have the opposite effect to that intended. Their daughters are not interested in their techniques or the tricks of the trade; they see only the social role that traps women into domesticity and have already decided that it is not for them.[1] It is not so much the ability to cook as a future that they are rejecting. 'My mother was always telling me to learn to cook. She told me that I wouldn't be able to

---

[1] Paradoxically, it has now become easier for women to pass on their culinary skills to their sons.

cook at all when I got married. I refused to learn: I was watching and could see what she was doing' (Biscotte). Madeleine, who is 60, was one of the few women interviewed who did, like the good girl she once was, learn from her mother who, in what was a real rite of passage, gradually let her take responsibility for the main Sunday meal. She has not been able to do the same for own daughters. 'They learned from books.' They wanted to learn for themselves. Her eldest daughter has just had a baby. Now that she has a family of her own, she is a very enthusiastic cook. But she has her own way of doing things.

Traditions are still passed on to some extent, but the opposite trend is more conspicuous. It encourages young people to learn to cook for themselves and girls in particular to refuse to accept that they have a duty to become good housewives. Even so, traditions are still being passed on, either implicitly or simply more discreetly. At the infra-conscious level, we accumulate a lot of schemata (not least those relating to table manners) that can be reactivated later in life. At a more conscious (but not necessarily intellectual) level, we notice countless details out of the corner of one eye and store them, to a greater or lesser extent, in our passive memories. Biscotte pointed this out when she told us what she said to her mother: 'I'm watching and I can see what you're doing.' She watched, and she was conscious of the fact that she was watching. Usually, children watch and learn without realizing what they are doing. 'Although you don't let on, you watch and that's how you learn. You actually remember all sorts of things' (Amandine). Luce Giard describes her own experience and beautifully captures how traditions can be passed on without anyone really noticing:

> I thought I'd never learned anything, that I'd never observed anything, because I stubbornly refused to be educated like a girl. I was as interested in that as I was in catching some disease. I'd always preferred reading or playing quiet games in my bedroom to being in the kitchen where my mother was working. And yet I did see and memorize what she was doing when I was a girl. And my senses remember the smells and the colours. I was already familiar with the sounds of cooking; the hiss of water as it comes to the boil, the sizzle of melting fat, the sound of hands kneading bread. A recipe or sometimes just a word was all it took to trigger a strange anamnesis, to reactivate bits of the old knowledge I'd inherited and the early experiences I'd remembered without really meaning to. I had to admit that, just like any other girl, I had learned the things women know. I'd acquired that knowledge while my mind was on other things. (Giard 1994: 16)

First steps

Teenagers who are still living with their parents are more interested in eating than cooking. They try out a few mad experiments but they also quietly observe a lot of details and may even learn to use some utensils (usually the microwave and sometimes the frying pan). When they subsequently move into a place of their own, the learning process speeds up. Within the space of only a few days, they have to learn to cook, though they may not be able to do anything more than fry eggs. 'The eggs stuck to the pan. I didn't know you had to use butter. I'd broken them very carefully, and I was feeling very proud of myself! But I didn't use any butter. You learn quickly, and I got it right the next time' (Cannelle). The young cook tries to make simple meals and to exploit the full extent of her knowledge (by trying to remember, by reading the labels on tins and by talking to friends). As she continues her apprenticeship she learns mainly by experimenting on a trial-and-error basis. She is self-taught and proud of it. She gradually begins to feel that she is getting the knack and that everything is becoming automatic and a real style of cooking begins to emerge. She thinks she has discovered her own style but in fact it has a lot to do with the way this period of self-education fits into contemporary culinary trajectories. Isabelle Garabuau-Moussaoui (2002a) outlines its main features: basic ingredients that are easy to deal with, knowing what things go together, sauces that go with anything, and spices. The basics consist of 'fluid' foodstuffs such as boneless meat and fish, fruit without pips and vegetables that do not have to be washed or peeled. Actually cooking them is a simple process and involves little more than boiling water for the pasta and cutting up fillets of meat. The skill lies in learning which things go together, discovering sauces based on cream or grated cheese and learning to use spices. Spices are often the main weapon in the young cook's armoury, and the spice rack is an important complement to his or her sense of personal identity. Tony knows more than most about cooking. He always has a supply of tomatoes and onions to complement his spice jars. His favourite stand-by is breast of chicken. He buys it by the kilo to last him the week but without any particular meals in mind. 'You can cut up a piece of chicken and make a fricassee. You can cook it Chinese-style, Mexican-style, whatever you like.' This means that there is less mental pressure when he has to do the shopping, as he does not plan meals in advance. 'We bought some rice, some pasta and some canned vegetables. A chicken. Some eggs. Things you can make without having to think: we'll have this when we make that recipe

one day' (Juliette, 22, cited in Garabuau-Moussaoui 2002a: 172).
Depending on the circumstances, these basic supplies and a few trim-
mings can be used either to make something quick and easy or used
in more unusual combinations. The creative crazes of adolescence
have not been completely forgotten. But for a young cook who now
has some experience to rely upon and who is eager to produce something edible, novelty is still the main guiding principle. 'I make it up
as I go along. I'm very imaginative, very adventurous' (Christine, 26,
cited in Garabuau-Moussaoui 2002a: 246). 'When you leave home,
there are fewer restrictions' (David, 21, cited in Garabuau-Moussaoui
2002a: 247). 'I'm a good cook but not a conventional one' (Thierry,
25, cited in Garabuau-Moussaoui 2002a: 247). Whilst young cooks
are keen to assert their individuality, they also quietly learn the basics.
They consult books and compare notes with friends. Sometimes, they
phone mum (or dad) if they have an emergency. 'I didn't know how
to cook pasta. No idea. So I phoned my mother. I used to ask questions like: "I've got pasta and some green beans. Would it be better to
fry them, or should I boil them?" Now, it's more a question of asking
for suggestions' (Marc, 22, cited in Garabuau-Moussaoui 2002a:
195). Family ties can work culinary miracles and traditions can be
passed on when parents have given up hope.

Everything falls into place

They have learned a few techniques but still have no sense of
organization and no fixed points of reference. Young cooks still act
impulsively and go in for passing fads dominated by an idea, a theory
or an ethics. 'I went through a pizza phase', says Juliette (22, cited in
Garabuau-Moussaoui 2002a: 173). 'And not so long ago, a blinis and
taramasalata phase.' Variations like this are still very close to being
sudden fancies. Clémentine is already at the next stage when it is the
way meals are organized that changes.

> 'For quite a long time, I did what I knew I could do which was not a lot.
> I soon realized I was getting nowhere. Then I tried to spend less money.
> I bought whatever was on offer in the supermarket, anything I could get
> cheap. I filled the freezer for the month. Things that were edible and things
> that were disgusting. I didn't make that mistake twice. Next month, I got
> out the little book my grandmother gave me when we moved in together.
> I really studied it and I made my first "proper housewife's" shopping
> list [the theatrical tone she adopts is a way of saying she is being ironic].
> Without bothering too much about how long it would take.'

And then she did begin to bother about how long it would take, still armed with the recipe book her grandmother had given her. Young cooks often go on using recipe books like this until everything becomes automatic. Candy remembers a time in her life when she read a lot of recipes: 'Oh yes! Cookery books, recipe cards!' Eventually, a real system is established and then stabilizes. 'It's also a habit you get into. Once you've found a way of doing things you can live with, it gets easier' (Clémentine). The former apprentice (and her partner, if she has one) acquires the knack of making a few things. She gets into the habit of making them. She remembers what she has to do and suddenly realizes that she has developed a style of her own. The mad improvisations of her teenage years are long gone and she really has learned to cook. The young kitchen hand has become a cook.

She may now turn to her parents again but not in the way that she used to phone them in an emergency to ask why her eggs were sticking to the pan. She now wants to rediscover something that is more emotional and more personal, and she is deliberately trying to establish some kind of link with the past. 'Learning to cook is important. Once you've done that, you can take that as a starting point and cook whatever you feel like cooking. I might fancy something one evening and ring my mum to get her to tell me how to make it' (Tony). The few recipes that have survived the breakdown of tradition and that have acquired a powerful symbolism thus come to function as a concentrated family identity that can stand the test of time (Attias-Donfut, Lapierre and Segalen 2002: 257). Sometimes they are all it takes to preserve the memory and reputation of a grandparent. Old Mrs Fargeau is convinced that the family will remember the recipe for her famous apple pie which her granddaughters love ('But Nana's is best. No one can make apple pie like Nana'), long after she has gone (Attias-Donfut, Lapierre and Segalen 2002: 257). The emotional and relational registers then have a decisive influence on how the system develops. The cook has learned her culinary scales and has acquired some rudimentary skills but that does not determine how she will cook in the future. Cooking now becomes a way of building a relationship and a family. Everything depends on how her partner and children react. A couple will try to discover things that they both like because sharing meals and pleasures strengthens their relationship. 'I cook the things we both like', says Tony. Unfortunately, couples do have their differences. Cooking now becomes not so much a matter of love as a kind of struggle over what they want their relationship to be. Convinced that she is in the right and, without realizing it, following Machiavelli's advice, the cook takes the view that the end justifies the means. 'You can persuade people to change their ways. When we first got together, he insisted on having meat at every meal, usually with potatoes. Things are fine now. People in the family get used to eating certain things' (Suzette). On the other hand, a cook who is not such a good strategist, or who faces more formidable opposition, may give in if her family refuses to change its habits. Hence the sad story of Amandine and her sons with their pizza and mayonnaise. And hence that of Maïté who began by making such a noble attempt to be a decent cook, though it has to be said that she did so out of a sense of duty rather than because she wanted to. Despite all her efforts, her family gave her no sign of satisfaction. Worse still, they began to complain and made it clear that there were not many things that they did like. 'They're not too keen on eggs, or chicken, and they don't like anything cooked in a sauce.' Maïté feels that she was quite right to give up the unequal struggle. 'They never ask for anything. Never.' Supply – the self-sacrifice – has to be a response to demand; there is no point in being a generous cook when no one will tell her what they want. 'The way we do things now suits everyone.' Maïté now eats like everyone else in the family and makes her own ham sandwiches.

Hers is a very exceptional case. As a general rule, the period when everything revolves around the children reinforces the culinary system (as does the gradual socialization of children over meals), though it may atrophy somewhat when the children leave home. The cook goes on experimenting and, thanks to a sort of Gaussian distribution, new points of reference are established and some of the old ones are forgotten about. In some cases, very early culinary experiments may have instilled certain habits but the cook no longer remembers where they come from because they have become an integral part of her system. The archaeology of the dishes we make and the way we make them can, however, revive a whole range of memories of important events which, although anecdotal, still have a foundational value. Candy says that her cooking is 'very traditionally French'. The interviewer asks her how that relates to her favourite speciality, which is paella. At first she says, 'It's a bit like French cooking.' And then she remembers something from another life: before they were divorced, her husband, who was very fond of Mediterranean and foreign food, introduced her to their spicy delights. That is what he left her: a piece in the jigsaw of the life she now leads. Paella has become a normal part of everyday life. Her system looks homogeneous but it is in fact a patchwork of pieces from a colourful life.

Sharing the work

Even though there was a failure to pass on culinary techniques for a few generations, the role of women remained exactly the same. A woman's place was definitely in the kitchen. She was the cook and had sole responsibility for feeding the family. The individualism of our second modernity has completely overturned the old hierarchies. This change results from several intersecting processes. The most important factor was of course the women's movement. Battles were fought in public and a quiet guerrilla war was waged in private. Women refused to obey their mothers' injunction to take on the sacrificial role. 'No, no, no!' said Biscotte. Women resisted the demands of their husbands when too much was asked of them. This struggle would not, however, have ended in victory if it had not been part of a much broader trend towards individual emancipation, especially where cooking was involved. Becoming an adult no longer means accepting a role, and especially not a sexually defined role. Young people (both girls and boys) are now primarily individuals who learn to construct their own lives and who are attempting to turn their dreams into projects. They do not start out by imitating role models; on the contrary, they want to subvert all models and to invent themselves. They want to eat pasta with chocolate sauce, and to have picnics on the carpet. During this somewhat fanciful biographical parenthesis, they are more interested in eating (or grazing) than cooking. This means that their practices are autonomous and ensures that boys and girls are equals.[2] When they really begin to experiment more (their experiments will eventually lead to the establishment of a system), games that involve odd combinations and lots of spices still have their attractions for many boys. It is not until later, when the system becomes a permanent feature of everyday life and when styles and methods become more settled, that men and women embark upon different trajectories, though they may be unwilling to admit that this is what they are doing. The men tiptoe away in search of more entertaining games and the women rediscover a sense of duty because there is no one else in the kitchen.

More couples are beginning to share the work but things are very

[2] Elise Palomares (2002) gives an interesting example of this, drawing on a survey carried out in Benin. In that country, gender roles are strictly defined. Indeed, the very fact that a woman cooks a meal for a man has great symbolic importance and is a sign that she will accept a proposal of marriage. 'The roles of cook and wife are inseparable' (Palomares 2002: 341). Yet young men (and especially students) are encouraged to pitch in when they are newly married or before any culinary system has been established.

slow to change. Because they have a long and influential history (which is recorded in infra-conscious schemata), there is still a definite tendency for certain gestures to be appropriated by women. This is especially true of anything to do with laundry. In European countries, between 1 and 3 per cent of men living with women do most of the ironing. When it comes to cooking meals, the task is shared on a much more equal basis. In roughly 1 household in 10 in Europe, it is the man who is in the kitchen and who cooks on a day-to-day basis. Even when men do not cook on a regular basis, it is quite common for them to pitch in. A comparative analysis of how much time is spent on cooking seems to lead to even more promising conclusions. In Scandinavian countries, for instance, 'the woman's share of the total time spent on preparing meals is two thirds' (EUROSTAT 2004: 50). Unfortunately, a closer analysis quickly reveals that, despite the rather deceptive statistical averages, there is still a lot of inequality. It is in countries where the total amount of time spent on cooking meals has fallen that most progress has been made. This has much more to do with the rise of individual autonomy and the increased availability of products that encourage us to make quick and easy meals than with any trend towards domestic equality between men and women, especially in the later stages of a relationship. 'Food preparation is a typical female task, especially in countries where more time is spent on it' (EUROSTAT 2004: 50). Once the family has a home of its own, and once meals become a central part of its life, it is usually the woman who does the cooking.

The division of labour

The sharing of domestic tasks is an ideology rather than a reality. This leads to many false interpretations. Everyone knows a few outstanding examples of men who are modern domestic heroes, and they are surrounded by so many myths that they have become the trees that prevent us from seeing the wood of a persistent inequality. We therefore have to get back to the real world, understand the complex dynamics of the resistance to change and the subtlety of particular developments. Equality is neither a minor issue nor a technical question. And nor is it reducible to a political clash between men as a group and women as a group. It involves the anthropological subjectivity of individuals who are trying to reshape their identities.

An overview allows us to make a schematic distinction between three types of men. Men who expect to be waited on and the modern heroes who cook represent the extremes. In the centre, we have an undifferentiated mass of 'helpers'. We will look at the modern stars last, as stars should get top billing. Before doing so, we will look at the largest category, namely the men who help in the kitchen. But we must first say something about men who expect to be waited on. This is how Hortense describes her husband: 'He expects to be waited on'. The contrasting gender roles model is still common amongst the older generations. The woman is responsible for looking after the house and her husband; the man brings in the money and expects to be waited on. Hortense shows no bitterness when she describes how useless her husband is in the kitchen; the tone is one of gentle mockery. 'Oh, he's useless in the kitchen. Absolutely useless. He can just about boil an egg. But now that I think about it, no, he can't even boil an egg.' And this sexual division of labour is not going to disappear of its own accord, as though by magic. There are still pockets of resistance, especially in more modest working-class milieus. This is not because of a culture specific to such groups but because of their social position. Terrified by the prospect of social exclusion, they have to cling to more traditional roles if they are to have any legitimacy at all. Which means real jobs for men and real families for women (Schwartz 1990). Women are wives and cooks and have no time to worry about their emancipation as individuals. This does not apply only to the old and the poor. The temptation for men to expect to be waited on is still very real in all milieus. It in fact seems to be becoming increasingly common, as a certain male chauvinism is now more fashionable because men are supposedly being emasculated. Laura's boyfriend had no compunction about asking her to do the cooking. 'For the first six months we were together, I didn't cook anything. It was all very simple: pasta, rice, fried eggs, ham, boiled potatoes and steak. He got fed up of eating that and nothing else. He gave me a cookbook called *I Can Cook*' (Laura, 25, cited in Garabuau-Moussaoui 2002a: 195). Presumably that was the last straw: they split up.

Women are no longer prepared to be trapped into a sacrificial role as soon as they embark upon a relationship. Why should they – and only they – devote themselves body and soul in an age in which individuals are autonomous and in which the sexes are supposedly equal? Their male partners have to show them every consideration or be very clever. Men often decide that they too would like to play at making different combinations of things and learn the secrets of seasoning. To begin with, the relationship is a happy muddle, with each partner vying to make the best sauce. But different positions soon begin to be defined and then become more stable: one partner (usually the woman) is a better cook than the other and more eager to cook. As they watch one another and learn to live together, there is more incitement for the more gifted and willing partner to do the cooking. They learn their respective roles from the little playlets they act out. Listen to Aurélie's story:

> 'The other day, he made a comment that I didn't take kindly. He said "The gas is too high, that's going to burn." I said, "Then you do it! If you think you can do better than me, I'll leave you to get on with it." I went outside for a cigarette and didn't come back for a quarter of an hour.' (Aurélie, 24, cited in Garabuau-Moussaoui 2002a: 191)

The stakes are high after exchanges like that. The words may be said in anger but they do not mean very much and may simply be designed to restore the speaker's psychological equilibrium (as seems to have been the case with Aurélie). This means that she accepts her role, even though she was half-convinced she had rejected it and that, despite their differences of opinion, she is prepared to do the cooking. What happens next depends on how her partner reacts. He may lend a hand and their respective roles may become less clearly defined. Or he may settle for the comfortable role of being the backseat driver. Aurélie presumably came back to finish cooking the meal and not to be waited on. The minor squabbles of everyday life gradually define gender roles that become permanent. Whereas the cook (who is usually the woman) takes centre stage, her helper hovers in the wings or makes brief appearances.

Helping

Today's men do not just expect to be waited upon and do help a little. They usually play a minor role, rather like semi-skilled apprentices, and feel vaguely guilty about not doing more. They help in quite specific ways. Their primary function is to act as assistant cooks; they stand in for their wives and cook for themselves when they are at home on their own and may even make simple meals for the children when the cook is away. 'He does his own thing when I'm away, but he doesn't help when I'm at home' (Anneth). 'He knows how to fend for himself when he's on his own but otherwise he does nothing. He takes the view that it's not his job' (Marjolaine). The old roles have not disappeared, and the husbands of Anneth and Marjolaine take advantage of the fact to ensure that they are not called upon to use their skills too often. Conversely, it is not unusual for women to defend their cook's prerogative tooth and nail. Madeleine's husband, for example, helps a lot in the kitchen (he is the son of a restaurant owner and would probably be happy to take on more responsibilities) but it is only when the interviewer presses her that she mentions this.

When he is not acting as a temporary replacement, the helper's main role is to do what the cook tells him to do. He either does so on a regular basis because certain tasks have been delegated to him or responds to specific requests for help when she cannot do everything. In some cases, the task in hand is so complex and the mental pressure is so great that the cook needs some moral support. Sometimes, she wants him to acknowledge her skills and devotion but she may just want not to feel so alone. In that case, the simple fact that he is there may be enough to make her feel less alone.

> 'Being all on my own in the kitchen is as boring as hell. Even if he does nothing and is just there, or if he sets the table or something, it makes me feel less alone. I don't like to be under the impression that I'm the only one to make an effort, even if it is no more than an impression.' (Clémentine)

She did try to delegate other jobs. But she likes to do things her own way and could not think of much for him to do. It does not take long to lay the table and she sensed that her partner was growing bored because there was no way for him to lend her any moral support. That is why they have got into the habit of having a drink while she prepares a meal. 'I enjoy having a drink with him while I'm cooking. Yes, I like that.'

Although head cooks are reluctant to hand over the controls, they often become irritable when their partners just sit there and expect to be waited upon. 'Sometimes I say to my husband, "Get me this or get me that." I don't dislike cooking, but I do like to have some help' (Charlotte). When she officially asks for help, it is as much because she wants to lighten the load as because it reminds her that she is secretly dissatisfied. 'And when he does help, it's because I ask him to. He never takes the initiative' (Clémentine). 'It gets done in the end, but he takes his time about it', she adds. The way in which he responds to the request for help has a decisive effect on what happens next. His failure to change might not have anything to do with men's refusal to change; some of the head cook's demands may involve tasks that are beyond her assistant, and she may fail to recognize that he has his own way of doing things. But it has to be said that it is not unusual for men to show little enthusiasm; whilst he may not expect to be waited upon, the helper may well drag his feet.

Although laying the table is his responsibility – and a very minor one at that – Clémentine's partner has not yet made a real habit of doing so. 'As a rule, he lays the table . . . when I ask him to! No . . . I do the washing up too. Because it gets on your nerves when you're always having to tell someone to do this, do that. And perhaps I'm waiting in vain. Perhaps he will never learn.' It could be worse. Some men use underhand tactics and make a show of being willing even though they have no intention of doing anything. Prune's husband is very shrewd. He does shout 'Don't you want a hand?' but he does so in a studied way. The question is phrased in negative terms; he is nowhere near the kitchen and makes it quite clear that he is busy with something else. Prune gives him the answer he wants to hear. And although she speaks softly, her husband pretends that he hasn't understood her meaning. Prune does not really need any help (which is why she does not make an issue of it) and has a real passion for cooking. She would, on the other hand, appreciate a few symbolic gestures to give her the impression that this is a joint enterprise. 'I'd like it if he took the initiative.' Dream on. Latent guilt is, unfortunately, not enough to inspire anyone to take the initiative. Passion is the only thing that can do that.

In fairness to the helper, it has to be said that his role is not always easy. Cooks are often so set in their ways that the helper is asked to do the boring jobs she does not want to do. Babette often asks her husband to peel the vegetables for her. The cry for help can take different forms and is often a request for moral support but the helper often finds it difficult to interpret. The cook may suddenly feel acutely alone but he has no way of knowing that. 'It's at times like that that I really would appreciate some help' (Marjolaine). But when her husband does offer to help, she immediately complains that he is getting in the way with his initiatives or opinions. 'No, I don't like it when he butts in and says things like "That's overcooked"' (Madeleine). And Suzette would rather not have any help at all: 'I don't ask for any help; I'd rather do it myself.'

A star is born

What the cook says to her helper (reprimands, setting him minor tasks, expressions of annoyance) has only a limited effect even though it stirs up his latent feelings of guilt. The outcome is often unpleasant for him and unsatisfactory for her. If progress towards a more equitable division of labour in the kitchen was left to her, we would still

214

be much further away from equality than we are today. What women say is less important than the emotional impulses that encourage men to become involved (Miles 2005). They have to want to be involved. They may want to cook because they feel creative, because they want to look good, or quite simply because they enjoy their food. Both girls and boys begin to cook as teenagers. During the long phase when they are teaching themselves to cook, they are as interested in eating as they are in making meals. Boys are more interested than girls in pleasure, more concerned about quantity and more focused on meals. It is often those primal needs that encourage them to cook. As we have seen, Clémentine despairs of her boyfriend because he even forgets to lay the table but there is still a ray of hope. 'He helps a bit – this is a very recent development – now that my cooking's improved a little. He's become more interested!' An interest in food is, however, closely bound up with a desire for self-fulfilment and to be creative, preferably under the admiring gaze of a larger audience. Men therefore tend to reserve their skills for special occasions. They do not make a discreet entrance but immediately take centre-stage because they are convinced that they are great cooks. Women have inherited a historical role that is based upon discretion, self-sacrifice and a sense of duty; the way they behave today is still greatly influenced by that role. Men, in contrast, have only just begun to cook and they do so in a very different way. When they do cook (as opposed to merely lending a hand in the kitchen), they do so in very specific ways. When a man puts on his chef's hat, he is not interested in making ordinary meals. Men intervene at specific points in time (and take their time over it) and in specific places (where they take up a lot of space). They talk a lot about what they are doing and expect positive comments, if not praise. Gilbert admits that he tends to take over the kitchen when he 'makes a proper meal' and surrounds himself with a whole range of utensils. His wife, who has been elbowed out, 'finds it difficult to make a cake when I'm making a proper meal' (cited in Welzer-Lang and Filiod 1993: 267). When she talks about her husband, Suzette gives a good description of these male characteristics but she is also careful to describe where she stands. She is initially somewhat condescending towards a man whom she first describes as her helper. 'He helps me from time to time. He might make a dessert, or help with the preparation, but nothing elaborate.' But, whether she likes it or not (and she is not in fact terribly keen), her husband really does want to do more. She then describes how he does specific things in specific places. 'He might grill the meat. He prepares it himself, seasons it, and grills or barbecues it. He only helps me in very specific areas.' In the earliest societies, men, who were the hunters, acquired the habit of grilling meat over the embers of a fire. This was one of their few domestic tasks, and very much the exception to the rule. The history that is recorded in the depths of our infra-conscious minds has a very long memory when it comes to men doing things in certain ways. Their fondness for barbecues is one example and this explains why it is not a culinary activity like any other. Grilled meat is a special case. In many couples, this may give rise to the impression that the man is involved and does have certain skills but that is no threat to the head cook's usual prerogatives. Suzette therefore has no problems with the barbecue. Things are very different where desserts are concerned, and crumble, in particular, is close to being a bone of contention. 'Oh, I leave him to get on with it, absolutely. If he's decided to make dessert . . . he's the crumble specialist . . . He hasn't even given me the recipe for his crumble. He enjoys making crumble. So I leave him to it.' Suzette leaves the kitchen and refuses to have anything to do with making crumble. Her life as a cook is strictly compartmentalized and crumble is something out of the ordinary. She sees it as a game and leaves her husband to play, just as she would leave a child to play. But at the same time she feels upset and irritated by her husband's willingness to be left to get on with it. He is in a world of his own and keeps the recipe to himself. And she gets really annoyed when he begins to show off like a third-rate actor. 'And when we have guests as well, he will say with pride that *he* made the crumble. *His* crumble!'

It is true that the way men boast and brag about their culinary exploits can get on the nerves of cooks who quietly get on with their job day after day. But we have to understand that these characteristics cannot be imputed to some male genius that is both universal and unchanging; they are products of a historical trajectory and a social position. Women have always cooked out of a sense of duty; men learned to cook at a time when individuals were becoming autonomous and they cook because they have developed a passion for it, because it is creative and because it is a personal challenge. There is no a priori reason why they should go on showing off about it for the rest of their lives; it is because they are just beginners that they behave like this. They may well begin to cook more modest meals on a day-to-day basis and may become chefs who organize everything. This depends on two things. They must obviously want to cook, and cooking must be more than a way of looking good at little cost to themselves. But their partners must help them to change. Now, the transfer of culinary power can be very problematic: the way men show off is often used as a very convenient excuse for putting them in their place. Take the example of Clémentine. She complains that her boyfriend forgets to lay the table and that she has to ask him to do even that simple task. And yet whilst he cannot be bothered when she asks him to help, he does sometimes show some ambition and suddenly becomes highly motivated. 'He decides he wants to make something, something special. You'd better watch out! The great chef is going to cook. It's quite a ritual!' She is critical from the outset and worries about the mess he will make (she will have to tidy up after him and do the washing up). She rules out the possibility of a fairer division of labour. 'And is it good?' asks the interviewer. 'Well, I suppose I have to say yes, it is, but, there again, he's a novice.' She feels no impulse to support his efforts and would rather he did more to help her and left things at that. Charlotte is not so sure. She is not sure what to make of her husband's vague attempts to become an excellent cook. At the beginning of the interview, she has nothing but praise for him 'Daube [beef braised in red wine] is his speciality. It's *his* recipe. I think he makes the best *daube* in the west of France.' She went on singing the praises of 'the best *daube* in the west of France' at several points in the interview. But once she had mentioned the more delicate aspects of her relationship with her husband, she changed her tone. 'It's not too bad. He makes it every six months. And takes over the kitchen for five or six hours. And that's not the only thing. *I* have to wash up afterwards!' Her husband is retired but she is still working. One *daube* twice a year is not enough to create even a semblance of equality. She sometimes thinks that his *daube* has a bitter taste: it is not the best in the west. Charlotte is constantly changing her mind. Sometimes the head cook uses her helper's minor failings as an excuse not to give up her power. But it is also true to say that the helper who develops a sudden passion for cooking never corrects his old faults, and that he is not prepared to do so. He is not making excuses. With the best will in the world, Charlotte cannot perform miracles and therefore cannot help her husband to do more than cook his *daube* every six months.

When men start to do the cooking

It is very unlikely that the helper's bursts of enthusiasm will lead to a role reversal once a couple have begun to become set in their ways. It is much too late for Charlotte, and probably for Clémentine too. As a rule, it is only when men take over the cook's role during the early stages of a relationship that they retain it for any length of time. That is a necessary but not a sufficient precondition, as it is not unusual for men to gradually relinquish the role after making a promising start. They are much more likely to go on cooking when they began to cook of their own accord much earlier in life because they wanted to and because they acquired certain skills in the process. Childhood, the years they spent living in their families of origin and the periods they spent living on their own before embarking on their current relationship are the decisive influences. Both Tony and Savarin, who were the male cooks interviewed, are typical examples and became accustomed to cooking long ago. 'I started to cook when I was fourteen. I used to make cakes. And then, when I was still living at home, I began to make four or five things simply because I enjoyed them.' Savarin explains how a combination of two things influenced his attitude towards cooking. 'I like to eat well. And I've always been used to eating proper home cooking.' Food, meals and cooking were important features of his family's culture. He might, like many teenagers, have rebelled against it but he liked his food too much. It was not long before he began to experiment for himself. By the time he was living on his own, he was already an accomplished cook, unlike the majority of single men, who live on snacks. 'Even when I got home at 9 or 10, I used to cook a meal for myself.' He has no memory of any biographical variations; he has always been the head cook.

The early stages of the relationship are also decisive. Savarin's girlfriend may well have found his approach to cooking irritating and it is still quite a man's style in that he shows off a lot (every meal is an event that has to be discussed and planned in advance). Tony's girlfriend also finds him irritating. But she has never challenged his authority in the kitchen. Whether it is the man or the woman who takes charge of the cooking is less important in itself than the reasons why they come to blows. The discussions would, for instance, have been much more heated if Tony had met Prune (and it is hard to say who would have won). But with his girlfriend, everything was clear from the start. 'Given that she can't cook, and is afraid to try new things. Sometimes, she does get the urge . . . but it all tends to be very basic. So she makes something simple because she knows how to.' He obviously has no intention of helping her to develop her skills and is happy to let her be his helper. Her job is to peel the onions and do the washing up. And to make the occasional fruit pie (her special 'something').

As with Savarin, modesty is not Tony's most conspicuous virtue, and it is possible that he attaches more importance to food and meals than his girlfriend would like, even though she keeps quiet about that. But he also has a real passion for cooking and it is not just a passing fad. And what woman would not be charmed by the way he turns every evening meal into a little party, makes certain that the atmosphere is right and even provides mood music and soft lighting? Men who develop a passion for cooking may well make a lot of fuss about it but they can sometimes perform miracles too. For historical reasons, women tend to cook out of a sense of duty rather than because they have a passion for it. But the meals that cooks make strengthen relationships and families, and it is that (rather than the food itself) that awakens women's passions. That is why they are willing to do what they are told when family life revolves around the children (once they are old enough to eat at the table) or even when the man takes charge during the early stages of the relationship. Nothing is decided until this crucial stage has been reached. Women's passionate interest in their families tends to reactivate the old division of labour and their sense of duty. Anything that gives women a specific role tends to promote an archaic inequality, even when their passions take the modern form of demands for specific rights or communitarian demands. Elisabeth Badinter (2006 [2003]) rightly points out that feminism finds itself in a dead end when it exaggerates the difference between the sexes. Major changes occur as a result of the interaction between individuals who are more autonomous and not defined solely by gendered roles. When it comes to the culinary division of labour, most progress is made when we are young or when we have reached the stage when individuals are less constrained by gender stereotypes.

From sacrifice to gift

Individuals are now less defined by set roles, and especially gender roles; they are people first, and men or women second. We therefore have to relativize the male/female opposition I have just described briefly, as it applies only at the most general level: every individual has a different history. And yet, after an intense period of inventive autonomy when we are young, the weight of the past we have internalized, combined with the continued existence of gender stereotypes, does recreate a sharp division between the sexes. Even though the male/female opposition is somewhat schematic, we can still learn a lot from it. We have already explained why men show off so much when they begin to cook. Women follow a very different trajectory. They have a long history of domesticity. They have been cooks for generations and their behaviours are defined by their role as cooks. Their acceptance of that role made life bearable, if not always easy. Their culinary skills and diverse impulses sometimes meant that they also derived a more personal pleasure from cooking. As their role as cooks became less strictly defined, women had to make more effort to perform what they now saw as a thankless task. Their sense of duty became more acute and turned into an ethics of self-sacrifice.

They are no longer under any obligation to play that role (at least in theory) but the idea of a 'duty towards the family' still has very female connotations. Women do make more sacrifices than men and are therefore more likely to feel isolated and to find things difficult, as when they are faced with having to peel huge quantities of vegetables or have to 'come up with an idea'. As Daniel Miller (1998) notes, shopping can be extremely problematic for the same reasons. In such sad circumstances, cooking is an absolute self-sacrifice and is something that is difficult and painful to do. What is the link between this and the more joyous forms of self-sacrifice which involve personal pleasure and making other people happy? In his analysis of the relationship between gifts and sacrifice, Alan Caillé (1995: 288) notes that sacrifice 'develops out of giving' but that it also perverts the gift relationship. Although it makes the act of giving more intense (or at least appears to do so), it does so in a very specific way because it is the product of the long history of the constraints that weigh down human beings. It is now possible for us to give gifts simply because we wish to, and to do so in a 'disinterested way that once seemed almost inconceivable' (Caillé 1995: 288). This makes us more human. Something that is given freely means more than a painful sacrifice and this is a remarkably efficient way of establishing social bonds. Cooks have an intuitive understanding of this. They try to escape becoming trapped into a sacrificial logic. They make 'quick and easy meals' and encourage family members to help themselves to whatever is in the fridge. This is primarily because they do not have a vocation for suffering. But it is also because they sense that nothing good can come of such sacrifices. Everyone now feels that it is the quality of the social bond that matters. We are no longer sure how it is forged. And pain often leaves a nasty taste in the mouth. Maryse's reaction to the idea of self-sacrifice is visceral. 'Ah. It's no sacrifice. I don't like that word. That's putting it too strong. No, it makes people happy, that's all. You do certain things. It's spontaneous, it's what you do. And it's quite natural.' She alternates between two themes: a sense of duty ('it's natural') and self-sacrifice for the sake of the people she loves ('making people happy'). She dare not pursue the logic of passion any further. Suzette does: 'When you cook, you do so to make other people happy in some way. That's why you have to do a little bit more at the weekend, for instance.' 'Do a little bit more' . . . we force ourselves in order to please others, in the same way that we force ourselves to make a sacrifice. But we enjoy doing so because it both gives us pleasure and gives them pleasure. 'I do it for the rest of the family. But it gives me pleasure. I enjoy doing something for the rest of the family' (Savarin). She gives them pleasure because doing so gives her pleasure.

'Hand-made' love

We do not begin to make meals because we feel some passionate impulse to do so. That is not how things work. Putting a meal on the table every day is just something that has to be done and it is always a race against the clock. All the interviewees made a clear distinction between cooking for pleasure and having to cook every day. And yet neither form of cooking is just an ordinary domestic chore. There is something different about it. This is because family life is built around the dining table. Charlotte and Hortense compare cooking with doing housework but they do so in order to demonstrate that they are two different things. 'It's hard to get very enthusiastic about housework. But when you cook, everyone gets together around the table' (Charlotte). 'No one notices when you do the housework. But when I call everyone to the table, they really appreciate what I've done for them . . . And besides, getting together over a meal is important' (Hortense). The other good thing about cooking a meal is that everyone can see how much work has gone into it (and may even compliment the chef). Charlotte makes the same point: 'When you make something really tasty, you feel good about yourself.' But, like Hortense, she does not wish to place too much emphasis on that: what really matters is that the family gets together over a meal. Prune sums up their feelings perfectly: 'Why do I like to cook? Because we're a family, so we get together over a meal and we like having a meal together.' She uses the word 'like' twice, and applies it to both 'cooking' and 'having a meal together'. But it is all about her love for her family too. The joys of cooking and the joys of eating add an extra dimension to the syncretism of meals. Family life becomes more intense when pleasures can be shared. Biscotte speaks nostalgically of a past which is, sadly, long gone: 'I used to have a house full of people who liked good things; I knew that they would like what I made for them, and I enjoyed that.'

Cooks are often not really sure whether they are cooking because they like it (because it is an achievement and because it tastes good) or because others enjoy the meals they make. They do not need to be sure. The fact that they cannot tell the difference between the two things indicates the extent of their commitment to what they are doing. This combination of pleasures is central to the process of cooking for love. The cook experiences a range of different pleasures but she also likes to communicate with the people she is cooking for. She will not continue the experiment unless they become 'subjects of desire' (Miller 1998: 149) who anticipate and respond to her enthusiasm. Daniel Miller rejects the essentialist concept of love, which he regards as an abstract and ethereal entity. Love is a product of the pragmatic realities of everyday life. An analysis of the 'material culture of love' (Miller 1998: 137) would reveal precisely how its elementary mechanisms work. I am obviously not suggesting that it all comes down to what happens in the kitchen, or that we should forget about what goes on in the bedroom, or about the cuddles and the pillow talk. But the kitchen is not a separate realm and what goes on there probably does more than it might to create love for both couples and child-centred families. Thanks to the magic of cookery and the relational and sensual alchemy of meals, love sometimes grows as we peel onions or knead dough. We make it by hand.

A way of saying 'I love you'

Love is also, and mainly, a product of more direct expressions of desire and affection, of feelings, and of verbal exchanges. Making a meal is, however, also an indirect form of communication. Cooking for love is obviously a way of expressing love. The sensual enjoyment of food, combined with sensual pleasures of seduction, is obviously one of its most demonstrative expressions (Etchegoyen 2002). But love can also take more discreet, ordinary and implicit forms. Saying 'I love you' to someone's face is not always as simple as it is in the movies, and silence is all too often golden. But sometimes we talk so much and repeat ourselves so often that it all becomes a matter of routine, and routine is the antithesis of love. The world of the spoken word is full of traps and obstacles; certain gestures are more eloquent and less likely to be misinterpreted than others. When we find it difficult to say something out loud, busy hands in the kitchen can send out a message and allow us to communicate by arousing desires and exchanging pleasures. 'I try to make people happy. It's a way of communicating.' Marjolaine is very clear about the 'communications' aspect of the meals she makes. Cooking is a substitute for language, a poor man's pleasure for those who cannot express themselves in any other way. 'Preparing meals to make other people happy is a poor man's pleasure. If I could, I would probably find other ways to communicate.' It is indeed an astonishing way of saying 'I love you.' Self-sacrifice for the sake of love is rarely the cook's sole preoccupation. She has to keep an eye on the clock, adapt to difficult situations and put up with minor irritations, as well as concentrating on the task in hand and she therefore dislikes being interrupted. Prune is, to say the least, hard to approach. 'I don't want anyone under my feet, and I need to be on my own. I like to be left in peace because, if I'm not, I can't concentrate and I lose my temper. Sometimes I tell them to bugger off!' And yet her love for her family is unconditional and all she dreams of is making meals that will make it happier. Prune also admits that she and her husband do not always communicate as well as she would like, even though 'my husband finds it easier to open up over a meal than when we're sitting on the sofa in front of the telly.' For her, cooking is an indirect way of telling her husband that she loves him and she uses it often and quite deliberately. But when it is used to say 'I love you', it is a language that can take strange forms – which can be aggressive – that have little in common with the conventional idea of love.

Cooks who sacrifice themselves to make meals are not saints. Meals help to forge a social bond because they are pleasurable and because they turn the dining table into a stage. But that is rarely the only thing they do. The cook has something else on her mind. 'You do it for the people you love. When you cook a meal, you add a bit of love.' Prune is being perfectly sincere and she does cook for love. And she finds just the right words to describe this substitute language: 'a bit of love'. She is, in other words, not fully aware of how much love she puts into it; she refuses to see how much cooking has to do with relationships. She simply adds 'a bit of love' to a pragmatic activity from which there is no escape. Cooking is a way of saying 'I love you' when we do not know how else to say it, and it is rarely seen for what it is. It is relatively easy to forget that it is a language, especially as the cook always has other things on her mind too. Prune, for example, cooks for herself rather than for her family. 'I find it relaxing, and I enjoy it.' The two things are not incompatible, as we are more sympathetic to other people when we are enjoying ourselves. They are less compatible when the personal pleasure comes from self-fulfilment through creativity, as it may become somewhat narcissistic. Suzette thinks in hierarchical terms. She 'wants to' primarily because she is cooking for her family 'when we all get together'. She also has more personal reasons for wanting to cook: cooking is both a leisure activity and an art form. And everything (self-sacrifice and personal fulfilment) has to be kept within certain very definite limits. 'But I do try to do things that don't require much preparation.' The gift is a calculated one. The cook who cooks for love refuses to let cooking become an overwhelming passion, as that would turn her into a domestic slave. The old image of the cook who is chained to the stove horrifies her. Cooks want no more of those inescapable constraints and dream of freedom and individual lightness. The high point of the cook's art is knowing how to combine controlled passion with a modicum of self-sacrifice, which is sincere at the time but always kept in check. Anneth imagines a happy family sitting around a table with 'dishes that are well-presented and in good taste.' Cooking is not a chore because 'that's why you do it'. At various points in the interview, she uses the word 'goal' to describe both a dish that has worked perfectly (culinary technique) and a happy family meal (family dynamics) because she constantly confuses the two things. She does, however, make it very clear that this 'finality' must not take up too much of her time. 'If I could find something I could prepare more quickly and get better results, that would be the perfect solution.'

Food and elective bonds

The cook keeps her passions in check because she is afraid of becoming a domestic servant, because there is never enough time and because everything feels difficult, because of the health risks inherent in a diet that is too rich and because of the way the people she is cooking for react. When they do say what they want, they do not always do so in the way that, in an ideal world, the cook would like them to. They can be cold or indifferent. As Maïté complained, 'They never ask for anything. Never.' They may be critical, make unkind comments or praise the cook's skills but criticize her choice of menu. But the main problem is that they contradict one another: the more people there are at the table, the less likely it is that they will all agree about anything. So how is it possible to create a meal that will allow them to commune with each other? How can Amandine fulfil her dream of a family that eats together when her son wants pizza with mayonnaise and when her husband insists on sticking to his Cretan diet? Even Prune is in two minds. 'My son is very difficult. As a rule,

I often plan meals around what he wants. He loves anything based on tomatoes, so I do lots of tomatoes for him. My husband isn't too keen on tomatoes, so I try not to give him any. So it gets complicated.' Her husband 'loves his food'. Cooking for love would be a dream, were it not for one problem. 'He shouts at me. He would like more variety.' He does not want to see their meals being de-structured by individualism but nor does he want them to feature too many tomatoes because he feels that would make him a second-class citizen. Prune has to choose and she finds that very difficult. In our society, likes and dislikes are highly individualized and family meals mean that certain choices have to be made (Muxel 1996). Even a tomato represents a relational choice. The cook's choices reflect the state of her emotional commitments. It is not just the food but the bonds themselves that are elective. And it is unusual for a cook to give her husband priority over her children. When a couple has a child, the hierarchy of family ties has to be reorganized. A married couple have become parents. And what they eat reflects that change.

A cook cannot respond to everyone's likes and dislikes in the same way. She therefore has to arbitrate and give priority to some of the people she is feeding rather than others. And, at least in official terms, her own likes and dislikes do not count. 'You put other people first. It's only natural' (Anneth). This is not exactly surprising to the extent that cooking for love obeys the same logic as the old sense of duty, and that logic is sacrificial. For centuries, mothers gave their children the best share, and wives did the same for their husbands. The hierarchy of who got the biggest portion and the things they liked best was institutional. Although it is now the cook who takes the decisions, the outcome is still the same: what other people like is more important than what she likes. She represses her own desires and eats meat when she would rather be eating fish (Montagne 2004). In his ethnographic study of supermarkets, Daniel Miller notes the extent to which women try to put themselves in the place of those they are cooking for and to anticipate their wishes. He concludes (1998: 32) that 'love grows as we do the shopping' because we forget about our own needs. Whilst this is true in general terms, his comment requires some qualification. The cook may well try to take other people into account but she can also be calculating and even manipulative when she wants to get her own way. This is, to say the least, perfectly logical in an age of individual autonomy. Altruism and selfishness are not opposites or a zero-sum game. They always coexist in subtle combinations and it is therefore interesting to look at some of these mechanisms.

Family consensus and education

Making meals is a constant battle. The cook is a strategist who, unfortunately, often reacts to expressions of indifference and complaints rather than trying to please everyone. Every meal is a new experiment that allows her to correct her aim, to stop cooking things that some family members will not eat and to try to find compromises. 'Children have to learn to eat a bit of everything, but you can't deliberately give them things they don't like day after day. When I used to do cauliflower, I always added a few potatoes' (Hortense). Every family gradually elaborates its own food culture in the course of the minor but constant heated exchanges that take place over meals. 'It's not as though we all liked the same things, but I do cook things we all like.' With loving care, the cook makes meals that bring the family together day after day and it is *what* she cooks that brings it together. The consensus that emerges is obviously not very balanced, as the cook has her elective affinities. Clémentine, for example, cannot resist chocolate cake and cannot say 'no' to her daughter. And thanks to the miraculous alchemy of food, they both like the same things. 'So I indulge myself for her sake. I make cakes that are fun, lots of things like that with chocolate.' Clémentine is not so self-indulgent when she cooks for her partner and often looks up quick recipes in the book her grandmother gave her. She has double standards. Cooks no longer want to make heroic sacrifices. Because they are carried away by the logic of pleasure, they would never dream of making things they themselves do not like. They take into account the likes and dislikes of their partners and children but they also take their own into account. They may well be generous but they refuse to be victims. They therefore have to strike a delicate balance. 'I loathe garlic but my husband loves it, so I add a little from time to time. But I would never be so bold as to put garlic in the lamb I'm roasting' (Paule-Dauphine). Can the cook be objective when she sees herself as just another mouth to feed? Cooks think so but they are not necessarily right. Listen to Eugénie. She begins by explaining her theory of what a fair consensus is. 'He prefers certain things to others, so they are the things I make. But we don't necessarily like the same things . . . so . . . well, I try to strike a balance to keep everyone happy.' The examples she then gives seem to contradict her egalitarian principles. Without realizing it, she bases her choices on a very personal notion of what a good diet means and then stresses that her husband does not put up much resistance. 'I can't really say he's very difficult.' He will, for instance eat the artichokes she keeps serving, even though he

226

loathes artichokes. 'He will eat them. He will eat what I put in front of him. Even though it's not exactly what he likes. He'd rather have potatoes.' Eugénie is typical of the many cooks who get their own way despite themselves and who take decisions on the basis of what they like, even when they think they are taking other people's views into account. This unwitting blindness is well intentioned: they are trying to tell them what they like in the hope that they will enjoy it too. 'I don't do it for my own sake; I want them to try something new' (Anneth). They want to enrich their shared family culture on the basis of what they know: they are trying to teach their families to be happy. And they sometimes succeed in doing so and their families are grateful to them for two reasons: they have tried something they thought they wouldn't like and they have brought the family closer together by getting them to try something new. 'I make what's good for my family but my likes and dislikes are the starting point' (Suzette).

Teaching the family to be happy can easily become part of a broader educational strategy. Immersed in the vast amount of literature on healthy eating that is now available (see Part I), cooks obviously use it to justify their own choices. They are now trying to improve their family's health rather than helping them to discover new pleasures. This higher purpose turns the battle over meals into a crusade and silences the cook's critics; she therefore pays less attention to their likes and dislikes. How, for example, could anyone challenge Marjolaine's decision to reduce the amount of sugar and fat her family eats? From the nutritional point of view, she is quite right to do so. She has also noticed that this restrictive discipline has other benefits: their new habits are having an effect on their sense of taste: 'I enjoy my food more; it has more taste.' Pleasure and health have become synonymous. But isn't she concentrating on her own likes and dislikes and using the health argument as an excuse to get them to eat the things she likes? 'Perhaps, yes, I probably am, but it's also for the good of their health!'

Manipulative tactics

Cooks often manipulate things so as to get their own way in much more specific ways. They are faced with a huge variety of products and the choices they make are based upon multiple criteria (different people like different things; a series of meals has to be structured; price, quality, nutritional value and ecological factors have to be taken into account). Everything is, in other words, much more complex than it used to be and no one will be completely satisfied, no matter what decision the cook makes. As we shall see, cooks resolve this difficulty by taking sudden decisions that make everything less complex, no matter which criteria they use. There is therefore a great temptation for them to serve up something simply because they like it, because it is good to think with or because it is healthy. That is how Suzette got her family to eat olive oil (which she now loves). 'Olive oil was a big problem, because the family don't like it. I do. I can get used to anything, provided it's healthy. It wasn't easy to persuade them to try olive oil.' Melba finds it hard to get her family to eat cod. She is very pleased to see that the latest nutritional advice (on Omega 3 oils) puts fish still higher up the health-food charts. In her view, cod is a treat. She begins the interview by reiterating her theory about the cook's self-denial and claims that her own likes and dislikes are irrelevant, especially where her children are concerned. 'I think all mums are the same.' She then adds that there are limits and that parents must not lose sight of the idea that children have to be taught to eat what is good for them. 'If I think it's good for them, I'll make it again, even if they don't like it.' And what is good for them (and her husband)? Cod. Even though they do not like cod. A few days ago, her husband went purple with anger: 'You really are impossible! Not that stuff again!' She thought she knew what she was doing and had served the cod in a sauce that should have made it impossible for him to know what he was eating. 'I didn't want to admit defeat.' She will now have to come up with a new trick. Hortense has exactly the same problem with a whole range of food. She tries all sorts of things, watches how her family reacts and then beats a strategic retreat in order to plan a new assault. 'It's only for a while. And then I'll be more careful about how I present it.'

Cooks use two main tactics to get their own way. They claim to be acting in the name of higher interests and to be educating their families about healthy eating, and they listen selectively when people tell them what they want to eat. They actually do take their likes and dislikes into account. But they have to cook for a number of different people who do not all like the same things. They all like a variety of different things. They have their favourite foods and their own preferences as to how they should be cooked. Those preferences may or not coincide with the cook's likes and dislikes. A clever cook can identify the common denominators and can thus create a common culture that appears to be based upon a consensual logic but which in fact actually reflects her own preferences. Some succeed in getting their own way most of the time but still take other people into account.

They make a note of and also exploit their family's likes and dislikes in order to make their own lives easier. Maryse has noticed that her husband is not too keen on dishes that come with sauces. 'It makes my life easier.' She has stopped making meals that take a long time to prepare, starting with the things she found difficult. Maïté is also very good at exploiting other people's likes and dislikes. She complains that the fact that no one ever tells her what they want means that she can no longer be bothered to cook. But she said that because she wanted to make a good impression on the interviewer. The fact that they do not ask for anything in particular works to her advantage and she knows how to exploit the situation. 'When you're cooking for the kids, it's not worth making anything complicated because they won't like it. I've always said that I'd rather make them what they like. And they don't like anything complicated.' They would rather have ham sandwiches.

Clémentine is one of the few people who were interviewed to admit that she has her own preferences, and one of the few who was aware of the privileges she enjoys because she is the cook. 'I don't eat at lunchtime, so I'm not very interested in other people's likes and dislikes. Look after number one! So if there are any leftovers at lunchtime, I might have a little something extra.' The evening meal is a very different matter. Depending on how she feels at the time, she may make something quick and easy or commit herself to making something special. This determines how she uses her grandmother's cookery book. When it is a quick and easy meal, cost and ease of preparation are the decisive criteria; when she is cooking for love, taste is what counts. 'The things I like. I say to myself, I'm the one who does the shopping, I'm the one who makes the shopping lists and I'm the one who does the cooking, so I'll cook what I like. At least I'll enjoy it.' Clémentine, it will be remembered, complains about her helper's attempts to cook 'He decides he wants to make something. Something special. You'd better watch out! The great chef is going to cook. It's quite a ritual.' To make matters worse, he always cooks fish. 'I don't like fish myself. Fish does not agree with me. If I'm still hungry, I make a snack meal of whatever's in the fridge.' She and her husband still have a long way to go before they can find things that they both like.

Compliments, but not too many

With few exceptions such as Clémentine, cooks do not actually realize that they are making the family eat what they themselves want

229

to eat; they quite genuinely believe that they put others first, And they do pay a lot of attention to what others say because it helps them to perfect their selective techniques. From the cook's point of view, there is no doubt about it: they are altruistic and do not often indulge themselves. No matter whether they cook because it is their duty or whether they have a passion for it, cooking is a self-sacrificial act and they do it for other people. What is there to prove that they are disinterested and quite devoid of narcissism? The fact that they like receiving compliments . . . but not too many.

Cooks like to receive a few compliments, as is only natural. Only Maïté, logically enough, does not expect to get any. 'Compliments or no compliments, it doesn't matter to me. I've done my good deed for the day. It had to be done, and now it's done. Over and done with.' Anyone who wants compliments has to make at least a minimal effort. 'If they tell me "that's nice", that's my little reward and it's nice. If they don't say anything, it doesn't matter to me' (Candy). She says that it doesn't matter to her but we have to understand what she is really saying. She obviously prefers to get her 'little reward'. But her goal is still the same: she wants to feed her family as best she can, irrespective of whether or not she gets her 'little reward'. It is when they do something out of the ordinary that cooks really expect compliments. They expect a reaction that shows that the family has noticed that she has made an effort. 'When I've spent a long time making something really tasty and no one says anything, I ask them: "Well, what do you think?" As a rule, I get the answer "It was good"' (Bélangère). A cook who is fully committed to the logic of self-interest expects to be 'recognized as someone who puts other people first' (Caillé 2004: 21). This means that the cook needs a sign; it may be very minor but it has to be clear. 'When I don't get an answer, I say "Well, was it good or not?" Not every time, of course, just now and then. "When we don't say anything, it means it's good." Does it, now? You might say "It's good", just once in a while' (Hortense).

The family's opinion is important for another reason: the cook simply wants to know if the food was good. When she cooks something out of the ordinary, everything becomes more complicated and it is much more likely that something will go wrong at the technical level. Praise reassures her. 'Getting compliments is not a matter of pride, but it does mean that it really worked, or at least that's how I understand it' (Candy). Cooks who are particularly anxious or uncertain as to how good they are are more grateful for the compliments they get. Madeleine, for example, has never learned how much salt she should use. 'I go from one extreme to the other' and the family diet alternates between food that is terribly bland and food that is far too salty. 'I'm always frightened I won't get it right.' She is not fishing for compliments; she simply wants someone to tell her that everything is fine.

Cooks do not, however, want to receive too many compliments. Everyone who was interviewed was quite definite about this. Charlotte is always telling her husband not to praise her too highly. 'Of course I like compliments, but not too many. My husband is always telling everyone: "Oh, she's a really good cook." I tell him, "Shut up. You're getting on my nerves!"' Charlotte is well aware of the fact that there is a big difference between the meals she dreams of making and the meals she actually makes. The way her husband praises her cooking does not ring true because he is exaggerating. That touches her guilty conscience and she makes a big effort when she would rather make something quick and easy. Compliments have to be tailored to suit the occasion. There is also another reason why cooks do not like to get too many compliments. If they are praised too highly, their egos feel flattered and that subverts the logic of the gift relationship because it proves that they cook for narcissistic reasons or because they have an ulterior motive. That completely blocks the dynamic that constructs families thanks to an exchange of pleasures. Paule-Dauphine explains very clearly why 'she really likes' getting compliments when she does not expect them: they have to be spontaneous. This is neither modesty nor politeness on the cook's part. The compliments cooks 'like to get' are egocentric only in a secondary sense. They are not the ones that are addressed to them directly. The signs they look out for (and acknowledge) are actually addressed to the other guests, and they are signs of enjoyment: 'It's not because I'm fishing for compliments, it's because I want them to enjoy it' (Tony). 'Do you find that flattering?' the interviewer asks Babette. 'No! It's because I'm glad they liked it.' Eugénie seems to finish her sentence for her: 'When they like it, it makes me happy, and I like that.' It is the way the pleasures that circulate create a bond that makes them happy. The best compliments are the spontaneous reactions of those who are actually eating the meal. 'Wow, that's good! You must make it again.' The most perfect form of praise can sometimes even take the form of a silence that is broken only by the sound of people chewing; some silences are very eloquent. 'When everyone wolfs it down and you hear nothing . . . I don't know, it's encouraging, it's their way of saying thank you for all the work that went into it. I appreciate that,' says Madeleine, even though she does like a few more explicit expressions of gratitude too.

Cooks do not make meals because they are fishing for compliments. 'If I don't get any compliments, I don't say anything' (Prune). They sometimes cook because, like Prune, they want to. Making others happy makes them happy. 'I do it mainly for myself. I enjoy my cooking.' If, however, pleasure is to circulate, this has to be a two-way process. 'If they're happy, I'm happy.' Cooks whose acts are altruistic also get their own reward.

For the family

It all starts because she wants to cook. There are of course times when she does not feel like it and forces herself to cook a meal simply because she has to. 'Because I have too, that's all. Because we have to eat; because I have to. Someone has to do it.' Maïté is not, however, overwhelmed by her sense of duty. 'Even if I had the time, I wouldn't do any more cooking than I had to. Once they've got their plate of pasta, that's all they want.' She cannot be bothered, does not want to cook and does not feel like it. 'I don't want to, that's all! Don't feel like it.'

It all starts because she wants to cook. What does she want to cook, and why does she want to? Cooks find it hard to say. Tony comes up with a lot of reasons. 'It's a form of relaxation. And it's good for me. Eating well and having a balanced diet is good for me. And it's kind of research.' Marjolaine gives only one reason but it is very abstract. 'It's my way of expressing myself.' 'Wanting to' is a complex phenomenon and it can mean a lot of different things. Various factors can stir the cook into action: the urge to be creative (the cook as artist), a wish to be famous (the cook as star), a more prosaic need to relax (like children, cooks play with their food). There may also be something even more indefinable. They may simply want to. Clémentine simply wants to cook when she is feeling good about herself. 'Well, if I'm happy, if I'm feeling pleased with myself, or I've had a good day, I might get us a drink, and make a meal that's a bit nicer than usual.' All these fragmentary desires fuse into a single impulse because she wants to do it for her family. 'Even if only one or two of the children are there, I'll set to work. Even though I don't like cakes, I'll happily make them.' Biscotte has to be 'persuaded' to cook, but she also has to be persuaded to eat. 'I'm not a big eater. I don't eat when I'm on my own. I won't let myself be persuaded, so I'm not hungry, so I don't eat.' Now that her family is gone, she is not hungry. 'When we were a family, I ate as much as they did, like them . . . I liked it, didn't have to force myself. But now, my stomach . . . Not hungry.' Having a family gives you an appetite.

A cook who is inspired by the family dynamic is a hungry cook. In the physical sense of the word. A rumbling stomach makes her even more eager than ever to cook; the need is both urgent and physical. 'My taste buds are salivating' (Savarin). When our taste buds are not salivating, we are less eager to cook (or to have a family). 'When I have no appetite, it really does feel like a chore. I'll make a quick meal, and it's over and done with quickly' (Marjolaine). Fortunately, Marjolaine does often 'want to eat and that makes me want to cook'. At moments like this, cooks begin to wonder if they might not be being a little selfish because they can already see themselves enjoying the fruits of their labours. 'Preparing a meal and then eating it is all part of the same pleasure. It's a sequence of events. And the meal is the end product. I get enormous pleasure from eating' (Savarin). Deep down inside, he knows that he is not being selfish and that it is the relational dynamic that makes him hungry. He is also hungry for something else: he wants to please and to give other people what they want. 'It's because I want to eat that I want to cook. And perhaps I want to do something for them. I want them to enjoy it' (Marjolaine).

Shopping

Unfortunately, doing the shopping also has its difficult moments and that rather spoils the beautiful harmony of the circulation of pleasures. That some things will be difficult is inevitable. And everyone agrees that shopping is the worst thing of all. 'It's the shopping that gets me down' (Hortense). For the moment, the cook is responsible for doing the shopping and she does not really understand why. Cooks themselves are surprised at how pressurizing shopping can be. This is the moment of truth. It is no longer possible to hide the fact that being the cook is an incredibly complex business because it means making choices based on the criteria of nutrition, taste, health and cost, planning the future of social bonds and deciding how much time she wants to devote to making a meal. She has to do all this within the space of a few moments but cannot think straight as she pushes her trolley down aisles lined with products that are just begging to be bought. No one ever told her that cooking a meal was such an intellectual business. She feels alone and she feels tired. 'The worst thing about it is having to know what you're going to buy, what you're going to eat on Monday, Tuesday, Wednesday . . .' (Clémentine).

The only solution is to fall back on the old sense of duty or even the ethics of self-sacrifice: she will put up with it for the sake of the family (Devault 1991; Miller 1998). But she cannot allow herself to see it that way. On the contrary: the person who has the responsibility for doing the shopping has to convince himself or herself that this mental fatigue is an aberration, a sudden and inexplicable personal weakness. And he or she tries to shake it off as quickly as possible.

How can she get over this feeling of irritation and forget about it? Cooks try to develop tactics that allow them to do so. Clémentine, who is still a novice, tried to vary her routine. When she tried to shop only once a month, the results were disastrous, so she went to the opposite extreme and began to shop every two or three days. And discovered that: 'It's a pain.' No sooner has she done the shopping than she has to start thinking about the next trip. She has therefore introduced a new schedule: she will shop once a fortnight. She may be in for a nasty surprise, as going shopping less often can be a new trap. It is certainly a logical reflex. 'Doing the shopping is the biggest pain of all. I try to do as little as possible' (Melba). She does it less often, but at considerable cost to herself: because she does all her shopping in one go, the mental pressure becomes even greater than it was. She feels it less often but the pressure is worse. Two factors increase the mental pressure that makes shopping such a pain: the structure of the household, and the relationship with time. The bigger the family, the more complex the intellectual task. 'When you have a big family, shopping is a real pain' (Olivia). Madeleine recalls how exhausted she felt when her children were still living at home and when she had to cater for all their needs. Now that she has only her husband to think about, things are much easier, especially as she now has all the time in the world. She often 'pops out to the shops', which also gives her the chance to go out for a walk and to chat to friends: shopping has almost ceased to be a problem. Except when she has to pop out 'at the last minute'. When that happens, she is astonished that she finds it hard; she thought it was just a bad memory. 'The worst thing about it is that you can't think of anything else.' This is not in fact surprising. The mental pressure is so unpleasant because there is a direct correlation between the intellectual complexity of the problems the cook has to solve (especially if she has a large family) and the time available for doing so. 'The shopping has to be done quickly. And I do mean quickly' (Maïté). The more she believes she can get the shopping out of the way, the more likely she is to feel, all at once, that it is difficult. Women with heavy work commitments as well as a lot of domestic responsibilities are the most obvious victims. The luxury of having a lot of time is the only thing that can reduce the stress of doing the shopping or even turn it into a pleasure. A few of the people interviewed gave lengthy idealized descriptions of how much they enjoyed going to markets. They would rather forget the horrors of having to shop on a day-to-day basis.

Lists

Cooks who are short of time therefore have to come up with more subtle tactics. The first is to make a shopping list. Shopping lists come in different shapes and sizes. A list of the basic products the household needs can be written on a slate or in a notebook kept in a drawer to ensure that they are not forgotten when the fateful day comes around. The lists that are made in advance are the most interesting. They may be long or short, vague or very detailed, or very specific when there is a big meal to prepare. But they all work on the same principle: they reduce the mental pressure by breaking the preparations down into stages. The cook does the intellectual work first to ensure that the actual experience of shopping is not too intense or too unpleasant. 'Without a list, you can never find your way around the shop . . . and I don't like that' (Amandine). The products that are to be found in different aisles are sometime listed separately so as to rationalize the way the shopping trolley is used (Lahire 2005 [1998]). For people who have enough time, making a shopping list can be an important activity in its own right and they plan their shopping trips in advance. 'I like to be organized. I don't like it when I've done the shopping and then remember that I've forgotten this or that. As soon as I get up in the morning, I start to think about what we should have for lunch' (Maryse). Even Maïté spends some time on her shopping lists because they make the shopping easier, even though she always buys the same things. 'I make my list on Friday evening, and make a note of what we're going to have on Saturday and Sunday.' Unfortunately, the cook is not out of the woods yet. Cooks who carefully plan ahead find it even more difficult to 'come up with an idea'; their plans are too detailed and drawn up too early. They solve one problem but create another. Besides, the lists are made because of the widespread illusion that everything can be planned in advance and that a list of things on a piece of paper provides the answer to all their problems. Lists are always incomplete. We have to remember that cooks have to construct a family; their lists (which are often very incomplete) simply mention a number of things to buy. That is why they in fact have two lists. One is written out in full on a piece of paper and lists the basics that must not be forgotten. The other is 'in my head'. 'I make a mental list: well, I'll make . . .' (Maryse). The mental list is at once less detailed and more ambitious. It covers a much broader spectrum and includes both images of the family and a variety of possible scenarios. Unless the cook is planning a big meal, the mental list is usually no more than an outline that allows her to know what to look for in the shop and it can be ignored if she comes up with a better idea. 'I always have some idea. But when I'm in the shop, I sometimes say to myself: "No. I'm not going to do what I planned." I sometimes change my mind, depending on what I see in the shops' (Hortense).

The cook gets to the shop, with or without a written list, and with or without some idea of what she is going to buy. At first, her list is a great asset. She heads for products that look reassuringly like simple objects. Even without a list, she often does not find walking down the aisles too unpleasant to begin with. A glittering world of foodstuffs and brands gives her all sorts of new ideas. There are things she has never heard of and they are all within hand's reach. Too many ideas, too many possibilities. She begins to feel the full weight of the mental pressure. But she is not here to dream and has to eliminate some possibilities. She has to construct and elaborate a plan for the future, and it has to be coherent and solid. She has to avoid nutritional and relational problems. She has to choose from the vast range of things that are on offer.

Special offers and rationality

Cooks choose on a rational basis. Their choices are based on contradictory criteria and there are too many things to choose from. When reflexivity extends beyond short and well-defined periods of time, it becomes the cook's enemy and increases the mental burden without providing a solution to her problems. She has to have a method. And although she may not be aware of it, it is a very sophisticated method. She is not aware of this because the first rule is to make things less complex by not thinking about their complexity. (This is why cooks are always surprised to find that shopping is a pain and why they do not want to think about it.) She has to act as though all this was just one more thing to put up with and as though it was not important. The truth is that her decisions will have a huge influence on the family's future. She convinces herself that she has a list of things to buy and that there is not much more to it than that. All she has to do,

236

it seems to her, is rely upon her usual points of reference (favourite brands, the variation principle, standard menus) and then make a few impulse buys to complete the list.

She cannot, unfortunately, completely forget the underlying complexities of shopping, as she would then have no guidelines at all. She is literally in two minds. Part of her is still the architect who uses meals to create a family life. Unreal images (evocations of an imaginary past and sense-perceptions that heighten them) constantly come into conflict with flashes of reflexivity. Her thoughts alternate between visions that are influenced by what the family wants and much more pragmatic calculations (what is already in the trolley, the things she has already bought, the things she has forgotten, coherent choices). Her dreams and her pragmatic calculations must eventually coincide, as must her dietary and relational concerns. The cook thinks about her family and imagines its future as she buys yoghurts and tins of peas. Paradoxically, having her partner or children with her does not help at all.[3] On the contrary, it makes everything worse. A partner will say what he wants while they are doing the shopping. The ensuing negotiations distract the cook's attention and do not really fit in with her overall plan. The cook has to concentrate on her future scenarios, even if it means losing her temper when the demands of her partner or family become unreasonable, or taking no notice of them. This is a major cognitive task and it is the real reason why she finds shopping so difficult. The cook refuses, however, to devote too much attention to this because she knows that she would become lost in its complexity. She does all she can to simplify the task of planning ahead. She does her best to be the impulsive individual who is seduced by the huge variety of things she sees in the shops.

The sales floor is a world of stimuli that trigger personalized images in the form of existential scenarios. The products on offer become the virtual organizers of biographical sequences. Some of the stimuli that are displayed so prominently make no impact because they do not coincide with her internalized sense of what is and what is not possible, or simply because the cook is thinking about something else. When the two do coincide, the cook experiences a sudden sense of relief. Her impulses are so obviously right that her choices are immediately obvious. Everything becomes less complex. Supermarkets are

---

[3] Long-distance consultations by mobile phone, which are now becoming more common in the shops, are not the same thing. In most cases, this means that the shopping has been delegated to a helper who takes order from the cook. On the rare occasions when it is the cook who calls home from the shop, the consultation is short and kept within reasonable limits, does not raise the tension and tends to reduce the mental pressure.

places where we suddenly fall in love with a camembert or a leg of lamb. A cook who surrenders to one of these very minor impulses tries to justify herself in such a way that the product she has chosen becomes the organizer and structures her later purchases and future meals. 'Some things are very attractive. Sometimes you see a cabbage, a lovely cabbage, and you say to yourself: "Oh, I could make a nice stuffed cabbage!"' (Clémentine). Clémentine's experiences of love at first sight are usually more restrained, especially when she is not really trying to plan her meals. 'I tend to buy things on impulse. Look, they've got veal. It looks nice. I'll have some veal!' Some shoppers, in contrast, do without lists and allow themselves to be swayed by their emotions. 'I have no idea what I'm going to make. And then I see something' (Paule-Dauphine). They wander down the aisles, hoping that something will catch their eye. Immediate sense-perceptions are the best answer to the sterile torments of reflexive complexity (Damasio 1995). Once something has caught her eye, the cook just has to construct a meal around it. 'I go shopping without having any idea of what I'm going to cook. As I look at what's on the shelves, I say to myself: well, that would be nice. Because I've seen something I like. That's what we'll have! It gives me an idea for a meal. I've got my menu now, I'll take this, and I'll take that' (Madeleine). Anneth has given up making lists and has adopted a new principle: 'I usually decide what to make while I'm doing the shopping.'

Shops are obviously not neutral territory. Behind the scenes, a lot of work goes into constructing displays that will catch the cook's eye (Cochoy 2002). How families interact is often decided by an end-display. And then, most important of all, there are the special offers, which can be incredibly attractive. There is nothing surprising about that, one might say. But they are not always attractive for the obvious reasons. Their success is often cited as proof that the cost-conscious customer is the personification of individual rationality. They actually prove the very opposite. The advertised savings are a wonderful excuse for not having to think and that has nothing to do with rational reflexivity. Special offers are the stars of the show and their appeal is irresistible. And the purchaser is a willing victim. The primary function of special offers is to reduce complexity to simplicity and to persuade the customer to buy something that will influence her subsequent choices. Several people actually said that they regularly bought special offers without looking too closely at the price. 'If something is on offer, I'll buy it without thinking too much about the prices' (Tony). 'I don't pay too much attention to the cost, but I do buy special offers' (Anneth). The good thing about special offers is that we do not have to think so much, and that makes every-thing easier. 'I see an offer, and say to myself: not bad, I'll take that' (Candy). We have little control over these reflexes (we simply say 'not bad'). This is a passive state of mind: we are waiting to be seduced. 'It's the offers that come to me' (Candy). Unfortunately, special offers are becoming more and more common; they have to compete and therefore become confusing. The respite was only temporary.

CONCLUSION

We have, for better or worse, entered the modern world of freedom and uncertainty, and that influences the way we eat. We are faced with such an abundance of food that we cannot decide what to eat but worry that eating too much might be bad for our health. We have access to a wealth of nutritional advice (if not too much of it) that provides warnings and allows us to form our own opinions. But opinions are not, alas, enough in this domain. Even a scientifically correct opinion is not enough. This is because eating is also a cultural and emotional business. We do not eat with our brains. Sharing meals with our families weaves the bonds that keep us together. As in the earliest societies, kinship is constructed 'by porridge' and by sharing food day after day. The history of meals has been extraordinarily turbulent. It stretches from the religious gatherings around sacrificial altars, in which men communed with the gods, to the starchy, formal table manners of the nineteenth century which developed an ethical model centred on the idea that the family could be reconstructed by disciplining bodies. The family sat facing one another over a table. Eventually, our bodies tired of that soulless rigidity. Our souls, for their part, were experiencing new desires. They wanted our hearts to beat as one or, should that prove impossible, at least communicate a little in a reassuring intimacy. They wanted to communicate in words but speech is not always an easy instrument to handle. And they wanted to communicate via their senses: food became an existential tool. The free individuals of modernity may, however, rebel against this fine familial model, especially when they are young, and may prefer to eat what they like when they like. Families have to make an effort to keep them at the table.

To be more accurate, it is whoever is in charge of the kitchen that has to make the effort, and even today that person is usually a woman. The family is quite content to be waited on and to discover the nutritional delights of the scene that is about to be acted out to the sound of glasses clinking and forks clattering. This essential scene lies at the heart of family life and it is all the more foundational in that it is becoming unusual in households where everyone often eats on their own. It therefore has to be a special occasion. Everyone in the family plays their part – chosen from a limited repertoire – but they are tempted to leave the table when the group pressure becomes too great, or to watch the television because they have nothing to say to each other. The awkward silences of the past have been replaced by the sound of the television. Having nothing to say to each other is not the worst thing that can happen; families may come to feel that they have nothing at all in common. They end up eating for the sake of eating in a world in which everything is tasteless, in an autistic world that is deaf to the normal emotions of people who are sitting around a table together. That is why food is not trivial. It is now a decisive element in the construction of the intimate, living entity that we call a family. Especially when the cook devotes her time, skills and emotions to producing something that does much more than just set the scene.

Everything rests, therefore, upon the shoulders of the cook. She has to make some very complex and difficult choices from the outset. She has to strike a balance between the family's likes and dislikes, and her own likes and dislikes. She has to choose between different dietary options, between spending and saving money, between abundance and self-control and between pleasure and nutritional value. She can either attempt to educate her family to eat well or leave everyone to their own devices and let them help themselves to whatever there is in the fridge. When she is alone in the kitchen (and sometimes in the shops), she senses that she is the secret organizer of everything that happens in the dining room. And she still has to take the most problematic decision of all: how deeply is she committed to cooking? And, thanks to an irony of history, that crushing responsibility became incumbent upon her at the very time when women were trying to get out of the kitchen. And at this point, we have to assume that the cook is a woman who has always been chained to the stove for life, whether she likes it or not. Women now find that this role is completely unacceptable. They want to reinvent themselves as free and autonomous individuals who are men's equals and on an equal footing with men. But it is still unusual for men to cook on a day-to-day basis. Fortunately, there is a solution and the growing number

241

and variety of products available on the market make quick and easy meals a real possibility. In extreme cases, individual members of the family can be left to fend for themselves with ready meals. Even the cook is becoming part of the general trend towards individualization and has to a large extent abandoned her old role. Like everyone else, women are now more interested in eating than in cooking. The fridge rules. A new dietary model is emerging and it both lowers the tension and loosens family ties. Life is becoming more liquid, just as food is becoming easier to swallow.

Such is the basic model and it is spreading inexorably. But as it tightens its grip, a counter-model is beginning to emerge, haltingly, and by fits and starts. The decision to cook a meal is prompted by emotional impulses and multiple and ill-defined desires. The new passion for cooking is a combination of a desire to be creative in aesthetic terms, gastronomic hedonism and a longing for greater conjugal and familial intensity. We want to feel emotions we cannot really express and we use food as a language of love because we have no other. Love is not just an abstract feeling that exists apart from the ordinary world. It is also something we construct day by day, sometimes with our hands. The cook's hands are doing something obvious. At the intellectual level, however, she has a lot of problems. Her brain hurts because she cannot conceal the fact that cooking is an extraordinarily complex activity. But her hands relieve the mental pleasure. Body and soul are focused on what she is doing with her hands. She is doing something that is very concrete but she is also very aware of its relational and emotional implications. A tasty meal can inspire love.

Sadly, there is nothing simple about the way we cook and eat our meals, which is based upon insoluble contradictions. It is therefore impossible for this history to end in the way that a fairy tale ends. For many different reasons (a cook who controls her impulses, guests who bicker or leave the table rather than expressing their admiration for the cook), the carriages always turn back into pumpkins. And there is another reason: if we grow too fond of our food, we unfortunately put on a few extra kilos and that is not good for our health. And it is a well-known fact that passions are always dangerous and can lead to excess. At this point, the reflexive individual inside the cook wakes up and represses her generous impulses. The cook goes on a diet and dreams of losing weight. The way we cook and eat is in perpetual flux.

A NOTE ON METHODOLOGY

The survey included 22 people who were interviewed using the comprehensive interview method (Kaufmann 1996). Esther Esnault and Cédric Touquet used all their ethnological skills to pay attention to the smallest details and to respect the simplest words. Data that is gathered in this way always has a particular flavour, depending on who asks the questions and how they asked them. In this case, it is very human and I am infinitely grateful to the interviewers.

A researcher who ventures into new territory must do everything possible to resolve a contradiction. He must at once keep the survey focused (otherwise there is a danger that it will become too general) and at the same time ensure that it is not so tightly focused that it becomes impossible to learn anything new. This sometimes takes him to unexpected places and that is often how the most interesting finds are made. I expected the survey to focus on domestic cookery. I expected to find the contradictory richness (the contradiction between quick and easy meals and cooking for love) that can be observed in the mind of any cook. But I had no idea that cooking could have such a material influence on how families are constructed. I had therefore planned to ask only a few questions about meals. When I came to analyse it, my data therefore proved to be somewhat inadequate.

I could have begun a second series of more focused interviews but what seemed to me to be a better alternative presented itself. I was working on the bibliography and discovered a whole series of fascinating surveys that dealt, either directly or indirectly, with meals and that were based on qualitative interviews. The data was remarkably rich and varied. Ignoring it was out of the question. Citing it in an allusive way was also out of the question. It was essential to recapture the immediacy and the lived quality of the interviews. That is what I

243

have tried to do and I would like to thank, amongst others, Julie Janet Chauffier, Karim Gacem, Isabelle Garabuau-Moussaoui, Mathilde Perrot, Esla Ramos and François de Singly for the quality of their work.

A failing (a blind spot in my survey) became a virtue. I was of course lucky, as one does not always find such a fine set of studies at the very moment one needs them. But the end product was much better than anything I would have obtained by carrying out a further survey of my own. Every method has its qualities and its failings. As the expression itself indicates, the comprehensive interview is by far the best way of understanding social processes. It is, however, productive only when it is used with great sensitivity. There is a danger (and this is the method's weak point) that the conclusion will be influenced by the researcher's a priori ideas. The main guarantee that this will not happen is the researcher's self-control but self-control is not always easy when the ideas are exciting. It is therefore sometimes helpful to compare our findings with other sources dealing with the same subject. No two researchers see their data in exactly the same way or from the same perspective. Comparisons are therefore very helpful.

We tend to take a very narrow view of things, and to assume that data can be analysed in the same way that a bag can be emptied: one survey = one result. That is a purely theoretical construct that serves the needs of the bureaucratic administration of both people and things. The bag is in fact bottomless, and the raw material is infinitely rich; we can always get it to say something else. I am increasingly convinced that we should not empty our bags too quickly because we always lose something of their untold wealth when we do so. We would do better to undertake fewer surveys and to analyse their anthropological wealth more thoroughly. My own view is that we should go back to earlier studies and rework them in the light of our own findings. Going back to more than one study is better still and that is what I have done here, even though I did not intend to. I had, fortunately, given enough consideration to meals when I formulated my questions.

BIOGRAPHICAL DATA

Anneth

49
Chemist's assistant
Married, one child living at home on a regular basis

Large fitted kitchen opens on to dining room (with table). Some meals also eaten at kitchen table.

Anneth does not dislike cooking and rarely finds it a chore (though she sometimes finds washing pans a pain). But when asked what she would do if every imaginable resource were available, she says that she would pay someone to do the cooking. The charms of cooking therefore have their limitations and are in fact largely imaginary: cooking means preparing a meal which she regards as a pleasant activity and a high point in the life of the family. That is what motivates her and sublimates her actions. It also dispels the feeling that everything is difficult.

Anneth feels that she has no gift for improvisation and prefers to rely upon recipes when she tries to make something she has not made before, which she does on a regular basis. She draws up detailed lists of what to buy. Usually, however, (when she is not making something new), she goes to the supermarket without any specific ideas in mind and relies upon the food on display for inspiration. Meals, which are the high points that structure the family, are planned within a few minutes and as a response to a wide range of requests. Although she rarely takes cost into consideration, a special offer may suddenly catch her eye: her other purchases are designed to make meals harmonious in both dietary and relational terms. Finds shopping difficult.

Amandine

45
Housewife
Married, three children living at home on a regular basis

Small but well-equipped kitchen opens on to dining room; no kitchen table. The dining table is close to the kitchen door, which opens so widely that it is almost part of the kitchen.

'When the children were younger, we used to get a bit worked up. But not now, not after all that time. If he doesn't want to eat what is on his plate, he goes to see what's in the fridge and that's all there is to it.' Although she loves cooking, she has thrown in the towel and makes special meals for her two sons (the eldest is 20): 'He always eats the same things. Breaded fish, burgers, pizzas, chips. And mayonnaise with everything, everything with mayonnaise.' Fortunately for Amandine, her daughter has not given in to the trend for domestic McDonaldization. She is still a faithful ally and likes most of the things her mother likes. Unlike her sons. And unlike her husband, who regularly develops a passion for new and sophisticated ideas. He would like her to do the same. 'The Cretan diet is all he's interested in, and it has been for sometime now. It's based on olive oil, fish, lots of vegetables and usually snails. And the snails have to be fresh. Well, I'm sorry, but I'm not going out collecting snails.'

Having to make three different meals means that she has to spend more time on preparation, and she would like to make meals that are quick and easy during the week. At the weekend, Amandine would like to have all the time she needs to make her culinary dreams comes true. But whose dreams are they? Her family likes such different things that making her dreams come true is, to say the least, a delicate task. So she invites friends for a meal in order to indulge her passion. Preparing such meals is an emotional business; she becomes very anxious and is worried that she will get something wrong. She and her husband have recently discovered the delights of wine. 'Good wine is delicious, fantastic.' Carried away by her enthusiasm, she has no qualms about introducing her thirteen-year-old daughter to the delights of wine: 'Oh, she loves it!'

Babette

52
Office worker in public sector (husband retired)
One child living at home on a regular basis

Smallish kitchen with lots of appliances (dishwasher, washing machine). There is only room for a half-sized fold-down table but the kitchen opens on to a veranda overlooking the garden.

'I think it's because I wanted to give my children the things I didn't have.' Babette has bitter memories of the lack of intimacy she experienced as a girl, and interprets slapdash meals as a sign of emotional deprivation. She therefore resolved that her life would be very different. Would unstintingly give the love she never knew (or thinks she never knew) by making delicious meals and devoting herself body and soul. That is why she finds nothing, or almost nothing, to do with cooking a chore. An hour . . . two hours . . . or more: she does not notice the passing time. The only thing that is really difficult is coming up with an idea. So she asks her husband 'What would you like to eat?' The inevitable answer is 'Whatever you like', which really gets on her nerves. Peeling vegetables is not her favourite job, so it is delegated to her husband, and this does something to reduce the feeling of annoyance. Everything else is a labour of love. She particularly enjoys adding a personal decorative touch and often does so at the last moment. Mealtimes provide an opportunity to enjoy both food and conversation. Even during the week, when only her husband is at home, she cooks, even though his state of health means that he more or less has to stick to a diet. Babette tries to make lighter meals that still taste good.

When she has guests at the weekend, or when the children are at home, the diet goes out of the window. She makes generous use of sugar, oil, butter and cream, as she always used to do. Her only goal is to make other people happy. 'They always think it's good when they come home.' The children are delighted. Especially when, like Proust's madeleine, some taste brings back forgotten memories. 'I made mashed potatoes the other day. My daughter said to me "Oh, that's good. It's been a long time since you made that." She really enjoyed it.'

247

Bélangère

44
Office worker
Married, two children living at home on a regular basis

Small kitchen arranged around a central table. Laminated dresser provides storage space. Hamster in cage.

Cooking is, she states, a real pleasure that grows as the meal takes shape. This is a preliminary to the delights to come. She loves the smell of cooking and is quite happy to nibble during the final stages (she uses the excuse that she is tasting to make sure she's got the balance of flavours right) but has no appetite when she sits down to eat. She enjoys the idea of the pleasures to come, but they always elude her and appear to be illusory.

The problem is even worse during the week, as she has to work against the clock. Coming up with 'an idea' is the hardest thing of all. Every night, Bélangère thinks about what to make the next day. And when she cannot decide, her mind goes blank because she feels mentally exhausted. So she asks her husband or her children. 'Oh, they're never any help! Sometimes I can't think of anything. So I ask them: "What shall I make?" And they say: "No idea".' She does not expect to get an answer, and that might make it even more difficult to reach a decision. She really wants to let off steam by letting everyone know how complicated her job is.

Bélangère also asks them what they think of the meal they are eating. 'When I've made a nice meal and when it's taken me a lot of time.' Nothing could be worse than a husband or children who do not notice the effort she has made. It is not that she wants expressions of gratitude or thanks. But the whole point of the meal was to make the family group happy. She needs to know that it has served its purpose.

Although she is always talking about pleasure, it seems obvious that her idea of pleasure is somewhat more contradictory, and that it is not very intense. It is a sort of dreary pleasure with no surprises, which no doubt explains why her tone is so monotonous and almost sad when she describes it. And when the interviewer asks her to describe her dream kitchen, she suddenly reveals that the kitchen has no emotional importance: she would 'get rid of everything' so as 'to have time to do other things.' This is a cry from the heart from a woman with mixed emotions and who is somewhat overwhelmed by her family commitments. When she talks about cooking, it is obvious that she is in fact talking about her family.

Biscotte

53
Housewife
Divorced

Large, well-equipped kitchen, with imposing table in the centre.

Her mother dreamed of training her for what she believed to be her future role as the perfect housewife: 'My mother was always telling me to learn to cook. She told me I wouldn't be able to cook at all when I got married.' Biscotte put up a passive resistance and simply watched her mother without doing any actual cooking; she was in no hurry to take on the traditional woman's role at a time when personal autonomy was the order of the day. When she married, she therefore had to learn to cook as a matter of urgency. Biscotte made an effort to remember everything she had seen her mother do and delved into cookery books to complete her education. She quickly learned to provide decent meals and remembers with nostalgia the happy family meals she enjoyed.

The rest of her story is much more turbulent. She suddenly found herself alone with three young children and developed a real passion for cooking. Working with her hands became a form of therapy that stopped her thinking. Although she is not very fond of cakes herself, she was always dreaming up new cakes to keep her children happy.

She lost her enthusiasm for cooking when her children left home. She once tried to make herself a 'proper meal'. But 'when I sat down at the table all by myself, I couldn't eat it.' So she prefers to live on snacks, such as a piece of cheese, some fruit or a yoghurt. And she has discovered that, as a rule, she is never very hungry. It is not just that she no longer has any interest in cooking or that sitting down at the dining table makes her mind go blank; she has no appetite. This presents a striking contrast with the scenes she remembers: 'I used to have a houseful of people who liked nice things, and I knew they would enjoy what I made. And I enjoyed it too.' She enjoyed the fact that they enjoyed it. But there was also the very simple and more personal pleasure of enjoying her food. Lost in her memories, she suddenly says something strange, using the present tense: 'I really like good things.' She in fact lives on snacks and no longer enjoys her food. A change of family context can be very disorienting when it comes to food.

Candy

42
Administrative officer
Divorced, two children living at home on a regular basis

Small kitchen with lots of pots and pans, dishwasher, washing machine, small table in front of the television.

Her life as a cook is strictly divided in two: weekends and weekdays. She refuses to refer to what she does during the week as 'cooking', buys ready meals and gets everything over with as quickly as possible. 'I work, I don't have the time.' At weekends, in contrast, she takes her time. 'I could spend my days doing other things, but I enjoy cooking. I find it relaxing.' During the week, she does her shopping quickly, and what she buys depends on what is on offer in the shops (provided that it does not involve much preparation); cost is her main criterion. At the weekend, in contrast, she begins to make very detailed plans on Friday, buys only what she needs for the recipes she is going to make, but buys only the best.

Mealtimes mean a lot to her, as they are the only times when she feels that her family comes to life. She tries to avoid watching television so that they can talk to each other and insists that her children stay at the table for at least a certain time. They nonetheless succeed in escaping. In other respects, she gave up long ago and usually cooks the things they like to eat.

Cannelle

23
Youth worker
In a relationship

Kitchenette, with open shelves for pans and crockery. Tiny table, with the two of them squeezed into five square metres.

Cannelle regards cooking as a work of art. 'You can't help yourself. It's an art form, and I'm not joking when I say that. A sudden fancy takes you, and you have to do it. I'm not saying it's a great work of art. It might mean no more than slicing the gherkins finely to make them look special.' It has to be said that she has made spectacular progress since she started (not so long ago), as she did not know that she had to put butter in the frying pan to make an omelette. Her starting point is simple and based on what she likes best in the whole world: potatoes. 'Potatoes, potatoes. It's not complicated. They just make me happy. That's all.' Using potatoes as a starting point, she lets her creative energy loose and has no inhibitions about experimenting with spices: 'I can do anything with my magic powders.'

Her meals are less spectacular. Although she cooks spicy food, the young couple's life together seems to be gradually losing its savour. Sometimes they even lapse into silence. Cannelle finds the silence unbearable and that creates a lot of problems for her. 'You find yourself sitting there like idiots who have nothing to say to each other. You say to yourself, "Come on, we're not a little old couple." But you do see yourselves as an old couple.' Fortunately, Saturday night fever makes her forget her momentary doubts. Cannelle outdoes herself and pays special attention to how the food is presented. Saturday night is party night and the drink flows. They talk endlessly. They feel as close to one another as they did at the beginning of their relationship; they are together again.

Charlotte

62

Civil servant in Department for Education (husband retired)

Well-equipped kitchen, with two work surfaces and side table. Plenty of appliances. Cat-litter tray and bowls for cat.

Charlotte does not have a lot of time, and weekday meals are over and done with quickly. 'It has to be said that I'm even more alone than ever, now that I'm with my husband all the time. We just have some soup, some bread and cheese, a yoghurt, and that's it.' She may not have time to cook but she does spend a lot of time during the week planning more elaborate meals for the weekend. She reads magazine recipes and regularly discusses them with her husband ('During the week, we discuss what we're going to eat on Sunday and exchange ideas'). They come up with various ideas, and she makes shopping lists two days ahead of time. When the moment of truth comes, however, it is not unusual for her to just open a tin when there are just the two of them. But not just any tin. She does not buy just anything: 'Something we bought in a country where we went on holiday.' But the discrepancy between the meals she dreams of making (she speaks lovingly of cooking) and day-to-day reality can make her feel slightly uncomfortable, reacting to what she sees as exaggerated comments:

251

'Of course I like compliments, but not too many. My husband is always telling people "Oh, she's a really good cook." I tell him: "Shut up! You're getting on my nerves."'

Her husband (who is now retired, whilst she still has heavy work commitments) likes his food and pops into the kitchen, 'to see what's cooking'.

'*Daube* is his speciality. It's *his* recipe. I think he makes the best *daube* in the west of France.' A few moments later, she comes out with a very different version: 'It's not too bad. He makes it every six months. And he takes over the kitchen for five or six hours. And that's not the only thing. *I* have to wash up afterwards.'

Clémentine

29
Artist
In a relationship, one child living at home on a regular basis

Poorly equipped kitchen. The cooker is old and of poor quality but has been beautifully painted. Painted fridge, mosaic table, beautiful crockery, but the pots and pans are not good quality.

Clémentine's culinary habits have recently changed completely. When she was single, she ate snacks whenever she felt like it and enjoyed her freedom. The early stages of the relationship did not lead to any major changes; the couple often ate together but at unpredictable times. It was after the birth of her daughter that she began to cook on a regular and organized basis. Given that she was not used to cooking, Clémentine experimented a lot (shopping only once a month, for example) before gradually establishing her own system. At the moment, she makes great use of the recipe book given to her by her grandmother; it encourages her to cook and allows her to be creative.

The results can be disappointing. The attitude of her partner takes away a lot of the pleasure, as he rarely makes any effort to help her. When he does cook, he cooks fish, which she loathes. Clémentine secretly takes her revenge by cooking her favourite meals. When the couple are on better terms, her unspoken disappointment gives way to the enjoyment of sharing something (a drink together while she makes dinner). At such times, the terrible chore undergoes a miraculous transformation.

Eugénie

62
Retired
Married

Kitchen organized around a small table. What was a fitted kitchen has been redesigned on more classical lines. One large oven and a small oven for day-to-day meals.

'Keep things simple.' 'Don't make life complicated.' She frequently uses these expressions which hammer home ethical principles that rule her life. And yet her life is not very complicated and, now that she is retired, Eugénie would have more than enough time to make more elaborate meals if she wished to. But she sees no need to change her habits ('I make the things I know I can make') or to spend her time making meals. At the same time, she does not dream of giving up cooking. 'If you don't cook, if you don't do the housework, what do you do?' She simply does what has to be done, as she has always done. When she finds things physically difficult, all she has to do is remind herself of her duty towards her family. That is enough to spur her into action.

The fact that the way she was socialized still determines the way she lives her life helped her to get over the shock of seeing her children leave home. Meals are certainly not what they used to be. Both Eugénie and her husband are worried about their health and are not as active as they used to be. They therefore eat less. She tends increasingly to make meals that are quick and easy. But they have the impression that they are sitting down to eat as they always have done . . . or almost. Some dishes have disappeared from the menu. So they invite the children for a meal, perhaps because they want to try these dishes again or perhaps because they miss having a family at home.

Hortense

62
Retired
Married

Hortense used to have a big kitchen (and a big garden). Sadly, it is now just a 'laboratory' space, with no dining table. It is, on the other hand, well equipped.

For Hortense, cooking is above all a family duty. 'It's part of life, it's only natural.'

She has therefore always found it easy to cook, even though she does find day-to-day shopping a chore; she has so many things on her mind that she can never make a decision. Since her children left home, she has learned that her 'duty' has a lot to do with the form the family takes. She no longer has the same enthusiasm. 'Now, when I decide to make a meal, simplicity is the decisive factor.' Two things make up for this loss of interest in cooking. Having an aperitif has become a weekend ritual. She also thinks more about dietetics and health. Her interest in meals as a family institution has given way to an interest in what she eats.

What she has to say about what she eats sounds very radical. She will not touch 'all that crap you get these days . . . GM crops and all that muck,' and cooks fresh vegetables bought from wholefood shops. She buys as little as possible from supermarkets and refuses to eat ready meals or frozen food (she makes an exception for fish). In her view, frozen foods and supermarkets are the worst things in the world. She is a little more embarrassed when she talks about vegetables. 'Canned vegetables. Oh, yes. You can get very good green beans in cans. On the whole, canned vegetables are very good. The ones that come in glass jars.' She used to have a large kitchen garden and grew vast quantities of green beans which she bottled. Although those days are long gone, she is still fond of beans and usually eats them that way. Even the most radical discourses have to take account of actual dietary behaviours.

Madeleine

60
Retired
Married

Old-fashioned kitchen with appliances and furniture that does not match. Table used only for breakfast.

Speaks in a monotonous voice as she describes the very simple meals she cooks; now that her children have left home, they take no time at all to prepare. 'It's cool, now.' It is in fact not that cool. The little mental effort involved in choosing what to make is still too much, given that she no longer has the energy to cook.

Madeleine suddenly begins to speak in the past tense to answer questions asked in the present tense. Her voice changes. She begins to sparkle and speaks more quickly. In those days, the whole family ate together and talked noisily about anything and everything (when she was a girl, her parents did not allow her to talk at mealtimes). Even the telly was banned to allow everyone to say something. On Sundays, she spent a long time cooking and even longer dreaming about what she was going to cook, even though there was nothing mysterious about her recipes: she got them from her mother. She was always short of time and had to buy in supplies for three days at a time but overcame that problem, just as she overcame many others. She has only happy memories. Cooking was never a problem.

Now that everything is 'cool', she is, paradoxically, beginning to feel an underlying anxiety. 'Now that the family circle is smaller, we are beginning to become a bit more set in our ways. There's no denying that.' The television is on, both at lunchtime and at the evening meal. Madeleine is now less inventive, has fewer guests and gets by on the basis of what she knows. She finds the lack of intensity unsatisfactory. She admits to liking her food and certainly enjoys the meals she makes. They have, however, lost something of their old sparkle. She tells herself that they have to be careful at their age. So why not learn to cook lighter meals, which they enjoy when they go to restaurants? She does not have the energy to cook anything new and finds it very difficult to summon up the energy, now that meals are no longer a central part of family life.

Maïté

50
Office worker in the private sector
Married, one child living at home on a regular basis

Fitted kitchen with everything she needs. Large fridge and breakfast bar.

Her mother was an 'excellent cook', and she remembers her making a whole range of things. Maïté herself takes no special pleasure in eating. Her personal likes and dislikes were probably a decisive factor in the sequence of events that determined how the family eats, which is to say the least unusual. When she was first married and when she had children, Maïté felt obliged to attempt to make proper meals in response to a hypothetical but unspoken demand from the family, even though she felt neither like cooking nor eating. Her efforts met with, at best, general indifference when they did not lead to complaints (and to make matters even more difficult, she and her husband worked different hours). She therefore decided to 'make what they like' and to let them 'fend for themselves' and organized a very loosely structured system based upon an unchanging diet. It was only at weekends that they all ate together. 'The way we do things suits everyone.'

The system centres not on the dining table or the cooker, but the fridge. From Monday to Friday, it is 'sandwiches' for all three members of the family (Maïté, her husband and their son). Everyone opens the fridge when they feel like it ('We eat in shifts'), takes whatever they can find and puts it between two slices of bread. They often eat standing up. 'At home, it's ham . . . lots of ham . . . lots of it.' At weekends, the whole family gets together (including the children who have left home). She does cook but 'just quick meals', and they are always the same: steak and chips, escalope with pasta. 'They never object, not a word. They eat whatever is in front of them.'

Marjolaine

52
Administrative officer (husband retired)
Married, one child living at home on a regular basis

Rather small but well-equipped kitchen with dishwasher and washing machine. There is only room for a tiny table against the wall.

'I'm not prepared to be his slave, but I do like to do things properly. I'm all in favour of more status for women, but family meals mean a lot to me.' Marjolaine is constantly torn between her contradictory ambitions and keeps a critical eye on what she is doing so as to strike a balance: 'I'm very careful about that.' During the week, it is not unusual for her to decide suddenly that she wants to be creative. 'I say to myself "Careful, you're making things difficult for yourself again."'

It is the weekends that are the real problem. Unlike many other people, her attitude changes for the worse at weekends. She certainly enjoys having a lot of people for meals (and her children come home for the weekend). But her love for her family is not enough to make up for all the work she has to put in. She gets no help at all from her husband (even though he is retired) and very little from her children. Because she has to do everything week in, week out, having to begin preparing the vegetables feels like a dreadful chore. 'That does get me down, when there are a lot of us and when there are lots of vegetables to peel. Things like that. And it's true that having a lot of people is a chore.'

Fortunately, and despite all the domestic chores she had to do, she almost always finds some way to motivate herself because she gets so much pleasure from eating, and especially from eating with the family. 'For me, meals have always been bound up with the idea of pleasure and having a party. And above all, the enjoyment of food. We enjoy being together, and that's important.'

Maryse

48
Unemployed
Married, one child living at home on a regular basis

The kitchen is small and crowded but there is a place for everything. There is a dining table but it is squeezed into the small space between the washing machine, the television and the bird cage.

She regularly watches a food programme on television and 'cuts out lots of recipes from the papers'. And it has to be said that when Maryse enjoys her food, she means what she says: 'When it's good . . . oh, I almost said something rude . . . it's . . . like an orgasm! When that happens, you really do appreciate being alive! The pleasure is orgasmic.' It is, on the other hand, very unusual for her to make the recipes she has seen or read. Why do something new? Why take unnecessary risks? As for day-to-day meals, she would happily eat 'shepherd's pie three times a week' if she was on her own. But she is not on her own. 'When there are two of you, you force yourself to make a meal.' The most important thing is to change the menu, whilst still upholding a family tradition. This limits the number of things she can cook. The same things turn up every week, the only element of surprise being that they do not always turn up in the same order. Changing the order in which they appear is the first thing she thinks of when she wakes up: what is she going to make for lunch?

Cooking takes up a lot of her time, and she also spends a lot of time thinking about it. She has no complaints. 'I enjoy it. I like taking my time. I should have lived in the 1950s. People took their time in those days.' Nowadays 'we live at 100 mph' and the fact that more products are available encourages laziness. It is sometimes difficult to resist the temptation to become sloppy.

Melba

45
Accountant
Married, two children living at home on a regular basis

Fully equipped kitchen opening onto dining room; dining table.

'In the evening, after a day like I've had, cooking is the last thing I feel like doing. Coming up with an idea and all the rest of it. Fed up with doing the shopping.' The more she tries to save time on preparing meals, the more time flies by, and she finds this both annoying and exhausting. Fortunately, her daughter, who really likes her food, comes to see what's cooking as soon as she gets home and that provides her with some welcome encouragement. Otherwise, it is only her sense of duty that forces Melba to cook. 'It's hard, it's often hard. You force yourself to make a meal.' And when it is just the two of them because the children are not there, 'it's something simpler'.

Meals are still important to her: 'Even if it is only for half an hour, it does mean that we all get together.' Weekend meals are more intense family occasions. In Melba's view, that is what a real meal should be. At the weekend, cooking is the opposite of what it is during the week. 'It can be a real drag, but it can also be very pleasant.' Melba is always looking at recipes (in the hope of finding an idea for 'something out of the ordinary'), spends a lot of time dreaming about all the wonderful meals she could make and is quite happy in her kitchen, with music in the background. The setting is not the same, and time, miraculously, stands still. Thanks to the magic of food, the woman who does not have a moment to herself during the week 'takes her time'. Time does not seem to mind.

Olivia

47
Office worker
Married

Large kitchen, fully equipped. The family eats at the large table in the middle of the room at weekends.

Although her memories are vague, she is categorical: her mother 'never cooked anything' and taught her nothing at all. Olivia therefore found herself at a complete loss as to what to do when she married (very young; she was 19). Her wedding presents included a big cookery book and that was no accident. Her role was now to be the cook, and she had to learn. She began tentatively and learned by trial and error: 'I remember burning a roast.' She very quickly acquired the knack and discovered that she derived great pleasure from cooking, and that it complemented her enjoyment of food. Although restricted by the social role she was forced to play, she discovered to her delight that she enjoyed both these things and that has had a lasting influence on her: cooking and food are now a very important part of her life.

Olivia is one of the few people to be interviewed who almost never found cooking a chore (big shopping trips are the exception to the rule). This is mainly because she is so good at time-management. She is so well organized that whatever she is making can be made in the time she has at her disposal and that she can always 'take her time', even when she has only ten minutes. Usually, she has much more time than that and does not mind how long she spends experimenting, or tasting and decorating her dishes. Time flies when we enjoy what we are doing.

Olivia is often on her own at lunchtime. Unlike many women, she does not take advantage of the fact to eat just a snack. On the contrary, she makes herself a proper meal and is happy to use large quantities of rich produce. She can afford to treat herself because her health is good and because she is not overweight. The same cannot really be said of her husband, who is overweight and who had to see a doctor who immediately put him on a strict diet. On doctor's orders, he stuck to his diet for a long time (even though she went on putting fatty meat into the 'low-cal' *pot au feu*). Now that his weight is back to normal, her husband has just told her what he would like tomorrow: prawns in cream, flambéed with whisky). It is hard to change a hedonistic way of life.

Paule-Dauphine

59
Housewife
Married

Large kitchen with a corner table and a bench seating up to ten.

'The number of times I say to myself "What am I going to make for lunch. What am I going to make?' It is only when she cannot come up with an idea that Paule-Dauphine really finds cooking difficult (and she finds cooking for a dinner party especially stressful). Inspiration usually comes to her so easily that she feels at a complete loss when she cannot think of anything. Her problem is not that she has to come up with something that is both new and complicated (she only does that for dinner parties and uses her recipes, which are filed in perfect order); she simply has to avoid making the same things too often. When she is at a loss, she turns to her husband and makes some suggestions, even though she knows they are not very convincing. He grumbles, but his criticisms are not meant to be unkind. 'Well, you think of something!' He tells her to do what she likes. 'I've already spent enough time trying to come up with an idea, and there comes a point when I've had enough.' There are limits to the amount of personal effort she is ready to put into giving her husband a nice surprise when she gets so little in return.

In order to rationalize things and to overcome her time-consuming doubts, Paule-Dauphine decides what to cook on the basis of simple criteria (fish three times a week, eggs from a market stallholder who does not have many) and a system of taboos (not too much starch, no frozen foods). She does, however, have a freezer. Statements of principle are more important than what she actually does. As everyone knows, cooking is the art of compromise.

Prune

33
On maternity leave
Married, two children living at home on a regular basis

Small kitchen with few utensils. Round table in the centre.

Prune has her own ideological set of beliefs. Nothing will change it, and it structures both her personal identity and her family life. She rules her family with an iron fist in a velvet glove: everyone has to be there for every meal and no one can watch television. This is a special moment and family discussions are sacred.

The way she cooks is sacred too. It developed out of the big family of her childhood and her memories of slowly cooked meals. The relationship with time is very important. As she is at home at the moment, Prune has a lot of time, and it is time that mysteriously gives her slowly-simmered meals their very special, personal taste. They taste of her: 'With a stew, it's you that adds the taste.' Because she is a great believer in passing on the family tradition and traditional cooking, Prune seems to be fighting a losing battle against every aspect of modernity. She dreams of having a garden in which chickens and rabbits can roam at will, and of making her own cheese the old-fashioned way. She refuses to eat frozen foods and will have nothing to do with certain appliances (she prefers her cast-iron casseroles to a pressure cooker), is critical of new dietary fads and chooses her words carefully when she talks about them. She happily admits that her cooking (thick sauces, lots of butter and fat) may be a little rich, but at least it is 'natural'. Even her sausages are 'natural' because she buys them from the butcher.

Her argument is so circular that it represents a sort of complete model for a social role that scarcely exists today. There is, however, one flaw in this idyllic vision and it takes the form of a paradox. At weekends, her relationship with time suddenly changes. Because she wants to be there for her family, she has less time to cook. She gets it over with quickly and does not have time to make proper meals.

Savarin

29
Computer technician
In a relationship, one child living at home on a regular basis

The kitchen is virtually an extension of the dining room and the table takes up part of it. Aquarium serves as a bar. Double sink.

Began to take an interest in cooking at a very early age and started to make cakes at the age of 14. He was not, however, too fond of cakes, and still isn't. But he does derive immense pleasure from anything that is not sweet. Savarin therefore soon began to try to make something more substantial and could cook well even before he left home. He continued to improve by fits and starts and is now an excellent cook. He does not recall any great changes when he moved in with his girlfriend. There was no discussion of a possible division of labour; both partners found it quite natural for him to go on doing something he was so good at.

What is more important, he never finds it a chore. For Savarin, cooking really is (almost always) a pleasure. The pleasure is closely bound up with the promises of the meal to come: his taste buds 'salivate'. This very physical enjoyment is the real explanation for his commitment to cooking and adds to its other attractions, which have more to do with the practical side of cooking (creativity, a satisfying

261

outcome). And, more generally, with the idea that he is doing it for his family. 'I do it for them. But I enjoy it too. I enjoy the fact that they enjoy it.' All these pleasures merge and heighten one another.

Like many other people, Savarin makes a distinction between cooking at the weekend and making quick and easy meals during the week. When he is pushed for time, he will heat up a frozen pizza or a plate of pasta. But it is fresh pasta: 'I love fresh pasta.' The idea of the treat in store takes away any regrets about not having the time to make something more elaborate.

Suzette

53
Primary schoolteacher
Married, one child at home for lunch

Large, fully-equipped kitchen, dining table and small television. Lots of utensils.

Suzette is astonished to remember that there was a time when she was an enthusiastic cook, when she never had any doubts and she did not care how long it took. And then the machine ground to a halt one day. She wanted to put herself first and do things for herself. When she found a way of doing so, everything to do with cooking became difficult. She was clumsy and lost her skills as she forgot her routines and as her memory of her culinary golden age became blurred.

For several years, she ate lunch on her own, as her son had left home and her husband ate at work. It would be more accurate to say that she had a snack. She enjoyed the pleasures of her existential lightness: there was nothing to prepare and she could do everything at her own pace. She was at peace with herself once more. One of her sons then announced that he would be coming home for lunch. She was upset and disappointed (how was she going to manage?) and felt guilty about being disappointed. But her family reflexes overcame her doubts; she wanted to make him a proper meal from the very start. Since then, her passion has grown by the day. She makes an effort to ensure that her son has a good meal. And doing so is almost as easy as it used to be.

The evening meal is more problematic. Her husband gets home very late. Suzette would like to eat when it suits her and sometimes thinks nostalgically of her solitary lunches. He would probably have no objections. He watches a lot of television and would be quite happy with a meal on a tray in front of the telly. Suzette resists these tendencies, which might drive them further apart. She is intuitively aware that the evening meal is one of the few things that is keeping the relationship alive. 'It's better when we're together; even if we don't have much to say to each other most of the time, we always have something to say at mealtimes.'

Tony

25
On job-creation scheme
In a relationship

Basic kitchen, but with everything he needs. The crockery does not match but there is a lot of it. Trestle table used for both food preparation and for meals.

For Tony, cooking is pure pleasure. When he has finished work, this is how he relaxes in the evening ('It's my tranquillizer') and he spends a lot of time in the kitchen. Time does not matter. There are no set mealtimes and they sometimes eat very late: 'We'd rather eat late than watch a film.' Every evening, he tries to create an 'atmosphere', lays the table and decorates it, provides background music and cooks recipes from all five continents. He has a liking for colourfully exotic things. They regularly have a drink before the meal. Without realizing it, they are in fact using this pleasant little ritual to signal the fact that they are a couple.

Tony shops for the whole week on Monday. He is quite flexible about what he buys and has only a few vague plans based upon all-purpose 'basics' (chicken breast), the variety principle and a few taboos (no frozen foods). Every evening, Tony improvises with what is there. What he cooks depends on the state of his fresh vegetables (which by the end of the week are not quite as fresh as they might be). This means that he can persuade himself that he has a healthy diet: 'I know my body will appreciate it.' His arguments are not very persuasive. They are his way of convincing himself that he is right but they have no scientific basis. But that does not matter. His convictions are quite in keeping with the little parties he organizes every evening. But what if the parties eventually become bad for his health?

REFERENCES

Andlauer, J. (1997), 'Les Saintes Tables: Préparer et manger le repas chez les contemplatives', *Ethnologie française* XXVII.

Aron, J.-P. (1975 [1973]), *The Art of Eating in France: Manners and Menus in the Nineteenth Century*, trans. Nina Rootes, London: Peter Owen.

Attias-Donfut, C. and Segalen, M. (1998), *Grands-parents: La Famille à travers les générations*, Paris: Odile Jacob.

Attias-Donfut, C., Lapierre, N. and Segalen, M. (2002), *Le Nouvel esprit de famille*, Paris: Le Seuil.

Aymard, M., Grignon, C. and Sabban, F. (eds) (1993), *Le Temps de manger: Alimentation, emplois du temps et rhythmes sociaux*, Paris: Editions MSH-INRA.

Badinter, E. (2006 [2003]), *Dead End Feminism*, trans. Joanna Borosso, Cambridge: Polity.

Badot, O. (2002), 'Esquisse de la fonction sociale de McDonalds à partir d'une étude ethnographique: modernisme et "transgression ordinaire"', in Garabuau-Moussaoui, Palomares and Desjeux (2002).

Bahloul, J. (1983), *Le Culte de la table dressée: Rites et traditions de la table juive algérienne*, Paris: Métailié.

Bastard, B. and Cardia-Vonèche, L. (1986), 'Normes culturelles, fonctionnement familial et préoccupations diététiques', *Dialogue* 93.

Bauman, Z. (2003), *Liquid Love: On the Frailty of Human Bonds*, Cambridge: Polity.

Becker, H. (1963), *Outsiders: Studies in the Sociology of Deviance*, New York: Free Press.

Bidart, C. (1997), *L'Amitié: un lien social*, Paris: La Découverte.

Bonnet, M. and Bernard, Y. (eds) (1998), *Services de proximité et vie quotidienne*, Paris: PUF.

Boudan, C. (2004), *Géopolitique du gout: La Guerre culinaire*, Paris: PUF.

Bourdieu, P. (1984) [1979]), *Distinction: A Social Critique of the Judgement of Taste*, trans. Richard Nice, Harvard: Harvard University Press.

Brenot, P. (2001), *Inventer le couple*, Paris: Odile Jacob.

Bromberger, C. (1998), *Passions ordinaires: du match de football au concours de dictée*, Paris: Bayard.

Bromberger, C., Ducet, C., Kaufmann, J.-C., Le Breton, D., Single F. de and Vigarello, G. (2005), *Un Corps pour soi*, Paris: PUF.

Bucher, A.-L. (1998) 'Éngendrer, nourrir, dévorer: les functions symboliques de la féminité', *Religiologiques* 17.

Burgoyne, J. L. and Clarke, D. (1983), 'You Are What You Eat: Food and Family Reconstruction', in A. Murcott (ed.), *The Sociology of Food, Eating and Diet*, Gower: Sage.

Caillé, A. (1995), 'Sacrifice, don et utilitarisme: notes sur la théorie du sacrifice', *La Revue du Mauss 5*.

Caillé, A. (2004), 'Présentation', *La Revue du Mauss 23*.

Caradec, V. (2004), *Vieillir près la retraite: Approche sociologique du vieillissement*, Paris: PUF.

Certeau, M. de, Giard, L. and Mayol, P. (1980 [1964]), *L'Invention du quotidien II: Habiter-cuisiner*, Paris: Gallimard, Foli-essais.

Chamoux, M.-N. (1997), 'La cuisine de Toussaint chez les Aztèques de la Sierra de Peubla (Mexique)', *Internationale de l'imaginaire 7*.

Charles, N. and Kerr, M. (1988), *Women, Food and Families*, Manchester: Manchester University Press.

Châtelet, N. (1977), *Le Corps à corps culinaire*, Paris: Seuil.

Cicchelli-Pugeault, C. and Cicchelli, V. (1998), *Les Théories sociologiques de la famille*, Paris: La Découverte.

Cingolani, P. (2005), *La Précarité*, Paris: PUF.

Ciosi-Houcke, L., Pavageau, C., Pierre, M., Garabuau-Moussaoui, I. and Desjeux, D. (2002), 'Trajectoires de vie et alimentation: Les pratiques culinaires et alimentaires révélatrices des constructions identitaires familiales et personnelles', in Garabuau-Moussaoui, Palomares and Desjeux (2002).

Cochoy, F. (2002), *Une Sociologie du packaging, ou l'âne de Buridan face au marché*, Paris: PUF.

Collignon, B. and Staszak, J.-F. (eds) (2004), *Espaces domestiques. Construire, habiter, représenter*, Paris: Bréal.

Conein, B. and Jacopin, E. (1993), 'Les Objets dans l'espace. La planification dans l'action', *Raisons pratiques 4*.

Corbeau, J.-P. (1989), 'Liens sociaux, individualismes et pratiques alimentaires', *Le Lien social*. Actes du XIIIe Colloque de l'AISLF, tome 2, Geneva: Université de Genève.

Corbeau, J.-P. (1992), 'Rituels alimentaires et mutations sociales', *Cahiers internationaux XCII*.

Corbeau, J.-P. (2002), 'Itinéraires de mangeurs', in Corbeau and Poulain (2002).

Corbeau, J.-P. and Poulain, J.-P. (2002), *Penser l'alimentation, entre imaginaire et rationalité*, Toulouse: Privat.

Corbin, A. (1986 [1982]), *The Foul and the Fragrant: Odor and the French Social Imagination*, Leamington Spa: Berg.

Corbin, A. (1990 [1987]), 'Backstage', in Georges Duby and Michelle Perrot (eds), *The History of Private Life, Vol. 4: From the Fires of Revolution to the Great War*, trans. Arthur Goldhammer, Cambridge, MA: Belknap Press of Harvard University Press.

Cosson, M.-E. (1990), *Représentation et évaluation du marriage des enfants par les mères*, Mémoire de maîtrise de sociologie sous la direction de François de Singly, Rennes: Université Rennes 2.

Cott, N. F. F. (1992), 'La Femme moderne: Le Style américain des années vingt', in Michelle Perrot (ed.), *Histoire des femmes en Occident. Tome V. Le XXè siècle*, Paris: Plon.

Coveney, J. (2000), *Food, Morals and Meaning: The Pleasure and Anxiety of Eating*, London: Routledge.

Csergo, J. (2004), 'Entre faim légitime et frénésie de la table au XIXe siècle: la constitution de la science alimentaire au siècle de la gastronomie', www.lemangeur-ocha.com.

Damasio, A. (1995), *L'Erreur de Descartes: La Raison des émotions*, Paris: Odile Jacob.

Darmon. M. (2003), *Devenir anorexique: Une approche sociologique,* Paris: La Découverte.

Defrance, A. (1994), 'To Eat or Not to Eat: 25 ans de discours alimentaires dans la presse', *Les Cahiers de l'OCHA* 4.

Desbiolles, M. (1998), *La Seiche*, Paris: Points-Seuil.

Desjeux, D. (2002), 'Préface', in Garabuau-Moussaoui, Palomares and Desjeux (2002).

Desjeux, D., Alami, S. and Taponier, S. (1998), 'Les Pratiques d'organisation du travail domestique: une structure d'attente spécifique', in Bonnet and Bernard (1998).

Desjeux, D., Zheng. L., Boisard, A.-S. and Yang, X.M. (2002), 'Ethnographie des itineraries de la consommation alimentaire à Guangzhou', in Garabuau-Massaoui, Palomares and Desjeux (2002).

Detienne, M. (1982 [1979]), 'Culinary Practices and the Spirit of Sacrifice', in Detienne and Vernant (1982).

Detienne, M. and Vernant, J.-P. (eds) (1982 [1979]), *The Cuisine of Sacrifice Among the Greeks*, trans. Paula Wissing, Chicago: University of Chicago Press.

Devault, M. (1991), *Feeding the Family*, Chicago: University of Chicago Press.

Diasio, N. (2002), 'Le Rien manger: Repas informels des enfants de 7 à 10 ans à Paris et à Rome', in Garabuau-Moussaoui, Palomares and Desjeux (2002).

Dibie, P. (1999), *L'Europe à table*, Paris: Filigranes.

Dibie, P. (2002), 'Les Périls de la table avant, pendant, après', *Internationale de l'imaginaire* 7.

Douglas, M. (1970 [1966]), *Purity and Danger: An Analysis of the Concepts of Pollution and Taboo*, Harmondsworth: Penguin.

Douglas, M. (1972), 'Deciphering a Meal', *Daedelus* 101.

Douglas, M. (1999), *Leviticus as Literature*, Oxford: Oxford University Press.

Dubet, F. (1994), *Sociologie de l'expérience*, Paris: Seuil.

Dubet, F. (2002), *Le Déclin de l'institution*, Paris: Seuil.

Durand, J.-L. (1982 [1979]) 'Greek Animals: Towards a Typology of Edible Bodies', in Detienne and Vernant (1982).

Duret, P. (2005), 'Body-building, affirmation de soi et theories de la légitimité', in Bromberger et al. (2005).

Duret, P. and Roussel, P. (2003), *Les corps et ses sociologies*, Paris: Armand Colin.

Durkheim, E. (2001 [1912]), *The Elementary Forms of Religious Life* (abridged edn), trans. Carol Corman, Oxford: Oxford University Press.

Durkheim, E. (2006 [1897]), *On Suicide*, trans. Robin Buss, London: Penguin.

Ehrenberg, A. (1995), *L'Individu incertain*, Paris: Calmann-Lévy.

Ehrenberg, A. (1998), *La Fatigue d'être soi: Dépression et société*, Paris: Odile Jacob.

Elias, N. (2000 [1939]), *The Civilizing Process* (rev. edn), trans. Edmund Jephcott, Oxford: Blackwell.

Etchegoyen, A. (2002), *Nourrir*, Paris: Anne Carrière.

EUROSTAT (2004), *How Europeans Spend Their Time: The Everyday Life of Women and Men*, Brussels: Pocketbooks.

Fagnani, J. (2000), *Un Travail et des enfants: Petits arbitrages et grands dilemmes*, Paris: Bayard.

Fehr, B. (2003), 'What has Dionysos to do with the Symposium?' *Pallas* 61.

Ferniot, J. and Le Goff, J. (eds) (1986), *La Cuisine et la table: 5,000 ans de gastronomie*, Paris: Seuil.

Fischler, C. (1993a), *L'Homnivore: Le Goût, la cuisine et le corps*, Paris: Odile Jacob.

Fischler, C. (1993b), 'Les Aventures de la douceur', *Autrement,* coll. 'Mutations/Mangeurs', 138.

Fischler, C. (1994), 'Magie, charmes et aliments', *Autrement,* coll. 'Mutations/Mangeurs', 149.

Fischler, C. (1996), 'Le Repas familial vu par les 10–11 ans', *Cahiers de l'OCHA* 6.

Fischler, C. (2003), 'Le Paradoxe de l'abondance', *Sciences Humaines* 135.

Flandrin, J.-L. (1986), 'Pour une histoire du goût', in Ferniot and Le Goff (1986).

Flandrin, J.-L. (1992), *Chronique de Platine: Pour une gastronomie historique*, Paris: Odile Jacob.

Fourier, C. (1967), *Le Nouveau monde amoureux*, Paris: Anthropos.

Frain, I. (2004), *Le Bonheur de faire l'amour dans sa cuisine et vice-versa*, Paris: Fayard.

Furst, P. (1974), *La Chair des dieux*, Paris: Seuil.

Gacem, K. (1997), *Les Repas domestiques: deux familles, deux systèmes, deux logiques*. DEA de Sciences sociales supervised by François de Singly, Paris: Université Paris Descartes.

Gacem, K. (1999), 'Les Succès du fast-food auprès des familles: Une pratique recréative', *Dialogue* 144.

Gacem, K. (2001), 'La Pesanteur des choses et des habitudes: l'exemple des repas familiaux', in F. de Singly, *Être soi parmi les autres: Famille et individualisation*, vol. 1, Paris: L'Harmattan.

Gacem, K. (2002), 'Monographie d'une famille recomposée à table: Construire un équilibre entre libertés individuelles et cohesion du groupe', in Garabuau-Moussaoui, Palomares and Desjeux (2002).

Garabuau-Moussaoui, I. (2002a), *Cuisiner et independance: Jeunesse et alimentation*, Paris: L'Harmattan.

Garabuau-Moussaoui, I. (2002b), 'L'Exotique est-il quotidien? Dynamiques de l'exotique et générations', in Garabuau-Moussaoui, Palomares and Desjeux (2002).

Garabuau-Moussaoui, I., Palomares, E. and Desjeux, D. (2002), *Alimentations contemporaines*, Paris: L'Harmattan.

Gardaz, M. (1998), 'Le Sacrifice de la chair et la nourriture des dieux hindous', *Religiologiques* 17.

Gauchet, Marcel (1998 [1985]), *The Disenchantment of the World: Political*

History of Religion, trans. Oscar Burge, foreword by Charles Taylor, Princeton: Princeton University Press.

Gaulejac, V. de (2005), *La Société malade de la gestion: Idéologie gestionnaire, pouvoir managérial et harcèlement social*, Paris: Seuil.

Gestin, A. (1997), *L'Investissement des étudiantes dans leur logement*, Memoir for MA in Sociology, supervised by François de Singly, Université Paris Descartes.

Giard, L. (1994), 'Faire-la-cuisine' in Certeau, Giard and Mayol (1980 [1964]).

Giddens, A. (1984), *The Constitution of Society: Outline of the Theory of Structuration*, Cambridge: Polity.

Goudineau, C. (2002), *Par Toutatis! Que reste-t-til de la Gaule?* Paris: Seuil.

Guilbert, P. and Perrin-Escalon, H. (eds) (2004), *Baromètres Santé Nutrition 2002: Photographie et evolutions des comportements alimentaires des français*, Paris: Institution Nationale de Prévention et d'Education pour la Santé.

Guittard, C. (2003), 'Les Saturnales à Rome: du mythe de l'âge d'or au banquet de décembre', *Pallas* 61.

Gusdorf, G. (1948), *L'Expérience humaine du sacrifice*, Paris: PUF.

Heilbrunn, B. (2004), 'Les Pouvoirs de l'enfant-consommateur', in F. de Singly (ed.), *Enfants–adults: Vers une egalité des status*, Paris: Encyclopaedia Universalis.

Herpin, N. (1988), 'Les Repas comme institution: Compte-rendu d'une enquête exploratoire', *Revue française de sociologie* 3(29).

Hubert, A. (2000), 'Alimentation et santé: la science et l'imagination', *Cahiers de nutrition et de diététique* 5(35).

Hubert, A. (2004), 'Introduction', 'Corps de femmes sous l'influence: Questionner les normes', *Les Cahiers de l'OCHA* 10.

Hubert, H. and Mauss, M. (1964 [1904]), *A General Theory of Magic*, trans. A. Brain, foreword by D. F. Pocock, London: Routledge and Kegan Paul.

Hubert, H. and Mauss, M. (1964 [1898]), *Sacrifice: Its Nature and Function*, trans. W. D. Halls, foreword by E. E. Evans-Pritchard, London: Cohen and West.

Jarvin, M. (2002), 'Les Représentations du "sain" et du "malsain" dans la consommation alimentaire quotidienne suédoise', in Garabuau-Massaoui, Palomares and Desjeux (2002).

Javeau, C. (1984), 'Les Manger et le vivre: aspects sociaux de l'appétit', *Actions et recherches sociales*.

Johns, T. (1999), 'The Chemical Ecology of Human Ingestive Behaviors', *Annual Review of Anthropology* 28.

Johnson, S. and Boswell, J. (1984 [1775/1785]), *A Journey to the Western Islands of Scotland and Journal of a Tour to the Hebrides*, Harmondsworth: Penguin.

Jolivet, M. (2002), *Homo japonicus*, Arles: Philippe Picquier.

Kaplan, S. (1996), *Le Meilleur pain du monde: Les boulangers de Paris au XVIIIe siècle*, Paris: Fayard.

Kaufmann, J. C. (1996), *L'Entretien comprehensif*. Paris: Nathan.

Kaufmann, J. C. (1997), *Le Coeur à l'ouvrage: Théorie de l'action menagerie*, Paris: Nathan.

Kaufmann, J. C. (2001), *Ego: Pour une sociologie de l'individu*, Paris: Nathan.

Kaufmann, J. C. (2002a), *Premier matin: Comment naît une histoire d'amour*, Paris: Armand Colin.

Kaufmann, J. C. (2002b), 'Secrets d'albums', Introduction to *Un Siècle de photos de famille*, Paris: Textuel.

Kaufmann, J. C. (2004), *L'Invention de soi: Une théorie de l'identité*, Paris: Armand Colin.

Kaufmann, J. C. (2008 [2005]), *The Single Woman and the Fairy-Tale Prince*, trans. David Macey, Cambridge: Polity.

Knibielher, Y. and Fouquet, C. (1982), *Histoires des mères, du Moyen Age à nos jours*, Paris: Hachette-Pluriel.

Labarre, M. de (2001), 'Les trois dimensions de l'expérience alimentaire du mangeur: l'exemple du sud-ouest français', *Anthropology of Food*. Special issue 1. www.aofood.org.

Lafortune-Martel, A. (1984), *Fête noble en Bourgogne au XVe siècle: Le Banquet du faisan (1454): aspects politiques, sociaux et culturels*, Montréal and Paris: Bellarmin and Vrin.

Lahire, B. (2005 [1998]), *L'Homme pluriel: Les resorts de l'action*, Paris: Nathan and Armand Colin.

Lambert, C. (1998) 'Rites eucharistiques dans les us et coutumes alimentaires au bas Moyen Âge', *Reliologiques* 17.

Latour, B. (1989), *La Science en action*, Paris: La Découverte.

Léger, J.-M. (1990), *Derniers domiciles connus: Enquête sur les logements nouveaux, 1970–1990*, Paris: Créaphis.

Lehuédé, F. (2004), 'Symboles d'un modèle alimentaire en déclin, les fruits frais n'ont plus la cote', *Comsommations et modes de vie*, CREDOC 178.

Lehuédé, F. and Loisel, J.-P. (2004), *La Convivialité et les arts de la table*, CREDOC (commissioned by Comité des Arts de la Table).

Lemarchant, C. (1999), *Belles-filles: Avec les beaux-parents, trouver la bonne distance*, Rennes: Presses Universitaires de Rennes.

Leroi-Gourhan, A. (1965), *La Geste et la parole II: La Mémoire et les rhythms*, Paris: Albin Michel.

Lévi-Makarius, L. (1974), *Le Sacré et la violation des interdits*, Paris: Payot.

Lévi-Strauss, C. (1969 [1962]), *Totemism*, trans. Roger Needham, with an introduction by Roger C. Poole, Harmondsworth: Penguin.

Maître, J. (2000), *Anorexies religieuses, anorexie mentale: Essai de psychanalyse sociohistorique*, Paris: Cerf.

Makarius, R. (1974), 'Préface' in Lévi-Makarius (1974).

Makarius, R. and Lévi-Makarius, L. (1974 [1961]), *L'Origine de l'exogamie et du totémisme*, Paris: Gallimard.

Marenco, C. (1992), *Manières de table, modèle des moeurs. XVIIe–XXe siècles*, Cachan: Editions de l'ENS.

Markus, H. and Nurius P. (1986), 'Possible Selves', *American Psychologist* 21(9).

Meissonier, J. (2002), 'Stratégies d'optimisation des temps quotidiens: Le Temps du repas', in Garabuau-Moussaoui, Palomares and Desjeux (2002).

Mennel, S. (1985), *All Manners of Food: Eating and Taste in England and France from the Middle Ages to the Present*, Oxford: Blackwell.

Miles, A. (2005), *Ces Hommes qui cuisinent*, Paris: Agnès Viénot.

Miller, D. (1998), *A Theory of Shopping*, New York: Cornell University Press.

Mintz, S. W. (1986), *Sweetness and Power: The Place of Sugar in Modern History*, London: Penguin.

Modak, M. (1986), 'Note sur les conversations de table en famille', *Dialogue* 93.

Montagne. K. (2004), 'Adaption de l'épouse cuisinière aux goûts alimentaires de son mangeur de mari', communication to XVIIe Congrès de L'Association internationale des Sociologues de Langue Française, Tours.

Motta, R. (1998), 'Le sacrifice, la table et la fête. Les aspects "néo-antiques" de la liturgie du *candomblé* brésilien', *Religiologiques* 17.

Muchembled, R. (1988), *L'Invention de l'homme moderne: Sensibilités moeurs et comportements collectifs sous l'Ancien Régime*, Paris: Fayard.

Muxel, A. (1996), *Individu et mémoire familiale*, Paris: Nathan.

Nourrisson, D. (1998), 'Le Buveur à travers les âges', in *Comprendre le consommateur*, Auxerre: Sciences humaines.

Palomares, E. (2002), 'La Pâte et la sauce: Cuisine, formation du couple et inégalités de genre à Cotonou', in Garabuau-Moussaoui, Palomares and Desjeux (2002).

Pellizier, E. (2003), 'Forme di Eros a simposio', *Pallas* 61.

Péron, R. (2004), *Les Boîtes: Les Grand Surfaces dans la ville*, Nantes: L'Atalante.

Perrot, M. (1990 [1987]) (ed.) *The History of Private Life, Vol. 4. From the Fires of Revolution to the Great War*, trans. Arthur Goldhammer, Cambridge, MA: Belknap Press of Harvard University Press.

Perrot, M. (2000a), *Présenter son conjoint: L'épreuve du repas de famille*, DEA de sociologie, IEP de Paris, supervised by Jean-Hugues Déchaux.

Perrot, M. (2000b), 'Femmes et nourriture', in *Histoire et nourritures terrestres: Les rendez-vous de l'histoire, Blois 1999*, Nantes: Pleins Feux.

Perrot, M. and Martin-Fugier, A. (1990 [1987]), 'The Actors' in Perrot (1990).

Pétonnet. C. (1968), *Ces gens-là*, Paris: Maspero.

Pezeu-Massabuau, J. (1983), *La Maison, espace sociale*, Paris: PUF.

Pfirsch, J.-V. (1997), *La Saveur des sociétés: Sociologie des gouts alimentaires en France et en Allemagne*, Rennes: Presses Universitaires de Rennes.

Picard, D. (1995.), *Les Rituels du savoir-vivre*, Paris: Seuil.

Pitte, J.-R. (2004), *Le Vin et le divin*, Paris: Fayard.

Porel, L. (2003), *Courir sous les arbres*, Paris: Éditions Société des Ecrivains.

Poulain, J.-P. (1997), 'La Nourriture de l'autre: entre délices et dégoûts', *Internationale de l'imaginaire* 7.

Poulain, J.-P. (1998), 'Les Jeunes Seniors et leur alimentation', *Les Cahiers de l'OCHA* 9.

Poulain, J.-P. (2002a), *Sociologies de l'alimentation: Les Mangeurs et l'espace sociale alimentaire*, Paris: PUF.

Poulain, J.-P. (2002b), 'La Décision alimentaire', in Corbeau and Poulain (2002).

Queiroz, J.-M. de (2004), 'L'Enfant au centre?' in Singly (2004a).

Ramos, E. (2002), *Rester enfant, devenir adults: La cohabitation des enfants chez leurs parents*, Paris: L'Harmattan.

Rawls, J. (1973), *A Theory of Justice*, Oxford: Oxford University Press.

Régnier, F. (2004), *L'Exotisme culinaire: Essai sur les saveurs de l'Autre*, Paris: PUF.

Richards, A. (2003 [1932]), *Hunger and Work in a Savage Tribe*, London: Routledge.

Rivière, C. (1995), *Les Rites profanes*, Paris: PUF.

Roche, D. (1997), *Histoire des choses banales: Naissance de la consommation dans les sociétés traditionnelles (XVIIe–XIXe siècle)*, Paris: Fayard.

Rowley, A. (ed.) (1997), *Les Français à table: Atlas historique de la gastronomie française*, Paris: Hachette.

Rozin, P., Kabnick. K., Pete, E., Fischler, C. and Schields, C. (2003), 'The Ecology of Eating. Smaller Portion Sizes in France than in the United States Help Explain the French Paradox', *Psychological Science* XIV(5).

Sabban, F. (1993), 'Suivre les temps du ciel: économie ménagère et gestion du temps dans la Chine du VIe siècle', in Aymard, Grignon and Sabban (1993).

Sabban, F. (1996), 'Art et culture contre science et technique: Les enjeux culturels et identitaires de la gastronomie chinoise face à l'Occident', *L'Homme* 137.

Sanitch, B. (1999), 'Reflections on References to Lévi-Strauss', Research Centre for the History of Food and Drink, University of Adelaide.

Sauvageot, A. (2003), *L'Epreuve des sens: De l'action sociale à la réalité virtuelle*, Paris: PUF.

Schmitt. J.-C. (1990), *La Raison des gestes dans l'Occident medieval*, Paris: Gallimard.

Schwartz, O. (1990), *Le Monde privé des ouvriers: Hommes et femmes du Nord*, Paris: PUF.

Segalen. M. (2003), *Eloge du marriage*, Paris: Gallimard, coll. Découvertes.

Serfaty-Garzon, P. (2003), *Chez soi: Les territoires de l'intimité*, Paris: Armand Colin.

Shorter, E. (1984 [1981]), *A History of Women's Bodies*, Harmondsworth: Penguin.

Simmel, G. (1997 [1910]), 'Sociology of the Meal', in D. Frisby and M. Featherstone (eds), *Simmel on Culture: Selected Writings*, London: Sage.

Singly, F. de (1996), *Le Soi, le couple et la famille*, Paris: Nathan.

Singly, F. de (2000), *Libres ensemble: L'Individualisme dans la vie commune*, Paris: Nathan.

Singly, F. de (ed.) (2004a), *Enfants–adultes: Vers une égalité des statuts?* Paris: Encyclopaedia Universalis.

Singly, F. de (2004b), 'La Spécificité de la jeunesse dans les sociétés individualisées', *Comprendre 5*.

Sjögren, A. (1986) 'Le Repas comme architecte de la vie familale', *Dialogue 93*.

Stevens, H. (1996), *Les couples et la politique: Double je ou double jeu?* Memoir for BA in Sociology, supervised by A. Quénin, Université de Versailles-Saint-Quentin-en-Yvelines.

Symons, M. (2004), *A History of Cooks and Cooking*, Champaign: University of Illinois Press.

Tchernia, A. (2000), 'Qu'est-ce qu'un grand vin au temps des Romains?', in *Histoire et nourritures terrestres: Les rendez-vous de l'Histoire, Blois 1999*, Nantes: Pleins Feux.

Thuillier, G. (1977), *Pour une histoire du quotidien au XIXe siècle en Nivernais*, Paris and The Hague: Mouton.

Tisseron, S. (1996), *Le Bonheur dans l'image*, Le Plessis-Robinson: Les Empêcheurs de penser en rond.

Todorov, T. (2001 [1995]), *Life in Common: An Essay in General Anthropology*, trans. Katherine Golsan and Lucy Golsan, Lincoln and London: University of Nebraska Press.

271

Tonnac, J.-P. de (2005), *Anorexia: Enquête sur l'expérience de la faim*, Paris: Albin Michel.

Touvenot, C. (1997), 'La Soupe dans l'histoire', *Internationale de l'imaginaire* 6.

Urvoy, D. and Urvoy, M.-T. (2004), *Les Mots de l'Islam*. Toulouse: Presses Universitaires du Mirail.

Valleur, M. and Matysiak, J.-C. (2002), *Les Addictions: Dépendances, toxicomanies: repenser la souffrance psychique*, Paris: Armand Colin.

Vanhoutte, J.-M. (1982), *La Relation formation-emploi dans la restauration: Travail salarié feminin, fins des chefs cuisiniers et nouvelles pratiques alimentaires*, PhD supervised by Henri Mendras, Université Paris X – Nanterre.

Verdier, Y. (1979), *Façons de dire, façons de faire: La Laveuse, la couturière, la cuisinière*, Paris: Gallimard.

Verdon, J. (2002), *Les Plaisirs du Moyen Age*, Paris: Hachette littératures.

Vernant, Jean-Pierre (1982 [1979]), 'At Man's Table: Hesiod's Foundation Myth of Sacrifice', in Detienne and Vernant (1982).

Vigarello, G. (1993), *Le Sain et le malsain*, Paris: Seuil.

Vigarello, G. (2004), *Histoire de la beauté: Le corps et l'art d'embellir de la Renaissance à nos jours*, Paris: Seuil.

Waysfeld, B. (2003), *Le Poids et le moi*, Paris: Armand Colin.

Weber, M. (1992 [1920]), *The Protestant Ethic and the Spirit of Capitalism*, trans, Talcott Parsons, London: Routledge.

Weber, M. (1992 [1922]), *Economy and Society*, ed. Guenther Roth and Claus Wittich, Berkeley and Los Angeles: University of California Press.

Welzer-Lang, D. and Filiod, J.-P. (1993), *Les Hommes à la conquête de l'espace . . . domestique: Du propre et du rangé*, Montréal: VLB Editeur.

Witherington, B. (2003), *New Testament History: A Narrative Account*, Grand Rapids, Michigan and Carlisle: Baker Academic and Paternoster.

Wolff, E. (1991), *Quartiers de vie: Approche ethnologique des populations défavorisées de l'île de la Réunion*, Paris: Méridiens-Klincksieck.

INDEX